"FIRST TH! ~~IRST"~~ FIRST"

RAF Hornchurch

1915-1962

Eric Smith

Ian Henry Publications

First published 1992
Second edition 2000

© copyright E R Smith, 1992, 2000

ISBN 0 86025 498 4

358.417094267

Printed by
Whitstable Litho Printers, Ltd.
Millstrood Road, Whitstable, Kent CT5 3PP
for
Ian Henry Publications, Ltd.
20 Park Drive, Romford, Essex RM1 4LH

FOREWORD
by
WING COMMANDER BILL STAPLETON, CBE

May, 1940, was a beautiful month. After a terrible winter of snow, ice cold and blackout, Yorkshire was at its best. RAF Catterick, with its lawns, shrubs, trees and highly coloured flowers, was an oasis in the world of shock and horror into which we had been precipitated. Only the snarls of the Rolls Royce Merlins reminded us that it was the base of 41 Squadron's Spitfires.

For nine months 41 Squadron had chased Heinkels away from reconnaissance missions or attacks on North Sea shipping, sometimes in atrocious weather. At night we had no lights to provide even a ghost of a horizon and we landed with the aid of only a totem pole and a couple of goose-neck flares. Although the withdrawal of the British Expeditionary Force never entered our heads, it was obvious that things were not going well in France and we were approaching a crisis. It caused little surprise when Norman Ryder, 'A' Flight Commander, burst into the Mess shouting, "The game's on, chaps, we're off south to Hornchurch NOW!"

A few personal belongings stuffed into the flare tubes was all the preparation allowed before eighteen Spitfires took off from the green grass of Catterick for Hornchurch in Essex. And what a change we found there; a seriousness and intensity different from the atmosphere in Yorkshire. 'Boy' Bouchier, the Hornchurch Station Commander, emphasised his strongly held beliefs, "They will attack with large formations - never relax - we have got to be ready for them." To us nineteen year olds it simply meant that he was truly past it! But how right he was. In the months ahead they were to attack with massive formations.

The lovely Mess at Hornchurch, with a dining room under the head chef of one of London's leading hotels, made us smugly pleased with our lot. Heroics AND superb food! What more could a young man want in the summer of 1940?

We flew our patrols over the beaches of Dunkirk. Thirty-six Spitfires, harassed by accurate ground fire, but effective in discouraging the Luftwaffe in their attacks on our troops. Our orders were to patrol the coast, but not go into France.

On 1st June, 1940, our second patrol of the morning, we were running short of fuel before Squadron Leader 'Robin' Hood called us over the R/T to return to Hornchurch. As one of the 'arse end Charlie' section, charged with protecting the Wing from being jumped, I made a final turn towards the beaches and saw a gaggle of impertinent black crosses emerge from the clouds. They were Ju88s, under the impression that the BEF had been left without air cover. I yelled over the R/T, "88s attacking!" and thirty-six Spitfires wheeled like one to get amongst them.

It was not a brilliant interception. Tactics, drills and command procedures had not yet completely evolved and we still lacked experience. However, it was heartening to see the Luftwaffe empty their bomb bays in one hell of a hurry and get out of the area at speed. I found myself alone after the melée, having chased an 88 into France. As I turned towards the coast I saw, unbelievably, an airfield packed with Heinkel 111s with no regard to dispersal. I dived into the attack, putting the wind up the German ground crews, who leapt off the aircraft and flung themselves flat. They need not have bothered: as soon as I squeezed the fire button I knew that I was out of ammunition. Not one round left in my eight Browning guns.

Dispirited, I climbed away, hearing the Hornchurch Controller calling me when, at 800 feet, I was hit, loudly and precisely, by flak which had been tracking me for some time. My elevators were ineffective, but as I reached sea level, I applied full rudder, causing a yaw which reduced the impact. I do not know how I got out; both legs were badly bruised and I couldn't move them. The enemy on the beach opened fire and I was convinced that I would soon be hit, when suddenly the firing ceased. Two burly figures swam out to me and helped me to the beach with every consideration. The officer who approached was taken aback by my abrasive comments on those who fired on shot down pilots: he apologised, explaining that mine was the first aircraft downed by this battery, who were a trifle trigger happy!

Then followed five years as a prisoner of war. I did not see Hornchurch again until 1951. Eleven years to the day, I landed there with the Air Officer Commanding in Chief, Flying Training Command, Air Marshal Sir Hugh Walmsley. What a series of coincidences: it was again the 1st of June, again a clear blue sky from which the sun shone brightly and there, on the tarmac, were three Spitfires.

I was choked - absolutely full. I tried to explain to Walmsley how I felt, but I should have known better. He was not the person to appreciate such poignant and emotional niceties.

Of the eighteen pilots who flew from Catterick to Hornchurch in 1940, eight were killed in action and two became prisoners of war (Norman Ryder and myself). Wonderfully, Wally Wallens, my great friend and section commander at the time I was shot down, survived the war after taking a 30 mm shell in the thigh - flying from Hornchurch during the Battle of Britain - and winning a Distinguished Flying Cross. They were - in truth - magnificent young men.

Which links me neatly to the author of this unique book. My first major appointment after release was to RAF Habbaniya, fifty miles west of Baghdad. It was a great RAF 'city' and had everything; hospitals, churches, cinemas, clubs, hounds and horses, pools, irrigated gardens, and so on. All this, in the middle of the desert, was a triumph of British engineering.

I loved 'Habb', as it was known. It seemed to be manned by a special sort of person - at all levels. And amongst these chaps was young Eric Smith, an exceptional member of my Unit. Some of the 'Duration of present emergencies' servicemen bitched about the loss of vital years from their careers. I well remember doctors prevented from becoming the world's greatest brain surgeons, and stockbrokers worried about the success of their partners, and embryo barristers convinced that they would never take silk because of this 'unfair' interruption to their lives.

But never, in the two years that we served together, did I hear one word from Eric Smith that didn't convey enthusiasm, cheerfulness and a willingness to get 'stuck in'. He was one of the called-up servicemen - and I am glad that there were many of them - who loved the Royal Air Force and made their contribution to the splendid achievements of that service.

He ran the Air Transport Unit Orderly Room faultlessly. I finished his release report with the words, "The Royal Air Force is losing a first class man". I am delighted to say that he has remained a first class friend, still passionate about the Royal Air Force and a dedicated researcher into its history. No one is better qualified than he to write about a piece of our history that is fast disappearing.

Bill Hassleble

Pilot Officer W Stapleton, 41
Squadron R A F, 1940

Wing Commander 'Bill' Stapleton
in retirement in 1990

INTRODUCTION

Forty-seven years span the time from when eight men and two BE2c aircraft opened the Royal Flying Corps airfield at Suttons Farm and the day when RAF Hornchurch closed for the last time.

The years between 1915 and 1962 encompassed enormous technical developments in aviation, developments that eventually outstripped the ability of the grass field to cope with military aircraft and which spelled its demise.

When it opened it was less than twelve years since Wilbur and Orville Wright had made their first flight in a powered aircraft at Kittyhawk, four years since Louis Blériot had made the first crossing of the Channel and three years since the Royal Flying Corps had been formed.

The BE2c aircraft that moved in had 90 horse power engines, open cockpits, few instruments and a speed of 82 mph. The pilots had no parachutes and no precedents to work to. Night landing aids comprised sawn-off petrol cans stuffed with cotton waste and set alight.

The airfield's most intensive years started a quarter of a century later. Between 1940 and 1944 the 'all Spitfire' station was in the thick of the battles fought out over the skies of southern England and mainland Europe. Dunkirk, the Battle of Britain, Ground attacks, Escorts to bombers, including those of the United States Eighth and Ninth Air Forces, all came the same to the airmen of Hornchurch and Fighter Command. Casualties, inevitably, were heavy. By 1940 90 hp had given way to 1030 hp; Twin Vickers had been replaced by eight Brownings; and open air flying had surrendered to the closed cockpit. At this stage Hornchurch was the ideal location for the fighter aircraft; its geographical position north of the River Thames and 15 miles east of London was unsurpassed.

By 1962, when Hornchurch closed, the latest fighter in the RAF's inventory was the English Electric Lightning, capable of Mach 2.3 (1,500 mph) with nearly 30,000 lb of thrust, with reheat. By then it was 17 years since the airfield had left Fighter Command.

But in the years that it served the Royal Flying Corps and the Royal Air Force, Hornchurch was in the forefront of the development of fighter aircraft and equipment, tactics and methods of control and communication from ground to air and air to air. Its history was full of incident that ran the whole gamut of human emotion that arise when two thousand young men are pitched together in desperate times of war. Triumph and tragedy, laughter and tears constantly overlapped.

My fascination with RAF Hornchurch started in 1938 when as an eleven year old, I watched the Gloster Gladiators taking off and landing at the time of the Munich crisis: it has remained ever since.

For gathering together the material for this book my thanks are due to the staff of the Public Record Office, who were always most helpful. For photographs, I am indebted to Ray Hill, Ron Cranham, Joe Crawshaw and my brother, Albert, for producing fine prints from unpromising material. Miss R A Mourant, the Head Teacher of Mitchell School, also supplied photographs and kindly gave of her time when I visited. Wing Commander 'Bill' Stapleton, my old boss at RAF Habbaniya in Iraq, who wrote the Foreword, also steered me in the right direction on the events of 1940, when he was shot down from Hornchurch.

I am also indebted to Squadron Leader D I Wynn of RAF Biggin Hill for information on the Hornchurch Gates, the Football Association for details of the war-time Cup Final in which Sergeant Leslie Smith appeared, the Fleet Air Arm Museum at RNAS Yeovilton for information on the FAA squadron located at Hornchurch, S Curtis, the Library Curator of the London Borough of Barking & Dagenham, for information on V-2 incidents, the Reverend Canon A C H Peatfield for information about the connection of New College Oxford with the lands on which RAF Hornchurch was built, Roger Custance the Archivist of Winchester College for historical information on William of Wykeham and Mrs D Bradd for Public Record Office abstracts.

For information 'from the other side' my thanks go to Kurt Puzicha of the Marine-luftschiffkameradschaft at Hamburg; this organisation, originally formed by airship veterans, exists to keep their memories alive. Kurt Puzicha supplied biographical details on the German airship personnel that were involved with the Hornchurch story. Other information from Germany was supplied by Kapitanleutnant Peter Brandt and Major Ostertag.

Finally, my thanks go to Christopher Whitehead of the Ministry of Defence and Squadron Leader C R Paterson of the Battle of Britain Memorial Flight and last, but by no means least, to Air Commodores James Leathart and the late Alan Deere, who, as young Spitfire pilots, played such a great part in the story of

RAF Hornchurch.

'OVERTURE'
THE GREAT WAR

Before 1915 Suttons Farm, Hornchurch, in the County of Essex, was a quiet agricultural oasis in open countryside. London's spreading carpet of bricks was forever edging outwards into Essex, but, as the Great War dawned, the outer edge of that carpet was still several miles away and there was little to disturb the farm's peaceful tranquillity. It was still rural Hornchurch and not yet urban Hornchurch.

That was soon to change. The little farm was to have fame thrust upon it as the land that gave birth to Royal Flying Corps, Suttons Farm, a fighter airfield that became front page news nationwide in the autumn of 1916 as the base that took the leading rôle in the destruction of the German airship menace: it was a threat that had terrified Londoners for eighteen months.

It then became embroiled in the turmoil of dealing with the Gotha and Giant bomber aircraft that replaced the airships and, as RAF Hornchurch, a quarter of a century later, in the Dunkirk operation, the Battle of Britain and sweeps over occupied Europe. In post war years it had many rôles, including being the home of the RAF's Aircrew Selection Centre. In its heyday, in the 1930s and 40s, it was one of the most popular airfields in the Royal Air Force and, being so near to London, it became a 'must' for royalty, military top brass, politicians and other distinguished British and overseas visitors.

The ebb and flow of threats to national security and the constantly changing nature of defence needs resulted in frequent changes at Suttons Farm/Hornchurch between 3rd October, 1915, when it opened, and 1st July, 1962, when it finally closed down. At high tides of national peril it fairly hummed with the hustle and bustle and intense activity of an operational fighter station. The noise of engines starting and aircraft taking off was ever present; but at low tides it was left sadly silent, unused and somewhat neglected.

Its story is, in essence, a saga of courage and tenacity of two generations of young fighter pilots who overcame great difficulties, successfully bearing the defence burdens of the day in two world wars, and of the far more numerous ground staffs of all trades who supported them. Five hundred young men made their final take-off from Suttons Farm/Hornchurch and died in the defence of their country. Happily, many others survived to enjoy the peace that they had fought so hard to secure, but they never forgot the happy, but desperate, days that they endured or the camaraderie that they enjoyed during the most profound period of their lives.

###

The origins of Suttons Farm go far back into history. A large area of land in and around Hornchurch (now in the London Borough of Havering) was Crown Land in the 12th century and, in August, 1158, the lands and income from them were given by Henry II to the monks of St Bernard at Montjoux in the Swiss Alps and they established a daughter house here. Within five years the monks had consecrated a Priory Church.

In 1385 the estates were confiscated and returned to Crown ownership and, in 1391, they were bought by William of Wykeham [1324-1404], a remarkable man who was variously Bishop of Winchester, Chancellor of England, King's Chaplain and Chief Warden of Dover, Hadleigh, Leeds and Windsor Castles. He founded Winchester College in 1379 and then used the Manors of Suttons and Hornchurch Hall as an endowment to found Seinte Marie College of Winchester in Oxenforde - an academic institution better known today as New College, Oxford. His idea was that Winchester College and New College, Oxford, would cover a student's education through his college and university years.

New College still owned the estates at Hornchurch five and a half centuries later when Suttons Farm was sold to the Air Ministry for the permanent establishment of Royal Air Force Hornchurch, and the College still exercises its right to nominate the incumbent of St Andrews, the Parish Church of Hornchurch. The 600th anniversary of the association of the parish and the university college, dating from the purchase of the lands by William of Wykeham in 1391, was celebrated throughout 1991. The advowson was under the auspices of Canon Peter Peatfield, an ex-New College, Oxford, man and a former Honorary Chaplain to the Royal Air Force in Malaya.

The scale of casualties that could be inflicted if the airships reached London in force was self-evident. The geographical significance of Suttons Farm, near to the River Thames, the main navigational aid to reach the capital, was to spell the end of its peaceful life. As the importance of aviation as a third element in the pursuit of warfare increased, it was to give the little farm a greater importance than it had enjoyed before over the course of so many centuries.

In the spring of 1915 more probing raids were made in the general direction of London, primarily to test out the location and strength of anti-aircraft batteries, searchlights and airfields. These probes included a raid on Maldon by L-6 (commanded by Horst Brandenfels-Buttlar). On his return to base he reported that at the time he bombed he could see a

The Royal Flying Corps was established by Royal Warrant on 13th April, 1912, two years before the outbreak of war and in 1914 most of its squadrons were sent to France to serve on the Western Front. The defence of the United Kingdom was left in the hands of the Royal Naval Air Service, supplemented by the few Royal Flying Corps aircraft that remained behind. Air attacks on England began on Christmas Eve, 1914, when a solitary aircraft dropped a bomb on Dover. Although it was known that Germany was in the van of airship development, particularly through the efforts of Count Ferdinand von Zeppelin, the potential seriousness of their menace was not at first evident. By January, 1915, the German Naval Airship

lighted city and searchlights ahead - obviously either Chelmsford or Colchester. There were also two raids on Southend by army zeppelin LZ-38 (commanded by Erich Linnarz) when the batteries at Shoeburyness and at Cliffe - on the Kent side of the river opposite Canvey Island - were identified.

Erich Linnarz dropped an oddly worded note, composed in his best schoolboy English that was found on Canvey. It read, 'You English. We have come and will come again. Kill or cure. German.'

He was as good as his word. On 31st May, 1915, LZ-38 became the first airship to reach London after skilfully plotting a course avoiding the known defences. Seven people died in the attack.

A Royal Naval Air Service pilot, Flight Sub-Lieutenant A W Robertson, made the first operational sortie from the newly opened Rochford

Division was ready to launch a bombing offensive from its base at Nordholz (the HQ of the Division near Cuxhaven), Hage, Fuhlsbuttel (now Hamburg Civil Airport) and Ahlhorn.

On the night of 19th January, 1915, two naval airships, L-3 (commanded by Hans Fritz) and L-4 (commanded by Graf von Platen) crossed the Norfolk coast and bombed Great Yarmouth, Snettisham and King's Lynn. The four people killed and sixteen injured were the first casualties from air attack in the country. Hans Fritz was still commanding L-3 a month later when it had engine failure and came down on the Danish island of Fanø, the crew being interned in Denmark for the remainder of the war.

Airfield, near Southend, and sighted LZ-38, but engine failure forced him to land on marshland at Leigh-on-Sea. LZ-38 escaped on this occasion, but retribution was swift. A week later two RNAS pilots from 1 Squadron at Dunkirk - Flight Lieutenants J P Wilson and J S Mills - destroyed the airship by bombing its shed at Evère in Belgium. LZ-38 had been in commission for only two months. But further airship attacks followed on London, with particularly heavy raids on two consecutive nights, 7th and 8th August, 1915.

An improvement in the defence procedures against airships was now imperative. At this time the Admiralty and the War Office were often at loggerheads over the question of responsibility for home defence. The Royal Naval Air Service was increasingly occupied with its own maritime duties, providing reconnaissance for the Royal Navy, escorts for shipping convoys and dealing with the ever-increasing submarine menace. It lacked the resources to take on the additional problem of dealing with the airships and it became clear that the larger and better equipped Royal Flying Corps would have to assume the primary rôle.

RFC reconnaissance parties were despatched into Essex to ascertain the best possible sites for air defence. After examining several candidates, the War Office requisitioned Suttons Farm, Hornchurch, then farmed by Tom Crawford, and another field at Hainault Farm, a few miles from both Romford and llford.

On Sunday, 3rd October, 1915, the Royal Flying Corps arrived at Suttons Farm and speedily erected two large canvas hangers for temporary aircraft accommodation. Supplies taken in included some bomb racks, a landing 'T' sign and a supply of aviation spirit in cans. Two RFC pilots, Lieutenants H O'Malley and E Powell flew

House in West Street, Prittlewell, destroyed in the bombing by Zeppelin LZ-38, 10 May, 1915

Joachim Breithaupt, L-15, after capture, 1 April, 1916 (*Imperial War Museum*)

their 90 horse power BE2e aircraft from Gosport to Suttons Farm and became the first operational pilots based there. The Royal Flying Corps did not overtax the local accommodation resources at this time as the airfield opened with just eight men, in total, including the two pilots. A telephone (rare in private homes in 1915) was installed at the farmhouse and another in the *White Hart* in Hornchurch, and the first personnel were billeted in these places. A few smaller tents were pitched on the airfield for the staff on duty.

The bomb racks were for the small bombs and grenades that were thought to be the best weapons to tackle airships. It was known that the airships were filled with inflammable hydrogen, but it was assumed that the inner hydrogen filled bags were surrounded by an envelope filled with inert gas and that any rupture of the bags by gun-fire would produce an innocent mixture of the two gases that would fail to ignite. Thus it was considered that the only way an airship would be brought down by machine-gun fire was if it was filled so full of holes that it lost a large proportion of its gas through leaks and, thereby, its buoyancy.

Pilots were armed with small grenades and incendiary darts, designed to penetrate the outer envelope and explode inside the hydrogen filled bags. The later 'Ranken' darts were the invention of Commander F Ranken, RN; they were hollow cylinders, the size of a large church candle, with a bullet nose. Stuffed with incendiary material and a strip of match friction, they were thought to be the ideal weapon for the task. The difficulty, however, was getting into the only possible position to attack the airships - on top of them and at the same speed for an ideal dropping position. The tactics for this were formidable and, of course, any weapons that missed the target were just as dangerous to people on the ground as they would have been to the airship.

The items brought into Suttons Farm were the immediate essentials necessary to start operations and, with their installation, Suttons Farm came into use as a primitive fighter station. Although the Royal Naval Air Service continued to play a part in air defence until March, 1916, the main burden of the day was now firmly in the hands of the Royal Flying Corps and initial control of Suttons Farm was exercised by the 5th Wing of the Corps, under the command of Colonel Holt at Gosport.

Early conditions at Suttons Farm were spartan: everything was 'portable' and 'temporary' and pilots were detached from Gosport for a few uncomfortable days at a time and then relieved so that they could return to their more pleasant base. O'Malley and Powell were relieved by Lieutenants Jenkins of 14 Squadron and Yates of 23 Squadron: Jenkins, in his turn, was relieved by a young pilot who was destined to ultimately become Chief of Air Staff, the highest possible post in the Royal Air Force. The eighteen-year-old John Slessor proceeded from Gosport to collect a new BE2c at Coventry and then flew it to Suttons Farm. On 13th October, 1915, he took off for his first anti-zeppelin patrol and, at 2,500 feet over Romford, caught sight of an airship high in the sky, illuminated by searchlights: it was L-15 from Nordholz, commanded by Joachim Breithaupt. Slessor had to continue his slow climb through a thick layer of cloud and, by the time that he emerged, L-15 had climbed away and made good its escape. He continued to search for it throughout the remainder of his two hours patrol, but never saw it again.

The Suttons Farm landing facilities were as primitive as the accommodation and comprised petrol cans, sawn off at the top, stuffed with an inflammable mixture of cotton waste and petrol and laid out as a flare path. As John Slessor made his approach, a well-meaning searchlight crew thought that they would supplement the Suttons Farm facilities, but only succeeded in dazzling his sight; he damaged the undercarriage of his BE2c in a heavy landing, but escaped injury.

The resourceful Breithaupt and L-15 returned to base and lived to fight another day, but his report highlighted the fact that defences around London were improving. He mentioned the many searchlights 'turning night into day', violent anti-aircraft fire and, most significantly, the spurts of flame from the exhausts of four aircraft as they tortuously climbed upwards towards his airship.

The scheme adopted by the War Office for the defence of the capital provided a cordon of aircraft at fields around the perimeter and ground observers on the coast and further inland in constant telephone contact with the War Office and reporting aircraft as they crossed the coast and their subsequent flight path; mobile and fixed anti-aircraft batteries and additional searchlights completed the scheme. In the Suttons Farm area searchlights were located at Becontree Heath, Buckhurst Hill, Chigwell Row, Upminster and at strategic points along the Thames. Aircraft were placed in pairs at Northolt, Hainault Farm, Suttons Farm, Hounslow, Joyce Green (Dartford), Farnborough and Brooklands. Each field had two pilots, aircraft riggers and fitters and a party of Royal Engineers for communications and aircraft retrieval, where necessary.

Further airship sightings by Suttons Farm pilots included a zeppelin unusually low at 8,500 feet, by Lieutenant E W Powell on the night of 31st March, 1916. It was almost certainly the elusive L-15, which crossed the coast at Dunwich, Suffolk, reached the Thames and was then fired on by the Dartford guns. It was still commanded by Breithaupt, but on this night he pushed his luck just a little too far, L-15 was also seen and attacked by Lieutenant Claude Ridley from Joyce Green and Lieutenant Alfred Brandon from Hainault Farm. Brandon managed to get on top of L-15 and dropped explosive darts and bombs on its back. In return, he received heavy machine gun fire from the zeppelin. No immediate results were seen, but the guns and aircraft had mortally wounded L-15; losing height all the time, the zeppelin circled around Foulness Island. Breithaupt was undecided whether he had enough buoyancy to attempt the sea crossing, but finally ventured out to sea. L-15 continued to lose gas at an alarming rate and dropped into the sea near the Kentish Knock lighthouse, 15 miles out from Margate. It remained largely intact on the surface and Breithaupt and most of his crew were rescued by an armed trawler HMS *Olivine*.

The exception was Signaller Albrecht, who drowned in an apparent attempt to destroy L-15 as the trawler approached: if this was so, it was quite unnecessary. Attempts were made by the trawler to tow the cumbersome zeppelin to shore and beach it, but, as the gas went on leaking, it sank lower and lower, until it foundered off Westgate, Kent, and sank to the bottom. Breithaupt and his crew were landed at Chatham and placed in the Royal Navy Garrison Detention Room.

Charles Wakefield (later Viscount Wakefield), the Lord Mayor of London, presented each of the anti-aircraft gunners with an engraved gold medal.

By now there were six aircraft each at Suttons Farm and Hainault Farm, still as detached units from other airfields, but on 15th April, 1916, they were merged into a newly formed 39 Squadron, commanded by Major T C R Higgins, with headquarters at Hounslow. Lieutenant William Leefe Robinson was one of the six pilots in 'B' Flight and took up his appointment with destiny in one of the most renowned episodes in Royal Flying Corps history. He was first in action against a zeppelin on the night of 25th April, when he sighted Army Zeppelin LZ-95 at height over Seven Kings. He was seen by the zeppelin which dropped water ballast and climbed away from him at a rate that the BE2c just could not match: the problem was that it took the BE2cs 40 minutes to slowly screw their way up to the operating height of the airships, usually 10,000 feet, and the airships had a far superior rate of climb.

Things were now improving at Suttons Farm. Timber and brick buildings were now replacing the canvas tents, detachments had given way to a regular Squadron and tactics were improving. In August, 1916, the Headquarters of 39 Squadron were transferred from the rather distant Hounslow to Woodford Green and a third Flight was established at North Weald Bassett. A Lewis gun was fitted to each of the BE2cs and the death knell of the airship was sounded with the introduction of a new and highly effective incendiary bullet, devised by Commander F A Brock of the Royal Naval Air Service: these bullets were loaded into the Lewis gun cartridge belts in sequences of three, with the similar Pomeroy incendiary bullet and a tracer bullet. With regular patrol lines established from Kent to Essex across the Thames, taking in North Weald Bassett, Hainault Farm, Suttons Farm, Joyce Green and Farnham, a defence line was established that became an excellent aerial shield for London. With aircraft already at height as the airships approached, the balance of power between the two was shifting in favour of the defenders. The die was now cast and, in the autumn of 1916, the inferno of the airships was about to begin.

The turning point and climactic moment of glory for the Royal Flying Corps came on the night of 2nd/3rd September, 1916, when Lieutenant William Leefe Robinson turned an airship into a blazing holocaust and millions of people in London and the

13

Captain Wilhelm Schramm, Commander of Airship SL-11, shot down at Cuffley, 3 September, 1916

Captain William Leefe Robinson, V C (*Imperial War Museum*)

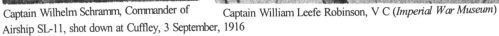

Capt. W Leefe Robinson and Lt. Frederick Sowrey in the Prince Henry Vauxhall car presented to the former by well-wishers

Home Counties watched it slowly sink to earth at Cuffley, Hertfordshire. The 21-year-old RFC officer changed the course of aviation history, being the first person to destroy an airship over the United Kingdom mainland.

Born on 14th July, 1895, in India, he was educated at St Bees School, Cumbria, from 1909 to 1914, before being commissioned into the Worcestershire Regiment on 16th December, 1914. Three months later an urge to fly prompted him to transfer to the Royal Flying Corps as an Observer with No. 4 Squadron at Amiens, under the command of Major C A Longcroft. On 8th May, 1915, he received a shrapnel wound during aerial combat and was sent home to England to convalesce. He took advantage of this respite to apply for pilot training and was accepted. From Farnborough he went to the Central Flying School at Upavon and, after gaining his wings, served briefly at Castle Bromwich and Joyce Green. On 2nd February, 1916, he arrived at Suttons Farm and soon assimilated the difficulties of flying by night.

Saturday, 2nd September was a miserable gloomy day at Suttons Farm, pouring with rain. Leefe Robinson was scheduled for a late patrol and rested on a camp bed in one of the canvas hangars. That night the Germans mounted their largest raid against London with 12 Naval airships and 4 Army airships. Each of the airfields forming London's defence line had aircraft up on two hour patrols. At 2300 it was Leefe Robinson's turn to take off and patrol the section straddling the Thames. With airships approaching London from all directions he first sighted a zeppelin caught in a cone of searchlights over Woolwich, but it climbed and was lost in clouds before he could get near. Shortly before his patrol was due to end, he spied another airship 12 miles away caught in searchlights over north London.

It was Army Airship SL-11, unusually a wooden framed Schutte-Lanz airship, not a metal framed Zeppelin, under the command of Wilhelm Schramm. After rising from its Belgian base and flying across the North Sea, SL-11 had crossed the Essex coast at Foulness at 2240 and passed over Coggeshall at 2300. It then made a wide sweep to avoid the known Thames defences and approached London from the north through Hertfordshire. Dropping bombs at Edmonton and Enfield, SL-11 was then coned by the Victoria Park and Finsbury Park searchlights whilst it was over Wood Green, and engaged by anti-aircraft fire. All this activity was observed by Leefe Robinson, who turned his aircraft and sped from Essex to north east London, preparing for an attack at 12,000 feet. On closing, his first two drums of Brock and Pomeroy were scattered and ineffectual, but then he took up a new position behind the airship and, from a range of 500 feet, he concentrated his fire on one spot.

Within seconds the whole airship was ablaze - an inferno in which Wilhelm Schramm and his 16 crew perished. The airship turned over and slowly fell to earth in a beet field behind the *Plough* public house in Cuffley. Strangely, the German Commander died not too far from where he was born - at Charlton in south London. SL-11 had only been in commission for a few weeks. The flaming airship was seen

15

Presentation of silver cup to Capt. W L Robinson, V C, at Hornchurch, 14 October, 1916.

Robinson being cheered by his ground staff at Suttons Farm

40 to 50 miles away, from Southend to Reading and Royston to Reigate. It burned on the ground for two hours. The excited Leefe Robinson fired off triumphant Verey lights into the sky and landed back at Suttons Farm at 0245. During his scheduled two hour patrol he had been aloft for the better part of four hours and his fuel tanks were nearly empty.

The crews of the other airships approaching London watched in shock and horror as the sky turned red, and their commanders prudently turned for home before reaching the capital. L-14 dropped its bombs at Thaxted in order to gain height and speed; L-16 turned at St Albans, dropping its bombs at Essendon; LZ-90 dropped an un-manned Observation Car and 3,000 feet of cable and a powered winch: the Car was designed to be lowered beneath the clouds when it was manned, it came to earth at Mistley, Essex. The biggest ever airship raid had ended, for the Germans, in tragedy and chaos.

SL-11 was the first airship brought down in full view of the people and crowds roared their delight into the night air. Special trains were laid on from King's Cross to carry 10,000 people to see the gaunt wreck of the craft. On the following Wednesday evening the bells rang out at St Andrews, Hornchurch, celebrating the triumph of their local hero.

Leefe Robinson was an immediate national hero and was summoned to Windsor, where he was presented with the Victoria Cross by King George V. He was also promoted from Lieutenant to Captain. His photograph was everywhere, in magazines and newspapers, and he was recognised by crowds wherever he went. The historic September night confounded the invincibility of the airship. The morale of hard pressed Londoners was given a tremendous boost.

The blackened, burnt bodies of the SL-11 crew were placed under a tarpaulin as a temporary measure, later being given a funeral with military honours by the Royal Flying Corps. The bodies were interred in the village churchyard at Essendon, between Hatfield and Hertford. Two sisters, killed when L-16 dropped its bombs on Essendon and turned for home, were buried in the same churchyard.

Although shaken by the loss of SL-11, the Germans persisted in launching zeppelin attacks against London, but within a month three more, all of the much vaunted 30's class of 'Super Zeppelins' were destroyed and crashed to earth over Essex and Middlesex. L-31, L-32 and L-33 were 650 feet long and 90 feet high and lifted 63 tons into the sky when they were loaded with fuel, stores, crew and bombs.

The night of 23rd/24th September, 1916, was the only occasion when two airships crashed in one night, both coming down in Essex, within 25 miles of each other. The first crashed at Great Burstead, near Billericay, the other at Little Wigborough, near Mersea Island.

L-32, up from Ahlhorn on its third combat flight, was commanded by Werner Peterson and it appears that, on this night, he had designs on Suttons Farm. Crossing the coast over Dungeness, he hovered and cruised around Kent before crossing the Thames between Dartford and Purfleet. This was a strange decision as it was certainly known to Peterson that this was a hotly defended area with searchlights, guns and aircraft in profusion. As expected, L-32 was quickly coned by searchlights and engaged by anti-aircraft fire: whenever the sweeping searchlights found an enemy airship the result was a classic *son et lumière* that intrigued the watchers on the ground. Undeterred, Peterson headed towards London on the Essex side of the Thames, dropping bombs on Aveley, Ockendon and Suttons Farm. At Woolwich he was again fired on and turned for home, but his escape route was now cut off.

Lieutenant Frederick Sowrey, on patrol that night from Suttons Farm in a BE2c, was directly in line to cut off Peterson's retreat. After turning around over Woolwich, Sowrey closed with L-32 and opened fire at 0045 with a mixture of Brock, Pomeroy and tracer ammunition. As in Leefe Robinson's case his first two drums had little effect, but the third burst caused a glow within the envelope that then exploded into an inferno. L-32 hung briefly in a perpendicular position before it drifted towards earth. With flames roaring, it passed low over the upstretched faces of the startled citizens of Billericay, before crashing two miles out of town at Snails Hall Farm, Jacksons Lane [now Greens Farm Lane], Great Burstead. Bits of the zeppelin dropped off on the way down. A propeller was found three miles away and two elevators and rudders were found in nearby Norsey Wood. Gondolas, engines and machine guns were scattered over a wide area across Snails Hall Farm and L-32 blazed for an hour before the flames subsided. John Maryon, the farmer, watched it all with a mixture of horror and amazement: he thought L-32 had been downed by anti-aircraft fire from the nearby battery at Vange, but there is no doubt that the zeppelin was ignited by the incendiary bullets from Lieutenant Sowrey's aircraft.

After landing back at Suttons Farm the elated and triumphant Sowrey piled into Leefe Robinson's powerful Prince Henry Vauxhall car (bought with donations from well-wishers). With Captain Stammers, Captain Bowers and Lieutenant Durston also aboard, they careered into the night to the scene of the crash, cheered on their way by the villagers of Hornchurch as they sped up the lane to the *White Hart*. They were followed hot-foot by Lieutenants Mallinson and Brock on motorcycles.

At dawn at Great Burstead the first grisly task was to remove the bodies of the airship crew and place them in a barn adjoining Jacksons Lane. One of the bodies was found far away from the wreckage: it was the commander, Werner Peterson, still wearing his Iron Cross, who escaped the agony of the flames by jumping from the zeppelin after it ignited.

As with the Cuffley airship, thousands of Londoners flocked to Billericay by special trains from Liverpool Street and walked the two miles to rural Great Burstead. They thronged close to the zeppelin's wreckage and even entered the barn to view the remains of the crew before a cordon of soldiers was posted round the scene.

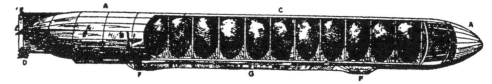

Fig. 81.—A Zeppelin Airship.

A.A. Rigid hull covered by fabric; B. Section showing the skeleton framework of hull; C. Arrangement of the interior gas chambers; D. Elevating-planes; E.E. Rudders; F.F. The two cars containing engines and crew; G. Passage-way between the cars; H. One of the propellers, of which the craft has four—two at the front of the hull, upon either side, and two at the rear.

(from The Aeroplane by Claude Grahame-White & Harry Harper, 1914)

Zeppelin L-32

Army sentries guarding the wreckage of L-32 at Snails Hall Farm, Great Burstead, 24 September, 1916

Lieutenant Frederick Sowrey received the Distinguished Service Order for his heroic action on that night. Intelligence Officers who rushed to the crash were delighted to discover a charred, but still readable, copy of the German Navy's Signal Code Book: it was a priceless discovery as the Codes had recently been changed.

The other zeppelin destroyed that night was L-33 on its first combat mission and under the command of Alois Bocker. Suttons Farm was not directly involved, the honours going to Hainault Farm and to the anti-aircraft guns. There was an element of farce about this incident, intermingled with the horrors of aerial combat. The story was quite exceptional and would hardly have been considered feasible had it been written as fiction.

After crossing Foulness Island L-33 was seen over Billericay and Wanstead. Bocker dropped his bombs in the East End at Bromley and Bow, causing fires and severe damage at the Homelight Oil Company in Old Ford Road and at Lusty & Sons Timber Yard in Bell Road, where 43,000 cubic feet of timber was consumed. The *Black Swan* in Bow Road, Stratford. was destroyed, and 11 people were killed in Bocker's attack. L-33 did not have it all its own way and was hit by anti-aircraft fire, prompting it to turn for home. Lieutenant Alfred Brandon, who had earlier shared the credit with the anti-aircraft guns for the destruction of L-15 at the Kentish Knock, was on patrol from Hainault Farm and engaged L-33 over Theydon Mount at midnight. It was not conclusive and he failed to set the airship alight, but further weakened it and L-33 was further damaged by the Kelvedon batteries, as it rapidly lost height and buoyancy. In the glare of Kelvedon's searchlight it was seen to release the last of its water ballast in a desperate effort to stay aloft, but Bocker was fighting a losing battle.

Nearing the coast at Mersea Island, L-33 hovered and then flew in a wide circle over the area at low altitude to the alarm of local inhabitants. The experienced Bocker hesitated, as he knew he had little chance of making the long sea crossing. As he circled, L-33 came so low that his shouted orders could be heard from the ground and the zeppelin finally came to earth intact in a remote area at Little Wigborough, close to a small pair of semi-detached farm cottages known as New Hall Cottages, occupied by farm workers' families. The huge airship straddled the lane leading from the cottages to Little Wigborough Parish Church.

A comic situation then ensued when Bocker, anxious that the 'super zeppelin' should not fall into British hands, decided to set it alight. Before igniting it he approached the cottages to warn the occupants that sparks might fly in their direction. The reaction of the families of Thomas Lewis and Frederick Choat to the fall of a 650 foot object in the middle of the night, virtually into their front gardens, is not easy to contemplate. It was no surprise that Bocker got no answer to his urgent hammering on the door. Although he intended them no harm, the families were not to know this and they huddled together and hid themselves as best they could within their homes. Fortunately they came through the experience unscathed and L-33 lit up the night sky,

Wreckage of L-33 and New Hall
Cottages, Little Wigborough today

Mrs T Lewis (right)
and her family

Kapitanleutnant Alois Bocker, Commander of L-33

Lieutenant Alfred de Bathe Brandon, who assisted in bringing down L-33 at Little Wigborough, 23/24 September, 1916

Peldon Special Constables; Edgar Nicholas standing extreme left

showering her sparks far and wide, but without setting alight to their homes.

Alfred Wright, a 45-year-old seedsman, living at Grove Farm a little further up the lonely lane towards Peldon, was not so lucky. As the airship ignited he mounted his motorcycle and shot off towards Mersea Island to alert the army camp there as to what was happening. Sadly, his motorbike collided with another vehicle in the darkness and he died on 13th November. His grave marker in Little Wigborough churchyard tells the story of that fateful night.

Satisfied that his airship was destroyed, Bocker assembled his men in column of three and marched them in good order up the lane towards Peldon. At the same time, Special Constable Edgar Nicholas, realising what the red glow in the sky signified, made his way by pedal cycle to investigate. The zeppelin crew - the only armed German military personnel to set foot in England in the 1914-18 war - and the British Special Constable finally came face to face and the German crew surrendered themselves without further ado. Continuing towards Peldon, with Constable Nicholas wheeling his cycle at the rear of the column, they were joined by Special Constable Elijah Traylor and Sergeant E A Edwards, a policeman from Hatfield Broad Oak who happened to be on holiday in the area. They took the crew to Peldon Post Office, where Bocker and his men were formally arrested and taken into custody by Constable Charles Smith of the Essex County Force.

At this point Alois Bocker asked Smith if he could make a telephone call and received the reply, "Certainly not!" Later newspaper reports fantasised on this and said that he asked to 'telephone a friend in London' or to 'telephone his sister in Colchester'. These reports aroused official interest, but, when asked again about the incident, the constable repeated that Bocker did not say whom he wanted to telephone.

An escort party of special constables was assembled to walk the crew to Mersea Island, where they were handed over to Colonel Oevee, in charge of the 83rd Battalion, who installed them temporarily in the Church House. One man had a fractured rib and was sent to the Military Hospital in Colchester. The Vicar offered cups of tea to all crew members, but Bocker refused his. During questioning of Bocker, a suspicion arose that one man might have died in the blaze or might still be loose. When asked how many men he had in his airship Bocker replied 'twenty-two', which was the normal complement of a 'super zeppelin' and the number who had perished at Great Burstead. However, he was corrected by his Deputy, Wilhelm Schirlitz, who said there were only twenty-one: it appears that L-33 must have flown with one crew member short on that night.

The story was still not quite over. A baby girl, born at Abbots Hall Cottages, Great Wigborough, was named Zeppelina, at the suggestion of Dr J H Salter of Tolleshunt D'Arcy, who was in attendance at the birth. She was duly christened Zeppelina Clark, later becoming Mrs Zeppelina Williams and living at Great Totham, not far from where L-33 came down.

Officers of 39 Squadron, RFC, 1916. L to r (standing) Capt. S R Stammers, Lt. Wulstan Tempest, Capt. William Leefe Robinson, Lt Frederick Sowrey, Capt. Frederick Bowers; (seated) Lt C L Brock, Lt C Durston, Lt P Russell Mallinson (*Imperial War Museum*)

Heinrich Mathy, Commander of L-31
Lt Wulstan Tempest, destroyer of L-31, 1/2 October, 1916

Lieutenant Alfred Brandon was also awarded the Distinguished Service Order, in recognition of the overall contribution he made in the zeppelin campaign. The remains of L-33 were cut up on site and taken to Maldon Railway Station for transportation.

The final airship to fall to a Suttons Farm pilot met its fate just eight nights later. It was L-31, commanded by Heinrich Mathy, up on its eighth combat flight from Ahlhorn. On the night of 1st/2nd October Lieutenant Wulstan Tempest, a friend of both Sowrey and Leefe Robinson, was scheduled to patrol on the by-now customary cross-Thames line from North Weald to Hainault Farm, Suttons Farm and Joyce Green. Although Tempest was based at Suttons Farm he took the opportunity to take his aircraft over to North Weald to start his patrol from there: this enabled him to spend the early evening having dinner with friends at nearby Epping.

L-31 approached by way of Lowestoft, Chelmsford, Kelvedon, Harlow, Ware and Cheshunt, where he shattered thousands of panes in the profusion of greenhouses there and destroyed 300 houses. Taking off on his patrol at 2200 Tempest sighted L-31 caught in searchlights over north east London and, from that point on, his actions were almost a repeat of Leefe Robinson's a month earlier. His take-off time, time of sighting the airship and its location were all similar. Fortunately for Tempest, the heavy anti-aircraft fire which was engaging L-31 abated as he neared the zeppelin. Mathy had obviously seen the exhaust flames of an aircraft approaching and dropped ballast and soared to escape. This time the tactic did not work and Tempest got in several heavy bursts at a height that would have been impossible the previous year.

The whole outline of the zeppelin was soon a flaming red, like a huge Chinese lantern, turning night into day. L-31 initially shot up 200 feet, paused in its agony and then roared down. Tempest feared being engulfed in flames at any moment and took hasty evasive action, but was relieved to see the incandescent mass roar past him. L-31 came to earth at Oakmere Farm, Potters Bar, only four miles from where SL-11 had crashed, and again the whole crew perished. The Commanding Officer again jumped to avoid the flames.

Embedded in the soil was an officer who was still breathing, but who expired almost immediately: identity tags showed it was the redoubtable Heinrich Mathy. He was, without question, the most resourceful of all the German airship commanders and his death had a most profound effect on the German Naval Airship Service.

With the improved performance of 'souped-up' BE2es, standing patrols with aircraft already at height as the airships approached and the introduction of incendiary bullets meant the airships stood little chance. The little grass field near Hornchurch Railway Station had played the lead in this national exercise and its fame spread far and wide. Leefe Robinson, Sowrey and Tempest were The ascendancy of the zeppelins, which had prevailed for eighteen months, was now over. The fatal flaw in their concept, that of being filled with two million cubic feet of highly inflammable and potentially lethal hydrogen was shown by three flaming masses in one month. The early advantages enjoyed by the airships was an ability to operate at

25

all presented with handsome silver cups on 14th October, 1916, at a special presentation in front of a large and enthusiastic crowd at the New Zealand Army Camp at Grey Towers. Thomas Gardner, JP, presided and the presentations were made by W H Legg, the Chairman of Hornchurch Parish Council. Even the under-privileged children of the Cottage Homes of the Parish of St Leonards, Shoreditch, which had a settlement in Hornchurch chipped in with their pennies and ha'pennies. At another ceremony, at the Homes, one of the lads presented Leefe Robinson with a silver ink-stand.

higher altitudes than aircraft could reach. Oxygen was available from long rubber tubes in all sections of the airships for crew members to take a gulp at when they soared to great heights.

They were susceptibile to bad weather, however, being buffeted by gales and accumulating masses of ice at high altitude, that necessitated off-loading all their ballast. Fierce thunderstorms could also have an unnerving effect on the crews.

The adulation showered upon the handful of RFC pilots who defeated the airship menace was well deserved. It required a rare brand of bravery to clamber into a 90 horse power biplane, in the dead of night, and climb away into a pitch black sky in search of a monstrous 600 feet long and well armed airship. They had no night flying instruments, no parachutes with which to escape from their aircraft, no precedents to work to and only primitive night landing facilities. These aircraft were flown by men whose great courage coincided with the needs of the hour. They made up the procedures for dealing with their formidable enemy as they went along.

###

Licking the wounds of the loss of four airships and their valuable crews in one month, the Germans changed tactics and, in general, concentrated the future operation of their airships on less well defended targets in the Midlands and the North. It was a blow to their pride, but London's respite from bombing lasted only through the winter of 1916. The Germans laid plans to resume attacks on the capital, but this time with bomber aircraft, instead of airships. On 28th November a single aircraft audaciously reached the city, dropped six bombs and made for home: its good fortune ran out when it was forced to land in allied territory at Boulogne with engine trouble. Paul Brandt, the pilot, and Walter Ilges, the navigator, became prisoners of war, but earned their niche in aviation history by being the first airmen to bomb London from an aircraft.

As 1917 dawned there were operational changes on both sides of the North Sea. The Royal Flying Corps, anxious to strengthen its night flying capability, set up an Operational Training Unit at Rochford for training pilots for Home Defence Squadrons. On the other side a special squadron was formed and equipped with large Gotha bombers to resume the air onslaught on London.

The Home Defence Squadrons in southern England at this time were -

SQUADRON	HEADQUARTERS	AIRFIELDS
37	Woodham Mortimer	Goldhanger, Essex
		Rochford, Essex

Gotha bombers parked outside the airship sheds at Gontrode, Belgium

Timber aircraft sheds, which replaced the canvas hangars at Suttons Farm in 1916 (*RAF Museum*)

39	Woodford	Stow Maries, Essex
		Hainault Farm, Essex
		North Weald Bassett, Essex
		Suttons Farm, Essex
50	Harrietsham	Bekesbourne, Kent
		Detling, Kent
		Throwley, Kent
78	Hove	Chiddingstone, Kent
		Gosport, Hampshire
		Telscombe Cliffs, Sussex

They were all equipped with a mixture of BE2c, BE12, RE7 and RE8 aircraft.

The Gothas flew with a crew of three and No.3 Squadron (Kahgohl 3) was a large force with 30 aircraft. Kahgohl 3 spread itself over three airfields in occupied Belgium - Gontrode, St Denis-Westrem and Maria Kerke. The Gothas were large biplanes with a wing span of 78 feet (a WWII Lancaster was 102 feet). They were capable of firing to the front, rear and below.

In a series of daylight raids, followed by a string of night raids, they tested the ingenuity of the British defences to their limit. Kahgohl 3's first mission was on 25th May, 1917 and, although London was the intended target, bad weather forced them to divert to Folkestone, where 95 people were killed in a heavy attack. On 5th June the Gothas struck at both sides of the Thames Estuary, hitting Sheerness and Shoeburyness, but this time one Gotha was shot down by anti-aircraft fire.

The most devastating raid of the whole campaign followed eight days later, when London was reached for the first time. Fourteen Gothas used the Thames as a navigational aid, but flew a few miles inland to escape the heaviest defences. They passed over Wickford, Brentwood, Romford and East Ham. Central London was bombed at noon, with heavy casualties at Liverpool Street Station, Fenchurch Street, Aldgate High Street and Finsbury Park. The most heart-rending scene of all immediately preceded this when, on the way in, a Gotha dropped a bomb on the London County Council school at Upper North Street, Poplar. Eighteen infant children were killed - only two of them being over 6 years old - and 34 more were injured, including a little girl who lost a leg. 54 infants at school on the ground floor of the building and the two teachers, Miss Watkins and Mrs Middleton, escaped, but the school caretaker, Mr Batt, had the terrible experience of finding his own six year old son dead.

The incident caused outrage throughout the land and there were emotional scenes at the mass funeral of the infants, as their horse-drawn corteges passed down East India Dock Road. Few episodes in the Great War aroused such horror and indignation and the route to the cemetery was lined with thousands of shocked East Enders. It had been an awe inspiring air raid which, in total, killed 162 people; the heaviest loss from

L-48 down at Theberton

Kapitan Ernst Brandenburg, First Squadron
Commander of Kaghol 3

Lieutenant Loudon Watkins, the Canadian
destroyer of L-48

any air raid in the war. Queen Alexandra sent a handwritten letter expressing her 'deepest sympathy with the parents, mourning the loss of their beloved children'.

From Suttons Farm Captain R Stammers and Captain Trygve Gran - an eminent Norwegian aviator - took off to tackle the Gotha formation. Gran attacked a Gotha at 12,000 feet over Romford on their inwards flight and another over the River Crouch on their return, but without apparent success. He was then, in turn, hit by 'friendly' anti-aircraft fire from the Shoeburyness guns and landed in a damaged state at Rochford. The fighter aircraft out of the 'BE' stable had proved their worth against airships; they were among the most celebrated of all RFC aircraft and were good gun platforms, but were now too slow and cumbersome to give much of a threat to the speedy and well-armed Gothas. A different aircraft was needed.

Ernst Brandenberg was awarded the coveted *Pour le Merite* for his dash in leading Kahgohl 3, but was injured a week later and replaced by Rudolf Kleine.

As an interlude to the Gotha raids, a rare airship raid in the south on 17th June, 1917, saw L-48, commanded by Franz Eichler, appear over Harwich, where the Royal Navy was based in strength. The lower half of L-48 was painted black as a camouflage measure, but it was seen and attacked by three different Royal Flying Corps aircraft. Captain Robert Saundby, up from Orfordness, Suffolk, and Lieutenant Douglas Holder with air gunner Sergeant Sydney Ashby in a two seater FE2b, also from Orfordness, got in attacks on L-48. But the credit for finally setting L-48 alight and bringing it down is usually given to Lieutenant Loudon Watkins - a Canadian serving with 37 Squadron at Goldhanger, Essex. Strangely, the three aircraft were never in sight of one another, although all three fired on L-48 at one time or another.

What is certain is that L-48 was set alight and became the fifth and final airship to fall to earth in the United Kingdom. Five members of the crew jumped to their deaths rather than remain with the blazing airship, as it plunged to earth at Holly Tree Farm at Theberton, Suffolk. The flames were seen by the crew of L-42 flying 70 miles further north. Amazingly, three crew members survived the burning of L-48, the only people to ride to earth with a blazing airship and live to tell the tale. Machinist Ellerkam, Machinist Ucker and Lieutenant Mieth were well enough to be interrogated at nearby Yoxford, before being transferred to a prisoner of war hospital. L-48 was carrying, for this trip, Captain Victor Schutze, the Commander of the Naval Airship Division, who died in the wreckage. L-48 was a brand new airship on its first combat mission. Thousands of sightseers descended on rural Suffolk from near and far to see the remains.

In June, 1917, changes were made in the Home Defence Squadrons to combat the Gothas. Six Sopwith Pups were allocated to 39 Squadron and Major J C Halahan assumed command from Major R G Murray. On 7th July 22 Gothas attacked London and killed 57, including a little boy of eleven who was being taken for a ride in a horse drawn van and perished with his father who was driving it. The casualties this time were mainly in the Stoke Newington area. Nine aircraft from 39 Squadron rose to take on the Gothas, but, although Lieutenant E S Moulton-Barrett fired three drums into one of them, there was no apparent result. Two famous London buildings were hit in this raid - the Royal Mint and the Central Telegraph Office, where a bomb crashed through the concrete roof to set the top storey alight, causing extensive damage. Cannon Street Station was also attacked.

The apparent immunity of the Gothas demanded prompt action and, three days later, 46 Squadron was withdrawn from its French base at Bruay to fly their Sopwith Pups into Suttons Farm. It was a crack squadron with several outstanding airmen, including Major Philip Babington, the Commanding Officer; Lieutenant Arthur Gould Lee; and Captain J T McCudden, whose Victoria Cross, earned on the Western Front, was gazetted whilst he was at Suttons Farm. Lieutenant Lee was probably the only aviator to serve at Suttons Farm and at the reconstituted RAF Hornchurch, where he became Station Commander from December, 1935, to April, 1937.

Major-General E B Ashmore was also recalled from France to take command of the newly formed London Defence Area, which had a line of anti-aircraft guns established 20 miles east of London, with the fighters having a free hand in this area.

The new system was put to the test on 12th August, 1917, when nine Gothas crossed the coast at Harwich to head for London. Defending aircraft, including 46 Squadron at Suttons Farm were, on this occasion, already on patrol at the right height, but the Gothas, sensing the danger, turned back before reaching the capital. London's gain was, however, Southend's misfortune: the seaside town was the largest astride the return route and the Gothas dropped their bombs there, killing 32 of its citizens.

At the end of August, 1917, 46 Squadron was posted to Ste Marie Cappel in France, being replaced at Suttons Farm by 78 Squadron from Chiddingstone. They were commanded by Major C R Rowden and equipped with Sopwith 1½ strutters, which were later replaced by Sopwith Camels. 78 Squadron remained at Suttons Farm for 2 years and 3 months - the longest period for any squadron in the Great War.

39 Squadron, until now the longest term tenants at Suttons Farm, had been split into three flights at Suttons Farm, Hainault Farm and North Weald Bassett. The eighteen aircraft were now concentrated as one squadron based on the latter, equipped with RE7s and FB2bs.

On 4th September 20 Gothas reached London and one bomb fell close to Cleopatra's Needle and the attendant lions on the Victoria Embankment, leaving permanent shrapnel scars on them. A passing bus was shattered. But with Sopwith Camels and Bristols increasingly available, daylight raiding became more hazardous. Five Gothas were shot down over the course of two raids.

At this time Women's Legion Auxiliaries, later to become the Women's Royal Air Force (WRAF), were posted to Suttons Farm. Some of the girls lived locally around

Hornchurch and were allowed to return home each night, much as they would have done in a civilian job. Others were accommodated at Bretons Farm, a couple of miles from the airfield towards Dagenham, where they slept uncomfortably on straw filled palliasses. The girls worked long hours as motor drivers, motorcycle despatch riders, clerks and telephonists. Their home at Bretons had attained a reputation for being haunted and it was with some relief that the girls welcomed the light of day and transport to their Suttons Farm duties.

An intensive period of raiding by Gothas followed in the autumn of 1917, with six attacks over eight nights. In one raid thirteen people were killed when a bomb exploded at the entrance to the Bedford Hotel in Southampton Row. On 24th September 78 Squadron sent up four aircraft at night from Suttons Farm, but it was anti-aircraft fire that shot down one of the raiders into the Estuary between Southend and Sheerness. Captain D J Bell exchanged fire with a Gotha over Gravesend, but inconclusively.

After two days respite there were heavy casualties again on 27th September, but on the following day the Germans were thwarted by thick cloud over Essex and Kent. The Notting Hill area suffered badly on 29th and on 30th three Midland Railway locomotives were badly damaged at Plaistow Locomotive Sheds. The final raid of this intensive series came the following night: the total casualty list for the six raids was 69 killed and 259 injured.

One effect of this was that up to 300,000 Londoners sought refuge in the deep Underground 'Tube' stations each night, with all the attendant disruption to their lives and to the Tube. At times the platforms were seriously overcrowded. However, there was only one raid in November and three in December. On 6th December a Gotha was hit by anti-aircraft fire from the Canvey Island battery and crashed after hitting a tree while trying to make for Rochford airfield. For this raid the Germans switched to incendiary bombs and many fires were started. The local airfields were now placed under the command of a newly formed 49 Wing, with headquarters at Upminster Hall, Hall Lane, Upminster, about two miles from Suttons Farm. Command of the Wing was given to Colonel Malcolm Christie.

On 18th December the first Gotha was brought down by an aircraft at night. The victor was the intrepid pioneer of night flying, Major Murliss-Green of Hainault Farm, who first sighted the Gotha over Goodmayes and engaged it in running battle as it headed for the coast. He finally shot it down into the sea off Folkestone. Another Gotha force-landed at Margate four nights later and was set alight by its crew.

Into 1918 and Suttons Farm became a two squadron airfield when 189 Squadron arrived from Ripon, Yorkshire. This was commanded by Major H S Powell and concentrated on night flying tuition. The Gothas were licking their wounds, but were supplemented by a new bomber coming into production, the Giant. In the first three months of 1918 there were only five, night attacks, but they caused another 128 deaths and 253 injured. The casualties included 38 killed in the Odhams Printing Works at Long Acre and 20 at the St Pancras Hotel, fronting the railway terminus.

On 7th March two pilots were lost in a tragic collision from neighbouring airfields in Essex. Captain A B Kynoch from Stow Maries and Captain H C Stroud from Rochford collided over Rawreth. The spot where Captain Stroud fell is marked by a propeller memorial in the Rawreth fields, the inscription reading -

This spot is sacred to the memory of Captain Henry Clifford Stroud,

Royal Flying Corps, killed in action on 7th March, 1918.

Faithful unto death.

His grave can be found in the small military section at Rochford Parish Church.

Hainault Farm accounted for another Gotha in this period. Captain G H Hackwill and Lieutenant C C Banks, both flying Camels of 44 Squadron, brought it down jointly. It crashed in flames at Frunds Farm, Wickford. It was only the second Gotha shot down at night.

On 10th March James McCudden flew a prototype Sopwith Snipe from Suttons Farm as a demonstration for senior RFC officers. The Snipe was planned as a successor to the Camel. McCudden flew it enthusiastically for 15 minutes, during which he showed its capabilities: the Snipe could climb to 10,000 feet in 11 minutes, compared with the 45 taken by the BE2c - and it was 40 miles an hour faster.

After the outcry following the Gotha raids, General Jan Christian Smuts was tasked with examining Britain's air defences. His conclusion was that the Royal Flying Corps and the Royal Naval Air Service should amalgamate under a newly formed Air Ministry and become the Royal Air Force. And so - *Per ardua ad astra* - the infant RAF arrived on 1st April, 1918.

At Suttons Farm, as elsewhere, things did not change overnight. RFC and RNAS had treasured traditions and hallowed histories forged in battle. It was some time before khaki uniforms and army ranks disappeared from Suttons Farm.

The last night raid mounted by Kahgohl 3 was on 19th May, 1918. This raid marked the final eclipse of the squadron and the superiority of the defences was demonstrated beyond argument. The largest force mounted for one raid comprised 40 Gothas and 3 Giants and, after taking off from their Belgian bases and crossing the North Sea, they were confronted by an even larger force of 84 RAF aircraft.

Captain D V Armstrong, in a 78 Squadron Camel from Suttons Farm, exchanged fire with a Gotha over Orsett and damaged it. It was possibly this aircraft that was later attacked by Lieutenant Anthony Arkell and Air Mechanic Stagg in a F2b of 39 Squadron at North Weald Bassett. In a letter to the author in 1976, the Reverend Anthony John Arkell said that he was convinced that the aircraft that he and Stagg shot down was not the aircraft damaged earlier by Captain Armstrong. In any event, the Gotha crashed in flames at Roman Road, East Ham, at the Becton end of High

Street South. Two of the three crew jumped to their deaths as the flames took hold of the Gotha. Other Gothas were destroyed by Captain C J Q Brand of 112 Squadron at Throwley and Lieutenant E E Turner with Air Mechanic H B Barwise of 141 Squadron, Biggin Hill. Three more fell to anti-aircraft fire, crashing at Maplin Sands, Foreness and Dover, while another force-landed at Clacton. Seven of the aircraft that attacked London that night failed to return and three more were so damaged that they crash-landed in Belgium. The London defences had once more regained the upper hand as the German losses of 25% of their aircraft were not sustainable.

The Gotha campaign had shocked Londoners as deeply as the airships attacks of two years earlier. At first the overall results in terms of Gothas brought down were, to say the least, disappointing, but defenders finally got on top and broke the back of the campaign during 19th May raid. It was the swan song of Kahgohl 3 and no more enemy bombers attacked London in the final six months of the 1914-18 War.

Although Suttons Farm, as a fighter airfield, did not enjoy the same overwhelming success in destroying Gothas as it had earlier shown in downing airships, it did participate in the attacks on the bombers during most of their raids. Even more important, it was the base that played a vital pioneering rôle in night flying, and then training others in the art. In the final analysis, it was this training that finally put an end to the activities of Kahgohl 3, once they had switched their attacks from day to night. In all, the airship and aircraft attacks caused the death of 1,414 people and material damage of £3 million [perhaps £300 million by today's prices].

As the war drew to its close through the summer and autumn of 1918, life at Suttons Farm returned to a less frenetic pace. The airfield was far more comfortable now, with the trappings of a more organised existence. The wooden huts, which were such an improvement on canvas tents, were supplemented by brick built buildings, including barrack blocks, an Officers' Mess, two hangars, an armament store, power house, radio mast, squadron offices, technical stores and workshops and a hostel for the WRAFs just outside the airfield entrance in Suttons Lane. The eight men who opened the airfield in October, 1915, had grown to 300 airmen and 24 WRAFS.

The base was still maintained in a state of operational readiness, as there was always the chance that the Germans might mount another large all-out attack, but as weeks turned into months without any enemy aircraft making an appearance, it began to look as though the base had met its last challenge in the war.

In 1918 the Essex squadrons were placed under two Wings, with 49 Wing at RAF Upminster, located at Upminster Hall (now the Golf Club) with Colonel M G Christie in command: this Wing controlled Suttons Farm, North Weald Bassett and Hainault Farm. 50 Wing was at RAF Great Baddow, under the command of Colonel Philip Babington, controlling squadrons at Rochford, Stow Maries and Goldhanger. Both Wings recruited WRAFs locally for service as cooks, drivers, clerks, typists, riggers and magneto repairers. 50 Wing was merged with 49 Wing on 23rd May, 1919, and 49 Wing ceased to exist in the autumn of 1919: they were, in essence, Administrative Wings and the squadrons they controlled did not themselves fly together as Wings, as the squadrons did in World War II.

In the high summer of 1918 an Inter-Squadron competition was organised covering aircraft maintenance, flying skills, wireless telegraphy, gunnery and formation flying. Ground competitions included parade ground drill and turn-out and transport. The competition finalists were 141 Squadron Biggin Hill, 61 Squadron Rochford and 50 Squadron Bekesbourne. The final was staged at Suttons Farm on 22nd September in front of a large crowd including Major Baird, MP, General Edward B Ashmore, the Commander of London's defences, and Lord Weir of Eastwood, who presented the trophies. The ultimate winners were 141 Squadron, which had formed at Rochford earlier in 1918 and then transferred to Biggin Hill. It was commanded by the same indefatigable Major Philip Babington who, in the previous summer, had brought 46 Squadron from France to Suttons Farm.

Further interest at the base was provided when 78 Squadron was re-equipped with Sopwith Snipes, the top fighter aircraft of the time. Suttons Farm still had its two resident squadrons - 78 and 189 - when the war drew to its close in November, 1918, and it took over a year to complete its wind-down, although demobilisation ate into its complement. 189 Squadron disbanded on 1st March, 1919, and on 31st December 78 Squadron suffered the same fate. Farmer Tom Crawford was advised that the farm would be restored as nearly as possible to the condition it was in when the War Office had taken it over. In fact, a few buildings were preserved, when they could be adapted for farm purposes.

London's air defences which had started with eight BE2c aircraft in 1915 had increased to eleven full squadrons - some 200 aircraft - by the end. The Germans lost six airships (five over land and one in the Thames Estuary) during the London campaign and twenty Gotha aircraft.

The Royal Air Force, with 3,300 aircraft and 300,000 men was the greatest air force in the world, but most of the aircraft were destined for the scrap heap and most of the men for a return to civilian life. At Suttons the decision not to retain the base in the post-war RAF meant that Tom Crawford was soon back in action with a new team of horses and sending his produce to Covent Garden from a now forgotten Suttons Farm.

The scrapping of the nation's air power was so ruthless that, in less than two years, there were no aircraft and anti-aircraft guns left in position for the air defence of London. The necessity to keep a reduced air defence system was not apparent and only three squadrons remained to cover the whole country. The Royal Air Force had all but disappeared and, but for the vision and determination of one man - Marshal of the Royal Air Force Lord Trenchard - it almost certainly would have done so completely.

Swords had been changed into ploughshares with a vengeance and, for the next few years, the only sorties made out of Suttons Farm were made by Tom Crawford's horse drawn wagons loaded with farm produce. The little grass airfield had demonstrated the usefulness of its geographical position for 4 years, 2 months and 28 days

POSTSCRIPT

And what of the airmen connected with Suttons Farm, neighbouring airfields, and their opponents?

ACLAND, William Henry Dyke

Commanded 39 Squadron from 9th August, 1917. Continued in the service during WWII and lived in Hertfordshire where he was an Alderman and then High Sheriff of the County. He was also Governor of the Police College. As Sir William Acland, he retired to the Isle of Wight, where he died on 4th December, 1970, at the age of 82.

BABINGTON, Philip

Commanded 46 Squadron when it arrived at Suttons Farm from France on 10th July, 1917. Continued in a distinguished career with the Royal Air Force to the end of WWII. He finished as Air Officer Commanding Flying Training Command and retired in the rank of Air Marshal in December, 1945. He lived at Chiddingstone, Kent, and died on 25th February, 1965, aged 71.

CHRISTIE, Malcolm Graham

Commanded 49 Wing (including Suttons Farm) from his Headquarters at Upminster Hall from the end of 1917. He remained in the Royal Air Force after the war and became Air Attaché in Washington from 1922 to 1926 and Air Attaché in Berlin from 1927 to 1930. He lived in London and died on 3rd November, 1971, at the ripe old age of 90.

GRAN, Trygve

Norwegian pilot with 39 Squadron at Suttons Farm, he had earlier participated in Captain Scott's ill-fated expedition in 1912 and was one of the search party that found the bodies. He made the first ever flight over the North Sea from Aberdeen to Stavanger on 30th July, 1914, and, but for the accident in timing his flight on the eve of the outbreak of the war when world attention was elsewhere, he would probably be as renowned today as Blériot or Lindbergh. Gran was an outstanding pilot and in his service with the RFC was awarded the Distinguished Flying Cross and shot down many enemy aircraft, flying from Rochford and North Weald, as well as Suttons Farm. He returned home to Norway and published a book on his life with 39 Squadron, written in Norwegian and translated as *Under the British Flag, 1914-18*. After a remarkable life he died at Grimstad, Norway in January, 1980, aged 90.

HALAHAN, John Crosby

Commanding Officer of 39 Squadron at Suttons Farm from 7th July, 1917. Continued in service with the Royal Air Force and, in World War II, with the Colonial Office. Lived at Bishopsteignton, Devon, and died on 22nd February, 1967, at the age of 89.

HIGGINS, T C R

The first Commanding Officer of 39 Squadron from 15th April, 1916. Served in the Royal Navy before transferring to the Royal Flying Corps. He continued in Royal Air Force service and was Senior Air Staff Officer in Iraq from 1926 to 1928. He retired in 1929, but re-engaged for service with the RAF Regiment in WWII. He lived at Bedford and died on 22nd September, 1953, aged 73.

LEE, Arthur Stanley Gould

A pilot with 46 Squadron when it was recalled from France and stationed at Suttons Farm. Arthur Lee continued in the service of the Royal Air Force and was in Iraq from 1925 to 1927. As a Wing Commander he returned to Hornchurch as Station Commander from 1935 to 1937. He went on to serve as Deputy Senior Air Staff Officer in Middle East Command in 1941-2 and in 12 Group Fighter Command, 1943-4. He headed the Mission to Marshal Tito in Yugoslavia in 1945 and retired the following year, writing many books in retirement. He lived in London, SW7, and died on 21st May, 1975, at the age of 75.

Lt C Durston, Lt F Sowrey, Capt W Leefe Robinson, Capt R Stammers, Lt W Tempest, 1916 (*RAF Museum*)

Werner Peterson, Commander of Zeppelin L-32

Lt Frederick Sowrey in the aircraft in which he destroyed L-32
(*National Museum of Canada*)

McCUDDEN, James
One of the Royal Flying Corps most outstanding pilots, he arrived at Suttons Farm with 46 Squadron and his award of the Victoria Cross, for service on the Western Front, was gazetted whilst he was in Hornchurch. He returned to France with 46 Squadron and was tragically killed on 9th July, 1918, taking off from Aix-le-Château.

ROBINSON, William Leefe
The first of the three Suttons Farm pilots to achieve national fame for shooting down a German airship. He left Suttons Farm on posting to take command of 48 Squadron at Bertangles, France. In March, 1917, he was shot down by Sebastian Festner of the famed 'Richtofen Circus' and became a prisoner of war at the infamous Holzminden prison camp. He returned home weak and depleted in health after the Armistice and became a victim of the influenza epidemic that swept the nation that winter. He died on 31st January, 1919, at the age of 23 and was laid to rest at All Saints, Harrow Weald, his coffin borne by his former RFC comrades. At St Bees School, Cumberland, a tablet was unveiled on 18th June, 1932, to commemorate Leefe Robinson and two other former pupils killed in the Great War. The memorial to him at Cuffley was subscribed for by readers of the *Daily Express* and it was restored on the 70th anniversary of his action in shooting down SL-11 (3rd September, 1986). His Victoria Cross was sold at a Christie's auction on 22nd November, 1988, together with other medals and memorabilia by his niece, Mrs Regina Libin, a retired headmistress of Haywards Heath. It realised £99,000 and the money was used to establish a cancer charitable trust appropriately named 'A medal for life'.

SLESSOR, John Cotesworth
An 18 year old pilot at Suttons Farm in the early days of detachments from Gosport, he was the first to encounter a zeppelin over Romford on 13th October, 1915. He remained in the Royal Air Force and, during a distinguished career, became Commander in Chief Middle East from 1944 to 1945 and finished in the RAF's supreme post, as Chief of the Air Staff, from 1950 to 1952. He lived at Yeovil, Somerset, dying on 12th July, 1979, at the age of 82.

SOWREY, Frederick
The second of the three at Suttons Farm who shot down an airship, Sowrey's being L-32 at Billericay on 24th September, 1916. He left Suttons Farm on posting to France and had great success with 19 Squadron. His victories included shooting down an Albatross from the famed 'Hermann Goering Squadron'. He remained in the Royal Air Force after the war, serving at Halton, Uxbridge and Tangmere, before retiring in the rank of Group Captain on 26th May, 1940. He served as a Gliding Officer with the Air Training Corps from October, 1943, and in retirement lived at Eastbourne. He died on 21st October, 1968, at the age of 75 and is buried alongside two brothers at Staines Cemetery. Lieutenant Sowrey received hundreds of congratulatory letters after shooting down L-32 and these are now in the archives of the Royal Air Force Museum at Hendon. The BE2c that he flew that night is now in the Canadian War Museum, Ottawa.

TEMPEST, Wulstan
The third of those at Suttons Farm who shot down an airship, Tempest's being L-31 at Potters Bar on 2nd October, 1916. He lived at Wash Common, Berkshire, becoming the first Commanding Officer of 211 (Newbury) Squadron of the Air Training Corps when the squadron was formed in 1941. After World War II he emigrated to Canada, dying there on 20th December, 1966, aged 71.

OTHER AIRFIELDS
There were several pilots at neighbouring airfields that overlapped into the Suttons Farm story. They included -

ARKELL, Anthony John
The 39 Squadron pilot who, with Air Mechanic Stagg [q.v.], shot down a Gotha at East Ham on 19th May, 1918. Anthony Arkell took Holy Orders after the war and was Vicar of Cuddlington from 1963 to 1971. In retirement he lived at Little Baddow, Essex, where he died in February, 1980 at the age of 81.

BRAND, C J Quintin
As a pilot with 112 Squadron at Throwley he destroyed a Gotha on 19th May, 1918. He remained in the Royal Air Force and, during a distinguished career, flew from London to Cape Town in 1920. In the Second World War he commanded No. 10 Group Fighter Command with Headquarters at Box, Wiltshire, from 1939 to 1941, the aircraft under his command featuring in the Battle of Britain. He retired in November, 1943, and died in Rhodesia on 7th March, 1968, aged 75, as Sir Quintin Brand.

HOLDER, Douglas
The Orfordness pilot who assisted in the destruction of L-48 at Theberton, Suffolk. Douglas Holder lived in

Chelmsford after the 1914-18 War and was an active prison visitor. He went on to become an Alderman and Deputy Mayor of Chelmsford and Deputy Lord Lieutenant of Essex. In World War II he was appointed the first Commanding Officer of 276 (Chelmsford) Squadron, Air Training Corps. He also sat on the Magistrates Bench. He died in 1978 aged 81. His gunner, Sergeant Sydney Ashby, did not survive the Great War, being killed in a flying accident in 1918.

RIDLEY, Claude
Ridley was the Joyce Green pilot who assisted in bringing down L-15 into the sea at Kentish Knock. He went on to become a Flight Commander with 37 Squadron at Stow Maries. He stayed on in the Royal Air Force, but retired from the service in 1929. During WWII he was re-engaged in the rank of Wing Commander for service with the RAF Regiment. He lived at Lewes, Sussex, dying on 27th June, 1942, aged 55. One of his memorials is an illuminated cross on the spire of Stow Maries Church, which he wanted to shine out over the fields that he knew so well. Details of his generous donation can be seen in the church. He is buried in Stow Maries churchyard.

SAUNDBY, Robert Henry Magnus Spencer
Saundby was the other Orfordness pilot participating in the destruction of L-48 at Theberton. He continued in service with the Royal Air Force in a distinguished career. In World War II he was Deputy Commander in Chief of Bomber Command, responsible to Sir Arthur Harris. He retired to Burghclere, near Newbury, Berkshire, in 1946, and thereafter devoted much of his time to the welfare of ex-servicemen. He also wrote several books. He died on 26th September, 1971, aged 85, as Sir Robert Saundby.

STAGG, A T C
Air Mechanic and Gunner to Anthony Arkell [q.v.]. Joined the Automobile Association as a patrolman after the Great War and lived at Romsey, Hampshire. He died in the 1970s.

WATKINS, Loudon Pierce
The Goldhanger pilot who is usually credited with the final destruction of L-48 at Theberton. He was a Canadian, one of three brothers who volunteered for service in the 1914-18 War. He arrived in England on 23rd December, 1915, and served in France before being recalled to England on 11th December, 1916, for Home Defence duties with 37 Squadron. He returned to France on 20th April, 1918, but was killed there when there was an engine malfunction in the FE2b that he was flying.

GERMAN AIRSHIP PERSONNEL

Schramm, Wilhelm, and crew of SL-11 - Cuffley, 3rd September, 1916
Peterson, Werner, and crew of L-32 - Billericay, 23rd September, 1916
Mathy, Heinrich, and crew of L-31 - Potters Bar, 2nd October, 1916
Eichler, Franz, and crew of L-48 - Theberton, 17th June, 1917

The seventy-one German crew members who perished in these incidents were originally interred in local churchyards at Essendon, Potters Bar, Great Burstead and Theberton, and there they remained at rest for fifty years. After World War II, however, there was a change of policy and, in July, 1966, the bodies were exhumed and re-interred at the German Military Cemetery at Cannock Chase, Staffordshire. This cemetery contains 4,925 German war dead, mostly airmen, who died in and around these shores in both world wars.

BOCKER, Alois
The Commander of L-33 which came to earth intact at Little Wigborough. He was placed in a prisoner of war camp, but later repatriated on condition that he did not fly combat again. He was then appointed Director of Airship Training at the large Nordholz base, near Cuxhaven, and finished the war there. He died in Köln in 1940.

BREITHAUPT, Joachim
The Commander of the elusive L-15 which finally foundered at the Kentish Knock. He remained a prisoner of war at Donnington Hall, Shropshire, until 1919 and then returned to Neuruppin. Between the wars he was at the Ministry for Aeronautics and by 1938 was a Colonel. He died in Bad Salzuflen on 18th July, 1960, aged 77.

ELLERKAM, Heinrich
One of the three who survived the flames of L-48. He was a prisoner of war until 1919, when he returned to become an inn-keeper in Hamburg. He died on 4th September, 1963, at Heidelberg.

FRITZ, Hans
Commander of L-3, the first zeppelin to raid England in 1915. He was a Captain at Stettin Naval Base in World War II until retiring from the Navy in 1942. He died on 23rd April, 1969, at Hamburg, aged 85.

KUHNE, Otto

Executive Officer to Breithaupt [q.v.]. He was repatriated to Germany after 18 months captivity on condition that he did not fly combat again. Later became a Lieutenant General and lived for a time at Hage, close to the airship base. He had a sister who lived at Bungay, Suffolk. Kuhne died at Gottmadinger-Bletingen on 19th March, 1987 at the ripe old age of 98.

LINNARZ, Erich

The Commander of LZ-38, which twice bombed Southend and was the first to reach London. Retired on 10th April, 1920, as a Major and obtained a post as a civil servant. In World War II he was a Lieutenant-General in the Army and, from 1st March, 1945, commanded 26 Panzer Division in Italy. He died on 23rd October, 1945 at the age of 66.

MIETH, Otto

Another L-48 survivor, Executive Officer Mieth was released in 1919. In 1928 he emigrated to Tanganyika as the director of a building business and was interned in Dar-es-Salaam in World War II - a prisoner in both wars. He managed a farm after the war before resuming in the building trade and died at Iranga, Tanganyika, on 30th April, 1956, aged 69.

SCHIRLITZ, Wilhelm

The Deputy Commander of L-33. After release in 1919 he returned to Germany and died in Kiel, aged 85, in 1978.

von BUTTLAR BRANDENFELS, Horst

The Commander of numerous airships, who first dropped bombs on Essex (Maldon) in the spring of 1915. He was the only airship commander to be awarded the *Orden Pour Le-merite*. He became Station Commander at Rhein-Main Airport and, during World War II, was Station Commander at Posen and Warschau airfields. He died on 3rd September, 1962, aged 73, at Berchtesgarden.

SQUADRONS AT SUTTONS FARM, 1915-1919

39 Squadron

Formed 15th April, 1915, it was split into Flights located at Suttons Farm, Hainault Farm and (from August, 1916) at North Weald Bassett. It was concentrated on the latter in December, 1917, and posted to France just before the Armistice. After the war it served in Egypt, India, Singapore, Malta and the Sudan. It left Luqa (Malta) for the United Kingdom on 30th September, 1970, and flew Canberras from Wyton for 13 years before the squadron was disbanded in 1983.

46 Squadron

Formed on 19th April, 1916, 46 Squadron arrived at Suttons Farm on 10th July, 1917, from France. It was posted back to Ste Marie Cappel, France, on 30th August, 1917, and disbanded on 31st December, 1919. It reformed in 1936 at Kenley and embarked its Hurricanes on the aircraft carrier HMS *Glorious* on 9th May, 1940, to participate in the Norwegian campaign. Returning from Norway *Glorious* was sunk by German warships and took 46 Squadron with it. It was reformed at Digby from 13th June, 1940, and returned close to Hornchurch when it fought out the tail of the Battle of Britain from Stapleford Tawney and North Weald. In post-war years it flew Meteors, Javelins and Andovers before the squadron was disbanded at Thorney Island on 31st August, 1975.

78 Squadron

78 Squadron disbanded at Suttons Farm on 31st December, 1919, but reformed at Boscombe Down on 1st November, 1936, as a Bomber Squadron. It flew Whitleys and Halifaxes throughout World War II from Yorkshire bases. After the war it became a Transport Squadron in the Middle East and then an Army Support Squadron. It disbanded as a Wessex Helicopter Squadron at Sharjah in December, 1971. It again reformed, in 1986, as a Chinook and Sea King Helicopter Squadron in the Falkland Islands. It is currently based at the new airfield at Mount Pleasant, Falkland Islands.

189 Squadron

189 Squadron disbanded at Suttons Farm on 1st March, 1919. It reformed at Bardney on 15th October, 1944, as a Lancaster Squadron in Bomber Command 5 Group. It transferred to Matheringham in October, 1945, and the squadron was disbanded there the following month.

'INTERLUDE'
THE INTER-WAR YEARS

At Suttons Farm Tom Crawford, with his land restored, enjoyed four more years of ploughing, sowing, harvesting and marketing his produce at Covent Garden, but then he received a visit from the men from the Ministry, giving him early warning that things would never be quite the same as before the war.

New airfields were needed for the additional squadrons and Air Ministry teams were despatched once again into Essex to search for suitable sites in a 10/20 mile radius east of London. Several fields were inspected in the Romford, Hornchurch, Upminster, Grays and Ockendon areas and, to Tom Crawford's dismay, Suttons Farm was visited on 24th November, 1922. The RAF found that their former airfield was now well established as a farm again, divided into three fields growing potatoes, turnips and clover. A few airfield buildings still existed, including the WRAF accommodation, now in use as an outhouse for the Romford Workhouse. Other buildings in farm use included the Motor Transport Shed, Guard Room and Blacksmith's Shop. The buildings were still only five or six years old, but they were generally in a poor condition and were unlikely to be integrated into a rebuilt airfield.

Although the Royal Air Force was decimated (and the WRAFs were completely gone by the end of 1920) it was fortunate that wiser counsels eventually prevailed. The future of the RAF was considered by three governments in quick succession in the early 20s: that of David Lloyd George, the short-lived Bonar Law administration; and the equally brief Stanley Baldwin government in the second half of 1923. When Sir Samuel Hoare became the Secretary of State for Air, he found that the RAF had only increased by two squadrons since 1920. A Committee was set up under the Chairmanship of the Marquess of Salisbury to study the question of defence and one of its tasks was to determine the future strength of the Royal Air Force. Its Report formed the basis of a Statement by Prime Minister, Stanley Baldwin, in the Commons on 20th June, 1923, and envisaged a Home Defence Force of 52 squadrons. This Expansion Programme remained a cornerstone of RAF policy for the next decade, until the emergence of the Nazi Party in Germany and the rebuilding of the Luftwaffe prompted a further major expansion programme in 1934.

None of the possible alternative sites was as suitable as Suttons Farm, however, and in a Minute to the Chief of the Air Staff, Air Marshal Sir Hugh Trenchard reported that an airfield in the vicinity of Suttons Farm was a necessity for national defence.

In July, 1923, compulsory purchase powers were sought and agreed by the Treasury. The owners, New College, Oxford, agreed to sell 120 acres of the farm, but requested that the boundary of the new airfield should be at least 300 yards from Suttons Farmhouse. This compromise was agreed by the Air Ministry as a goodwill measure, but it meant that the layout of the airfield had to be re-planned, additional land to the south had to be purchased and the centre of gravity of the airfield was switched from the Suttons area to that almost opposite, adjoining South End Road. Although re-building did start as early as May, 1924, the changes inevitably resulted in a delay to the original schedule and it was to take four years before the airfield was re-opened.

The rebuilding was thoroughly done, up to the highest standards pertaining at the time. A main roadway ran down from the main entrance to the 'C' type hangars which were installed at nearly all the RAF Stations built in the 1920s and 30s. There were gabled hangars, 175 feet long, with doors 35 feet high on runners. Just inside the gates, on the left, was the Guard Room with a flagpole flying the RAF ensign. Side roads led off to the left and right of the main road, leading to Sergeants' and Airmen's Messes, two storey accommodation blocks, fuel store, Motor Transport Shed, Parachute Store and Operations Room.

Although the use and function of the various buildings inevitably changed over the years, that was the basic layout. Armouries, stores and all the administrative and technical buildings required at various times sprang up on an 'as required' basis, and the Squadron Orderly Rooms and Crew Rooms were located in lean-to buildings at the hangars themselves. Neat flower beds, shrubs and lawns abounded throughout and the general standard reflected the neatness and tidiness associated with a highly disciplined Royal Air Force airfield.

On the opposite side of South End Road, furthest from the flying field, was the Officers' Mess, resplendent with a large dining room, ante-rooms and ranges of bed-rooms. Outside it was adorned with lawns, gardens and tennis courts. On the adjacent land were neat well-built Married Quarters.

It was an excellent RAF Station, one of the many technically efficient and domestically comfortable airfields built between the wars. It was light years away from the few tents pitched on a bleak field in October, 1915. A hard surfaced perimeter track ran around the grass take-off and landing flight paths: there were no hard surfaced runways. In front of one of the hangars was the Watch Office, an elevated glass enclosed building having an unobstructed view across the operational area and controlling take-offs and landings. Pilots also reported in and out as radio-telephony was not yet in general use. During World War II the Watch Offices became more familiarly known by their American terminology - Control Towers.

That was the airfield which finally re-opened as Royal Air Force Suttons Farm on 1st April, 1928.

The first resident squadron to move into RAF Suttons Farm was 111, which arrived from RAF Duxford with Armstrong Whitworth Siskins, under the command of Squadron Leader Keith Park, a distinguished officer who was destined, twelve years later, to command the 23 Spitfire and Hurricane squadrons comprising No. 11 Group - Fighter Command, in the Battle of Britain.

It was the general practice at RAF stations at that time for the Commanding Officer of the squadron to also become the C.O. of the station, in those cases where there was only a single squadron at the station. In this way Squadron Leader Park also became the first Commanding Officer of the rebuilt RAF Suttons Farm. Were there two or more squadrons at a station a separate Station Headquarters was established and an independent Station Commander appointed in the rank of Wing Commander or above: this was eventually to become the situation at Hornchurch when a second squadron arrived.

The Siskins were only one step ahead of the Sopwith Snipes with which Suttons Farm was equipped nine years earlier. Both were biplane fighters of similar size. The Siskin had a more powerful engine and superior speed, but both aircraft were essentially an airborne gun platform for the same armament - twin Vickers machine guns firing .303 bullets.

After only two months the name of RAF Suttons Farm was changed to the more realistic and accurate RAF Hornchurch and the airfield came within the administrative control of 'Fighting Area' of the 'Air Defence of Great Britain'.

RAF Hornchurch was still in the midst of its settling down routine when it received the first of what was to be many distinguished visitors from overseas. On 28th June, 1928, General Italo Balbo, the Commander of the Italian Air Force (*Regia Aeronautica*) led a formation of eleven aircraft on a non-stop flight from Rome to Hornchurch. It was an impressive feat in 1928. The Italians were met over the Essex coast by 5 Siskins of 111 Squadron who escorted them on the final stage of their journey, a goodwill mission from a former Great War ally.

Italo Balbo was to become famous for leading large formations of aircraft between the wars and his name caught on. The term 'Balbo' was later adopted by the RAF when, for a brief period in WWII, they experimented with flying two Fighter Wings - up to seven fighter squadrons - in formation together. 'Balbo' was the name given to the combined 70 or 80 aircraft. Five years after leading what was, for him, quite a small formation into RAF Hornchurch, Italo Balbo was made Governor General of Libya, then an Italian colony.

The brand new layout of the airfield was very striking and must have caught the admiration of General Balbo. It is doubtful whether he was equally impressed by the Siskin aircraft. Although they were popular 'planes in the RAF and probably as good as the biplane fighters of most other countries, they did not represent a great technical advance over the previous decade.

Although British peacetime technical development in fighter aircraft was as slow as everyone else's and the RAF continued with biplanes of wood or metal, wire and canvas, the intrepid RAF fighter pilots performed wonders with their aircraft and their quality was in marked contrast to the apparent visual obsolescence of their machines. The Armstrong Whitworth Siskin was a prominent feature at every Hendon display between 1927 and 1931 and was a superb aircraft for aerobatics. It equipped ten fighter squadrons of the RAF.

1929 was a further settling down period for RAF Hornchurch and 111 Squadron. They practised formation flying and spent time preparing a routine for Air Shows.

The Command of the Squadron (and with it, of RAF Hornchurch) changed twice during the year, with Squadron Leader F O Soden assuming command in March, followed by Squadron Leader L H Slatter in October. 111 Squadron also worked in co-operation with the Army on manoeuvres and in calibration of their anti-aircraft guns. With nearby Hornchurch Station only 14 miles from Fenchurch Street and the City - just a half hour journey in the train - and with an inter-change at Barking to the District Line of London Transport giving access to all parts of London, the station was hardly cut off from civilisation, despite its rural setting. This, in combination with the pleasant peacetime routine of a fighter airfield, made Hornchurch a popular posting in the expanding Royal Air Force.

In the Air Defence of Great Britain Exercises they were joined by the Siskins of 19 Squadron (Duxford) and the Gloster Gamecocks of 23 Squadron (Kenley).

The 1930s at Hornchurch proved to be a decade in which the airfield was at the forefront in each technical development and operational improvement affecting fighter aircraft in combat. It was a decade that finally broke away from the Great War concepts of aircraft, their size and shape, armament, speed and methods of control, both from air to air and ground to air. With aircraft it started with the Siskin and graduated through the Bristol Bulldog, Hawker Demon, Gloster Gauntlet and Gloster Gladiator to finally emerge at the ultimate in the Supermarine Spitfire. Hornchurch was the third station to be equipped with the revolutionary new aircraft, behind Duxford and Catterick, but after it received them it housed three out of the six Spitfire squadrons then available to the Royal Air Force.

The thirties started with 450 horse power and 156 miles per hour and finished with 1,030 hp and 355 mph. Armament practices were established each year and the Hornchurch squadrons were detached to Suttons Bridge Armament Camp, Lincoln-shire, used as such by the RAF between 1926 and 1939: it was tucked away in isolated fen countryside on the Lincoln-Norfolk border, one end of the landing strip was in fact in the latter county. It was a situation where aircraft started their touch-down on one county and rolled along to complete it in another. 111 Squadron first tested a new type of reflector gunsight at Suttons Bridge.

Another feature in the annual routine was the Air Defence Exercise where bombers from an anonymous European mainland country attempted to attack Hornchurch, London and other strategic targets in the south, whilst the fighters attempted to make contact and intercept them as near to the coast and as far away from their intended targets as possible. These exercises proved very useful in evolving defensive tactics and experimenting with new items of equipment as they came along. They were variously Northland v Southland, Eastland v Westland, Redland v Blueland, etc. At the start of the decade the potential enemy was purely mythical, but by the time that it drew to a close events that cast a dark cloud over Europe left no room for doubt as to whom the real enemy was going to be.

Practice for, and appearance at, the annual Air Display at RAF Hendon - originally known as the RAF Tournament - were other parts of the routine and the Hornchurch squadrons regularly performed with distinction at these events. Night Flying Trials were another regular event, as were the Empire Air Days, when the airfield was thrown open to the general public to enjoy aerial displays and fly-pasts from widely different aircraft and interesting exhibitions of static aircraft and air force equipment on the ground. Hornchurch broke the attendance record for Empire Air Days in the 1930s and that was solely from the people who paid to go in. Due to the location of the airfield along South End Road, thousands more regularly lined the roadside and watched for free, whilst scores of youngsters clambered over the wire perimeter fence to get a close up view of the Royal Air Force at work, Station personnel enjoyed the benefits of a very comfortable camp, but outside they enjoyed that most traditional of British institutions, the local pub, with The *Good Intent* on their doorstep and the *White Hart* and the 1680s built *King's Head* in the village. The Towers Cinema became an attraction in the thirties, as did forays to Barking, London and Southend, usually by train.

Towards the end of the decade improved aircraft with higher speeds and better armaments were coupled to a new system of aircraft control based on the wonderful new invention of Radio Direction Finding (RDF), later popularised by the name of Radar. The invention was the brainchild of Sir Robert Watson-Watt and, by virtue of towers established along the coast, gave eyes to the defenders long before enemy aircraft crossed the shore. With the Radar system linked to Sector Control Rooms in charge of the fighter squadrons, the defensive structure for World War II was finally put into position. Hornchurch became a Sector Station and its Controllers had operational command of the squadrons, not only at Hornchurch, but also, at various times, at Bradwell Bay, Eastchurch, Fairlop, Manston and Rochford.

The thirties were indeed a decade of revolutionary improvement in the design, performance and control of fighter aircraft and RAF Hornchurch was one of the leading test beds and exponents in the shop window of the RAF during this period.

1930 was full of interest at RAF Hornchurch. On 15th January, 54 Squadron re-formed and was also equipped with Siskins: it was scheduled to receive the new Bristol Bulldogs, but it was found to be necessary to make modifications to these aircraft before bringing them into service. The arrival of 54 Squadron made Hornchurch a two squadron station and a Station Headquarters was set up to accommodate the first non-squadron Commanding Officer to take control of the airfield in the person of Wing Commander E R Manning, who arrived on 4th April. 54 Squadron was destined to spend the next 12 years at Hornchurch, if one includes detachments to the satellite field at Rochford and to Catterick for 'rest periods' during the Battle of Britain. It was the squadron to serve the longest in the history of RAF

Hornchurch and came to be regarded as 'Hornchurch's Own'. It had disbanded at Yatesbury in 1919 and had not featured in the RAF's inventory in the meantime.

There were now over 400 airmen at Hornchurch and 111 Squadron was pioneering the experiments with radio-telephony in the air. 54 Squadron only had to wait three months for its Bristol Bulldogs, the first arriving on 8th April. They were to become a very familiar sight at Hornchurch over the following six years. The Bulldogs had an 18 mph advantage over the Siskins that they had displaced, but in size, power and armament were very similar. They were tidy looking biplanes with the usual open cockpit and they flew from Hornchurch until the autumn of 1936.

On 17th April Lieutenant Y Kobayashi of the Japanese Naval Air Service was flying a Siskin which burst into flames in mid-air. He had arrived at Hornchurch six weeks previously for a training course. He successfully baled out of the blazing aircraft, but was badly injured and had to be taken to the Victoria Cottage Hospital in Romford. His Siskin crashed near the airfield and burned out. Twelve days later there was another accident, when Flying Officer Byrne of 54 Squadron had the horrifying experience of seeing the wings of his Bulldog starting to disintegrate during a dive, probably due to the fracture of a bracing wire. Byrne baled out as the wings dropped off and was not hurt. One other less happy task of the station was to provide firing parties, pall bearers and escorts for military funerals and, on 26th July, Sergeant S Rutledge, RAF, a former member of the Old Sarum School of Army Co-operation, was laid to rest at Rainham, his home village, just south of the base.

In the 1930 Air Defence Exercises (Redland v Blueland) 54 Squadron did not participate, but 111 Squadron was detached to RAF Cranwell, the home of the RAF College and, on this occasion, the capital of 'Redland'. It was not all fun and games for the pilots. In their open cockpits they had to endure freezing conditions and the perpetual smell of oil. Even the routine act of getting off the ground and proceeding in the correct direction was not without occasional difficulties. The fighter pilot had to be pilot, navigator, wireless operator, flight engineer and air gunner rolled into one composite being.

On 28th July, 54 Squadron deployed to the Sutton Bridge Armament Camp for two weeks air gunnery and bombing, the complement of the squadron at this time being

S/Ldr W E Bryant	P/O N C Singer	Sgt A A Forbes
F/Lt F W Moxham	P/O K W Brett	Sgt N T Phillips
F/O C M Chambers	P/O D R de Sarigny	Sgt E G Watson
F/O E J Finnegan	Sgt S Trout	Sgt E Womphrey

On 1st October of this eventful year, the airship R-101 passed over the airfield at 2,000 feet, in full view of the station personnel and the local villagers. It was like a slow moving huge silver cigar and was in view for several minutes. It was 777 feet long, as big as an ocean-going liner. R-101 had been plagued by constant re-design and modifications and handled poorly even on this, its last successful flight.

Hornchurch Airfield entrance soon after re-opening, circa 1928

Three days later it slipped its moorings at RAF Cardington at 7.30 pm and encountered severe weather which gave it a buffeting and, in face of strong winds, slowed its ground speed to 25 mph. Six hours later it was struggling over France and losing height. It passed Beauvais Cathedral at the same height as the spire to crash a little further on at Allone. Only eight of the 54 people aboard survived the disaster and Lord Thompson, Secretary of State for Air, and Sir Sefton Brancker, Director of Civil Aviation, were amongst the dead. In the Lying in State at Westminster Hall, RAF Hornchurch provided 3 officers and 18 airmen as ceremonial guards. The permanent memorial to the victims is in the churchyard of the little parish church at Cardington. The disaster signalled the end for the development of large British airships and a decision was taken to break up the R-100 and abandon all further work.

Wreckage of airship R-101, 4 October, 1930

Squadron Leader E R Openshaw took command of 111 Squadron at the end of the year.

####

1931 saw 111 Squadron change from Siskins to Bulldogs early in the year and, for the next three years, RAF Hornchurch had two Bulldog squadrons regularly operating from the base. 111 continued to develop radio-telephony procedures in ground-to-air and air-to-air contacts with its new aircraft and prepared for an appearance at the Hendon Air Display.

Hendon had caught the public's imagination; it was a colourful happening and revealed the best of an increasingly efficient, progressive and disciplined service. It had started in 1920 and quickly became the highlight of the aviation year and a popular excursion for aviation buffs from a wide area. The 60,000 crowd who attended the first display grew steadily year by year.

In the Air Defence Exercises Nos 3 and 17 Squadrons brought their Bulldogs in to Hornchurch from RAF Upavon and 207 Squadron brought its Fairey 111F light bombers in from RAF Bircham Newton. These latter were small two seater bombers that had no difficulty in flying in and out of Hornchurch. In further trials this year, the two squadrons tested out new oxygen equipment and a new turn indicator was tested by Keith Park, now a Wing Commander.

Hornchurch had now been re-opened for three years and had settled down to the peacetime routine for fighter stations in the Royal Air Force.

####

1932 was a further consolidating year for the two squadrons and ran its now-familiar course of Air Defence Exercise, Hendon Air Display, Night Flying Trials, Armament Practice Camp and local Air Displays. At Hendon, 54 Squadron flew in formation and then looped, rolled, dived and even flew upside down, almost as one aircraft.

Squadron Leader S L Pope arrived to take over command of 54 Squadron and another arrival was Pilot Officer John Grandy, a fledgling pilot who had just earned his Wings at No. 5 Flying Training School at Sealand, Cheshire. 35 years later, as Sir John Grandy, he was appointed Chief of the Air Staff, the highest post in the Royal Air Force, a position he held for three years.

The Air Defence Exercise again showed that the fighters nearest the coast had little chance of making an interception. By the time the bombers had been 'observed' crossing the coast, it was too late, and they were well on their way to inland targets before ground controllers could get the fighters airborne. As a result, a lesson was taken from history and the squadrons were in future put on 'standing patrols' reverting to 1914-18 practice when dealing with the zeppelin campaign. Siting the 'standing patrols' entailed a certain amount of guesswork with respect to which part of a long coastline the bombers would choose to cross, but with the increasing use of radio-telephony, controllers were able to give the squadrons already patrolling at height, information on the position and course of in-coming bombers and the percentage of interceptions rose perceptibly. Radar itself was still a few years away.

54 Squadron Bulldogs at RAF Hornchurch, mid-thirties

74 Squadron Gauntlet in 1937. The 'Tiger' Squadron's stripes can be seen on the fuselage

In 1933 the first signs of things to come cast their shadows when Adolf Hitler became Chancellor of Germany late in the year and the Nazi Party became all-powerful in the Third Reich. The Royal Air Force was still a small body with less than 30,000 'regulars', backed by 12,000 reservists. The regulars numbered only a thousand more than they had after the reduction in the early 20s.

The Air Defence Exercises in July were the largest to date, with bombers attacking by night as well as by day and claiming the destruction of most of the fighters that managed to intercept them. The fighters, by contrast, naturally claimed that they had shot down most of the bombers. The fact that the umpires could not squeeze in with the fighters and had no option but to fly with the bombers might have had something to do with their siding with the bombers claim and over-ruling the fighters.

On 22 July Wing Commander C H Nicholas assumed control of the station and further changes saw new Commanding Officers of the squadrons; Squadron Leaders I M Rodney and E R Openshaw taking over 54 and 111 respectively. It was the last year that the two squadrons operated their Bulldogs in tandem from Hornchurch for the whole year.

The importance of the fighter stations was underlined when the Under Secretary of State for Air, Sir Philip Sassoon, visited Hornchurch on 2nd November; the first of many visits he was to pay.

From this year on the Air Defence Exercise participants would be in no doubt as to which country the mythical Eastland, Southland or Blueland actually represented.

On 14th October the German delegation walked out of the Geneva Disarmament Conference and Germany left the League of Nations. It was an ominous sign and, ten days later, Winston Churchill warned the House of Commons and the nation that Germany was secretly on its way to becoming the heaviest armed country in the world. This finally pushed a reluctant government off the fence and a further major expansion of the Royal Air Force was authorised.

Over the next three years the fighter defences were steadily expanded as new squadrons entered service. 1934 saw the break-up of the 54/111 squadron duo, 111 being posted on 12th July, to pastures new at RAF Northolt, to make way for the re-formation at Hornchurch of 65 Squadron, which had last seen service with Sopwith Camels at Yatesbury in 1919. 65 Squadron, led by Squadron Leader F O Soden, was equipped with Hawker Demons, two seater fighters with a pilot and an air gunner, which had first entered RAF service three years earlier. It was a variant of the Hawker Hart bomber and had little advantage over the Bulldog in speed and performance. In armament, however, it was, at last, a breakaway from the two synchronised Vickers guns firing forward that had been a feature of fighters since the Great War. The Demons still had two Vickers but, in addition, had a Lewis gun aft.

The air gunners were usually Leading Aircraftmen (LACS) and were drawn from ground tradesmen. The minimum rank of Sergeant for air crew personnel was still six years away and it was now possible for two crewmen in the same aircraft to be as far apart in rank as Squadron Leader (pilot) and Aircraftman 2nd Class (air gunner). The volunteers for air gunner duties received a little extra in the way of 'flight pay'.

Empire Air Day, in May, attracted 4,335 spectators. In the summer of 1934 a 54 Squadron Bulldog made a forced landing at Popards Farm, Rainham, one thousand yards from the flight path, but little damage was done to either aircraft or pilot.

The day after 111 Squadron moved out, the Prince of Wales arrived at a somewhat depleted Hornchurch by air and, after a short reception, left by car to visit the new Ford Factory at Dagenham. Fords had just moved their production line from Manchester to the Thames-side site and provided much employment for newcomers to the vast Becontree Housing Estate: London's 'carpet of bricks' was now creeping ominously closer to Hornchurch.

65 Squadron completed its re-formation and, from 1st August, it was again an operational force. On 27th September, the Chief of the Air Staff, Sir Edward Ellington, visited the station to inspect the two operational squadrons, 54 with its Bulldogs and 65 with its Demons.

1935 opened with more top visits, from Sir Philip Sassoon and Air Chief Marshal Sir Robert Brooke-Popham.

RAF Hornchurch benefited from the opening of a new railway station at Elm Park on 13th May; this was between the existing stations at Dagenham and Hornchurch and was on London Transport's electrified District Line, extended from Barking to Upminster in 1932. Air Force personnel usually patronised this station from now on and it also helped to increase the habit of locals and Londoners taking weekend strolls along South End Road, outside the perimeter fence in the hope of seeing the airfield in action and some take-offs and landings happening. To the man in the street flying was still a novelty and there were still a substantial number of people who had never seen an aircraft on the ground; to them the open view across the operational area of the airfield was an irresistible attraction. Motor car loads also arrived, occasionally in such numbers that parking restrictions had to be introduced.

In May, 54 Squadron was detached temporarily to RAF Roborough, near Plymouth, for affiliation with the Southampton Flying Boats of 204 Squadron, based at Mount Batten. The flying boat squadron had made a formation flight around the Baltic two years earlier.

The 1935 Air Defence Exercises (Northland v Southland) took on an added significance in view of events in Europe and again envisaged London being attacked by formations of bombers. 65 Squadron remained at Hornchurch, but 54 Squadron moved to RAF Kenley for this exercise. The lessons of the previous year had been learned and, as Southland bombers approached the coast, the fighters, already patrolling at height, moved in accordance with the Controller's instructions to intercept them, and their place on patrol was taken by other squadrons taking off and climbing to height. Three quarters of Southland's bombers were successfully intercepted by superior numbers of fighters. The standing patrols, radio-telephony and plotting tables had proved their worth.

On 4th October the Abyssinian War started and created a crisis in the Middle East, resulting in the movement of many RAF squadrons to the area. 65 Squadron technically remained at Hornchurch, but was reduced to a cadre and lost most of its personnel; it was not restored to full strength again until July, 1936.

Just before Christmas a new Station Commander arrived - none other than Wing Commander A S G Lee, who, as a young Lieutenant in the Royal Flying Corps, had served at Suttons Farm with 46 Squadron.

###

On 2nd February, 1936, a sombre note was struck as the Station Commander, Adjutant and a party of airmen attended the Memorial Service for King George V held at St Andrews Church.

The Air Defence Exercises were held for five days in mid-February, when Ford Motor Works, and RAF Hornchurch, were 'targets' for the bombers.

1936 was an exciting year for technical development in the RAF: the first Radar Stations opened in Suffolk, at Orfordness and Bawdsey Manor; they opened in great secrecy and few, outside of those who needed to know, knew of their existence. Bawdsey Manor finally closed down in March, 1991.

On 5th March the first Spitfire flew its first test flight from Eastleigh, near the Supermarine Works at Southampton. It was not then known as the Spitfire, simply by a production number. This test flight signalled the beginning of the end of biplane fighters in the RAF and the change over from twin synchronised Vickers to eight Browning machine guns firing from the wings.

At the Empire Air Day held that spring Hornchurch attracted a crowd of 14,750 spectators, a new record, and a further 10,000 had a free look 'over the wire' or lining South End Road. Music was provided by an Army band and the Dagenham Girl Pipers. A Short Scion - a two engined high wing transport - took off and landed innumerable times, giving short flights for spectators.

In June 54 Squadron started to say 'good-bye' to its Bulldogs after six years of faithful service. The Bulldogs seemed reluctant to go and the last not leaving until September. 65 Squadron similarly converted from Demons to Gauntlets.

It was in this year that the 'Air Defence of Great Britain' (a clumsy title for an administration) was abolished and replaced by four, much more understandable, functional Commands - Bomber, Coastal, Fighter and Training. They were to become familiar names and remained unchanged for 30 years, except for a short period in WWII when Fighter Command reverted to 'Air Defence of Great Britain'. Hornchurch was one of the foremost fighter stations to come under control of Fighter Command when its headquarters was established at Bentley Priory.

Pilot Officer Donald Finlay, who arrived for duty with 54 Squadron on 16th February, was appointed as Captain of the British team in the Berlin Olympic Games. He had won the hurdles at the AAA Championship at the White City for five consecutive years. In the Olympics he won the Silver Medal, behind the American, Forest Towers, in the 110 metres hurdles, breaking the British record in so doing with a time of 14.6 seconds. He also helped Hornchurch win the Air Council Cup and

ADGB Cup at Uxbridge.

Additional buildings were now complete at Hornchurch, including a third 'C' type hangar in the space that had been left for it and an improved watch office and, from this period on, the three years grace that lay ahead were filled with new tactics, intensive training and an ever-growing sense of the urgency that was needed to overcome all the difficulties of defending the urban sprawl of London.

To add to the encroachment of suburban London a 150 foot high chimney stack was erected at St George's Hospital, just 800 yards from the airfield and night flying had to be banned for six months from August, until the chimney was adequately lit. This chimney can be seen in the background of many of the wartime photographs taken at RAF Hornchurch.

At the end of 1936 Sir Hugh Dowding, the Air Officer Commander in Chief of Fighter Command, visited Hornchurch to inaugurate the new Sector Operations Room which, from its inception, raised the status of Hornchurch to one of the seven Sector airfields in 11 Group, Fighter Command.

Squadron Leader C A Bouchier visited the College of Arms to agree the design of an official squadron badge for 54 Squadron. The finalised badge officially described as a 'lion rampant semée de lys', symbolised the Squadron's service in France. The lion rampant in blue represented the Coat of Arms of Flanders and the fleur de lys in gold that of France, the fleur de lys being 'powdered' upon the lion. The tongue and claws were in red, symbolising the Squadron's offensive spirit and the service colour marking of the Squadron.

54 Squadron

65 Squadron was also entitled to a squadron badge at this time and that designed by the Chester Herald, Mr J D Heaton-Armstrong, was approved by King George VI. It depicts 15 swords and a lion passant. The swords commemorated the shooting down of 15 enemy aircraft by 65 Squadron on the Western Front on 4th November, 1918.

The badges of the two Squadrons were presented to their Commanding Officers, Squadron Leaders C A Bouchier (54) and C F Grace (65) by Air Vice Marshal Leslie Gossage, the AOC of No. 11 Group Fighter Command at a Ceremonial Parade in January, 1937.

Practice for the Hendon Air Display in June started in earnest. 54 Squadron in March, 1937, comprised -

Commanding Officer S/Ldr C A Bouchier
Adjutant P/O S Gemmell

    'A' Flight   'B' Flight

P/O R C Love	Sgt H Stringer	F/O D O Finlay	Sgt H Hastings
P/O P E Warcup	Sgt S Richens	P/O K R Russell	Sgt J Phillips
P/O P A Burnell-Phillips	F/Sgt D Stannard	P/O L H Schwind	Sgt V Penford

Only Sergeants Phillips and Hastings were still in the Squadron at the out-break of war.

There was another switch around of aircraft as 54 and 65 both converted from Gauntlets to Gloster Gladiators and 74 Squadron converted from Hawker Demons to Gloster Gauntlets. The first Gladiator was collected from Gloster Aircraft Works on 27th April and most surplus Gauntlets had been flown to other squadrons by the end of May. The loss of 74 Squadron's Demons meant that the air gunners who had been at Hornchurch for four years and accompanied 74 Squadron on its sorties were now redundant and they were either posted out to other squadrons or reverted to their ground trades.

On 25th May, a 74 Squadron Gauntlet unaccountably dived into the small civilian airfield used by Romford Flying Club at Maylands, Harold Wood, and the pilot, Sergeant Boxall, was killed.

At the Coronation of His Majesty King George VI NCOs and airmen from Hornchurch joined those lining the processional route to Westminster Abbey and, nearer home, three aircraft carried out a mock night attack in conjunction with search-lights on Romford Stadium, as part of Romford's Coronation Day celebrations.

At the Empire Air Day 17,073 spectators paid for admission, while the usual non-payers lined the road outside or made unauthorised entrance somewhere around the perimeter fence. Air Defence Exercises concentrated on the cramming of new tactics and the Radar Stations at Bawdsey, Dover and Canewdon were all involved. These exercises put the new control system to test, but, even though interceptions increased, the biplane fighters were finding it increasingly difficult to outpace the bombers, particularly the new Blenheims coming into service.

Distinguished visitors included the Maharajah of Nepal, accompanied by the Nepalese Prime Minister, Nagendra Men Singh. Sir Philip Sassoon, Viscount Swinton and Air Chief Marshal Sir Hugh Dowding also visited, while in the autumn a high ranking delegation from Germany descended from the skies; it was a visit from former 1914-18 adversaries in the form of Luftwaffe Generals Milch, Stumpff and Udet, accompanied by the German Air Attaché, Major Polte, who arrived on 23rd October.

They saw no eight gun monoplane fighters at Hornchurch, but rather the Gloster Gladiator biplanes which, with a maximum speed of 254 mph, were out-paced by the Luftwaffe's new Dornier and Heinkel bombers. They were met at Hornchurch by Air Vice Marshal Sir Victor Goddard and inspected the squadrons escorted by an interpreter. When they reached Pilot Officer Robert Stanford-Tuck's aircraft (65 Squadron) General Milch stuck his head into the cockpit of the Gladiator and showed a keen interest in the new gunsight. This interest was very professional; four years

Bristol Bulldog of 54 Squadron, RAF Hornchurch, after making a forced landing at Popards Farm, Rainham. Summer, 1934

54 Squadron lined up for Defence Exercises, August, 1939

earlier he had researched into the subject of potential British industrial targets in time of war and the report of his committee, *Studie Blau*, provided the detailed information that formed the basis of the Luftwaffe's attacks during World War II. The use of interpreters had led the German delegation to believe that their British hosts, including Air Vice Marshal Goddard, did not speak any German. In fact he did and recalls that, when they drove through London's East End in a limousine after leaving Hornchurch, General Milch looked out of the windows and said, "*Vas fur ein Ziel* [What a bombing target]". The faces of the other Germans creased with embarrassment when they realised from his facial expression that AVM Goddard was not perhaps as ignorant of the German language as Milch had assumed.

Armistice Day Church Parades were another regular feature in the Hornchurch calendar and, this year, Squadron Leader Bouchier and one hundred airmen took part in the British Legion Parade to St Andrews Church, where a service was held at the War Memorial and then on to the Towers Cinema, where a second service was held.

Personnel changes this year included Wing Commander M B Frew becoming Station Commander and Squadron Leader D Cooke assuming control of 65 Squadron.

1938 was marked with three unfortunate accidents.

On 18th January Flying Officer Robert Stanford Tuck, Sergeant Geoffrey Gaskell and Flying Officer Adrian Hope-Boyd were flying in formation; when over Uckfield, Sussex, they started to move into line astern, in the order of Hope-Boyd, followed by Gaskell, with Tuck bringing up the rear. They struck a gust of rough air, resulting in the heavy slipstream from Hope-Boyd throwing Gaskell over, with Tuck's propeller shearing through the fuselage of Gaskell's Gladiator. Sergeant Gaskell was still in his cockpit when his aircraft crashed at Ridgewood, just outside Uckfield. Stanford Tuck, who was able to bale out, was kept in hospital for a week and returned to Hornchurch with a limp and a permanent scar on the side of his face. Stanford Tuck had, by this time, earned a well deserved reputation as one of the several potentially brilliant young pilots in the three squadrons at Hornchurch. He was particularly good friends in 65 Squadron with John Welford, Jack Kennedy, George Proudman and 'Chad' Giddings, none of whom survived the war.

Later that spring 65 Squadron was involved in another collision when three Gladiators piloted by Flight Lieutenant L C Bicknell, Pilot Officer P R Austin-Sparkes and Pilot Officer A H Boyd were flying near North Weald, when they touched wings. Bicknell managed to bale out unhurt, but Austin-Sparkes was killed: Boyd was not involved in the collision.

Finally, on 11th June, Sergeant Marsh was killed in a flying accident whilst over the Isle of Sheppey.

Visitors to Hornchurch in 1938 included the Sultan of Muscat and Oman, Sir Kingsley Wood, the Rt Hon Leslie Hore-Belisha and one of the most famous female aviators of the day, Jean Batten, who arrived on 28th May, Empire Air Day, in her famous Percival Gull and autographed programmes. It teemed with rain until 3.30 pm and the attendance was reduced to 11,230 paying spectators, although they were thrilled by the sight of three Gladiators, in their 'swan song' air display, flying in formation, upside down and not too many feet above the ground, linked together by 20 feet of toughened rubber. The Hawker Hurricane made the first of its appearances at Hornchurch in this display.

Hornchurch was, by now, indisputably Fighter Command's 'shop window' to show off distinguished visitors, from home and abroad particularly those from countries perceived as potential allies in the conflict that seemed to be looming ahead.

The Air Defence Exercises, held in August (Eastland v Westland) were the largest to date and more valuable lessons were learned. It was a real test for the Radar Stations and Sector Rooms working together and the results indicated that 10% of the 'enemy' bombers would have been destroyed - an unacceptable rate of loss in the long term.

1st August, 1938, was a Bank Holiday and, on the following Friday, Hornchurch was brought to a state of 'Immediate Readiness for War'. All personnel were recalled from leave and the Operations Room was manned for 24 hours a day. Although the squadron pilots flew over the secret Radar Station at Canewdon, they were unaware of the implication of its masts.

The Gloster Gladiator was a docile and gentle aircraft and a superb machine for aerobatics. In the hands of 54 Squadron, under the leadership of Flight Lieutenant P E Warcup, the Gladiators won the 'Aerobatic Cup' before a gathering of Members of Parliament at Northolt. But, in truth, they belonged to an earlier era of aerial combat and were rather out of their class by 1939.

The continuing rise of Adolf Hitler and Nazi Germany took another step in March when, after the resignation of Austrian Chancellor Schuschnigg amid threats from Hitler, the German Army crossed the border. The *Anschluss* annexing Austria to the Third Reich met with little resistance, but served as another warning to the West of what was to come. Amidst wild celebrations, Hitler announced that the Third Reich would last for a thousand years. General Stumpff was now Chief of the Air Staff and, in preparation for the *Anschluss*, he arranged for an operational plan to be drawn up for the Luftwaffe, in case the British should intervene.

With the conquest of Austria under his belt, Hitler turned his attention to Czechoslovakia, where, in the Sudetenland, there was a large population of German descent. 15,000 of these demonstrated after the annexation of Austria, giving Hitler the pretext he needed.

It is a matter of history that the Prime Minister, Neville Chamberlain, was given one of the greatest ovations ever accorded to an English statesman when he alighted at Croydon after returning from Munich and waved the agreement of a peaceful solution to the Czechoslovakian crisis. It ceded Bohemia & Moravia to Germany, being signed by Chamberlain for Britain, Edouard Daladier (France), Benito Mussolini (Italy) and Hitler (Germany). To thunderous applause he said, "I believe it is peace for our time." Cynics were sceptical, but at least it gave Britain a further year in which to prepare. There can be little doubt that the Gladiator biplane fighters, with which nearly all fighter squadrons were then equipped, would have been swept from the sky by the Luftwaffe Me109s. In that year the stock of Spitfires and Hurricanes was increased sixfold from 90 to over 500.

The first outstanding event in the epic year of 1939 was the re-equipment of all three squadrons with the Supermarine Spitfire. 14th February was an historic day at the base when the first was flown in for use by 74 Squadron. In an intensive operation spread over the following eight weeks, ending early in April, 74, 54 and 65 Squadrons changed from Gloster Gladiators to Spitfires (in that order).

65 Squadron, the last to change, collected its first Spitfire from Eastleigh on 21st March and Flight Lieutenant A N Jones piloted it to Hornchurch. The first squadrons in the Royal Air Force to have received Spitfires were 19 and 66 at Duxford and 41 at Catterick. The three Hornchurch squadrons were the fourth, fifth and sixth in the RAF to be re-equipped: the transition was effected without fuss and with few problems. The pilots enthused and Alan Deere gave an early indication of the concentration that was needed. He climbed to 27,000 feet through thick cloud and spent so much time watching his instruments that he forgot to switch his oxygen on. He went unconscious and, after an uncontrolled dive of four miles, he found his senses in time to level out and regain his composure just above the sea.

The Supermarine Company, which produced the Spitfires at Woolston, near Southampton, merged fully with Vickers (Aviation), Ltd, in 1939, as the 25 years of the biplane fighter in the service of the Royal Air Force was drawing to its close. It was to be a few more years before the last passed out of service and Hornchurch flew many of its Gladiators up to Turnhouse to equip the reservists of 603 (City of Edinburgh) Squadron of the Auxiliary Air Force, who were still flying Hawker Hinds.

Another 'new' aircraft was seen when the Imperial Airways air liner *Hannibal* arrived with 22 Army officers on board. It had been the first of eight Handley Page 42/45 biplanes to be delivered to Imperial Airways eight years earlier and operated regularly on the London-Paris route. It was probably the biggest and certainly the first four engined machine to land at Hornchurch.

The arrival of the Spitfires boosted the attendance at the Empire Air Day to a record 45,000 paying spectators, probably 60,000 in total, all anxious to see the famous new aircraft which had revolutionised Fighter Command.

In the Air Defence Exercises 25 Squadron (Blenheims) moved to Hornchurch from Hawkinge. A new feature of this year's exercise at Hornchurch was a broadcasting system, manufactured by 'Tannoy' which was installed to enable the Controller's instructions to go out across the airfield to all dispersals, crew rooms and hangars. It proved of great value and became standard practice at all Fighter Command airfields. So well known did the loudspeaker system become that it was universally known by the manufacturer's name 'Tannoy', in

The WRAF, now known as WAAF (Women's Auxiliary Air Force) was re-formed on 28th June: it was a service that peaked at 175,000 in 1944, with girls who did valiant service on barrage balloon sites, in Fighter Command Control Rooms and at Sector Stations, as motor transport drivers, cooks, clerks, wireless operators and several other trades. Their jobs were not without risk and WAAFs worked and died in the service of their country.

much the same way as 'Hoover' covers a multitude of vacuum cleaners.

In August, 1939, Sgt Cyril David Gower, flying in formation over Grays, was caught in the slipstream of Flight-Lieutenant Wilfred Cressey, commanding 74 Squadron, and crashed to his death in the grounds of John Henry Burrows Intermediate School.

Prominent visitors this year included Major Horn, now a veteran, who had led 54 Squadron in the 1914-18 War and was in command when it went to France.

The Hornchurch squadrons were widely dispersed around the perimeter of the airfield as summer turned to autumn, causing the pilots some discomfort, but leaving them in no doubt as to their importance to the war effort and, in particular, to the defence of London. The dispersal underlined the feeling in Fighter Command that the greatest danger to Spitfires lay in attack from the air against aircraft on the tarmac.

Many individuals who were to become household names throughout the British Isles had arrived as fledgling pilots in the past few years. Into Hornchurch came 'Sailor' Malan, Robert Roland Stanford Tuck, 'Paddy' Treacy and Donald Finlay in 1936; James Leathart in 1937; Alan Deere, John Freeborn, Johnny Allen, Basil 'Wonky' Way and Charles Kingcombe in 1938; and George Gribble, Desmond McMullen, Derek Dowding (the son of the Air Officer Commander in Chief Fighter Command) and John Mungo-Park in 1939, to name a few. Other great names were to arrive after the war started.

Sixty Spitfire pilots were now based at Hornchurch and destiny had brought each and every one of them to this place at this time to re-ignite the honourable endeavours of the humble grass field from 1915 and start it on an even greater struggle to finally cement its place in history.

Twenty-two of the sixty would make the supreme sacrifice for their country before the war was over. And this was only from the three squadrons that started the war. Add the many squadrons that arrived at Hornchurch after 54, 65 and 74 departed and a total of 481 were to die from the Hornchurch Sector in the conflict.

A great sense of urgency and expectancy prevailed as Hitler marched into Poland on 1st September and every ear in the nation was tuned to a radio on 3rd September when the Prime Minister made his broadcast saying, "I am speaking to you from the Cabinet Room at Number 10, Downing Street. This morning the British Ambassador in Berlin handed the German Government a final note stating that, unless we heard from them by eleven o'clock that they were prepared at once to withdraw their troops from Poland, a state of war would exist between us. I have to tell you that no such undertaking has been received and that consequently this country is at war with Germany. May God bless you all. May He defend the right. It is evil things that we shall be fighters against - brute force, bad faith, injustice, oppression and persecution. And against these, right will prevail."

65 Squadron pilots, RAF Hornchurch, 1939: Gordon Olive, Norman Jones, George Proudman, Sam Saunders, Jack Kennedy, John Welford, 'Chad' Giddings

65 Squadron Spitfires flying from Hornchurch

PILOTS IN OPERATIONAL SQUADRONS AT RAF HORNCHURCH AT THE OUTBREAK OF WORLD WAR II

S/Ldr C E Sampson	F/O W E Measures	P/O J B Nicholas	Sgt G Bushell *
S/Ldr D Cooke *	F/O A W Ridler	P/O G V Proudman *	Sgt J Davis
S/Ldr H M Pearson	F/O R R S Tuck #	P/O D S Ross *	Sgt Edwards
F/Lt R S Blake	F/O W H Walker	P/O Temple-Harris	Sgt J L Flinders
F/Lt J A Leathart	F/O F H Welford *	P/O Thom	Sgt P S Hayes *
F/Lt A G Malan	P/O J L Allen	P/O B A Way *	Sgt Hawken
F/Lt C G Olive	P/O Browne	P/O R E West *	Sgt J R Kilner
F/Lt B A Saunders	P/O Chambers *	P/O R G Wigg	Sgt R R McPherson *
F/Lt W P Treacy *	P/O A C Deere	P/O S B Grant	Sgt E Makins
F/O A H Boyd	P/O D H Dowding	F/Sgt G W Couzens	Sgt P F Morfill
F/O V Byrne #	P/O J C Freeborn	F/Sgt W H Franklin	Sgt E A Mould *
F/O H S Giddings *	P/O G B Kingcombe	F/Sgt D Hastings	Sgt J Phillips #
F/O D S Hoare #	P/O D G Gribble *	F/Sgt E Mayne	Sgt S Perfect
F/O J C Kennedy *	P/O J D McKenzie *	F/Sgt N T Phillips	Sgt W M Skinner #
F/O Mainwaring	P/O J C Mungo-Park	Sgt F Buckland *	Sgt P H Tew

Of the sixty above, twenty-two were killed in action (marked *), while five others came down in enemy occupied territory and were made prisoners of war (marked #).

AIRCRAFT AT RAF HORNCHURCH, 1928-1939

	Siskin IIIa	Bulldog	Demon	Gauntlet	Gladiator	Spitfire 1
Manufacturer	Armstrong Whitworth Aircraft Ltd	Bristol Aeroplane Co. Ltd	Hawker Aircraft Ltd	Gloster Aircraft Co. Ltd	Gloster Aircraft Co. Ltd.	Supermarine Division of Vickers Armstrong Ltd.
Entered RAF service	Mar 27	Jun 29	Mar 31	May 35	Feb 37	Jul 38
At RAF Hornchurch	Apr 28	Apr 30	Aug 34	Aug 36	Apr 37	Mar 39
Until	Dec 30	Sep 36	Apr 37	Jun 37	Apr 39	Mar 44■
Engine	Armstrong Siddeley Jaguar	Bristol Jupiter	Rolls Royce Kestrel	Bristol Mercury	Bristol Mercury	Rolls Royce Merlin
Horse power	450	490	485	645	840	1030
Wing span	33'2"	33'11"	37'3"	32'9"	32'3 "	36'10"
Wing area	293 sqft	306 sqft	348 sqft	315 sqft	323 sqft	242 sqft
Length	25'4"	25'2"	29'7"	26'2"	27'5"	29'11"
Height	10'2"	9'10"	10'5"	10'4"		10'4"
Weight	2061 lb	2412 lb	3336 lb	2775 lb	3450 lb	5332 lb
Max speed	156 mph	174 mph	182 mph	230 mph	253 mph	355 mph
Ceiling	27,000 ft	27,000 ft	27,500 ft	33,500 ft	33,000 ft	34,000 ft
Armament	Twin Vickers	Twin Vickers	Twin Vickers Fwd; Lewis Gun Aft	Twin Vickers	Four Brownings	Eight Brownings
Remarks			2 seater pilot/Air Gunner	Last open cockpit fighter	Last bi-plane fighter	

■Spitfires seen at H'ch until 1959, but not in operational Fighter Squadrons after 1944

PRE-WORLD WAR II PERSONALITIES AT HORNCHURCH (1928-1939)

ALLEN, John Laurence
'Johnny' Allen joined 54 Squadron at Hornchurch on 5th December, 1938 and, on 21st May, 1940, he scored the Squadron's first victory over Dunkirk. Two days later he teamed up with Alan Deere to escort Squadron Leader James Leathart - flying an unarmed Magister - to the besieged Calais Marck airfield to retrieve Squadron Leader F L White, the Commanding Officer of 74 Squadron, who had been shot down and was stranded there. Between them Allen and Deere destroyed three Me109s and damaged three others during this gallant mission. On 25th May he baled out over the sea and was rescued by a destroyer. He received the DFC from King George VI at Hornchurch on 27th June. On 24th July, 1940, his aircraft was hit and the engine cut out intermittently. He crashed at Cliftonville, while trying to make Manston, and was killed, aged 24. He is buried at Margate Cemetery.

DEERE, Alan Christopher
'Al' Deere, a New Zealander, joined 54 Squadron at Hornchurch in September, 1938, flying Gladiators. With Johnny Allen he assisted in the Calais Marck rescue and received the DFC from King George VI at Hornchurch on 27th June, 1940. He took command of 602 (City of Glasgow) Squadron at Catterick in January, 1941, and visited the United States of America on a liaison tour in 1942. In 1943 he was Wing Leader at Biggin Hill and became Station Commander there in July, 1945. He later commanded the Polish Fighter Wing flying Mustangs at Andrews Field (Braintree) before becoming Station Commander at Duxford. In post-war years he was ADC to the Queen in 1962 and retired from the RAF on 12th December, 1967, as an Air Commodore. His autobiography *Nine Lives* devoted much attention to his time at Hornchurch. He died in 1995, aged 77.

DOWDING, Derek Hugh Tremenheere
Derek Dowding, the son of the AOC in C Fighter Command, joined 74 Squadron at Hornchurch in July, 1939, and served with distinction in the Dunkirk operations and the Battle of Britain. He left 74 Squadron in August, 1940, and later became a Flight Commander with 135 Squadron and served as a Test Pilot in the Middle East. He remained in the RAF after the war and retired on 17th November, 1956, as a Wing Commander.

FINLAY, Donald
P/O Donald Finlay joined 54 Squadron at Hornchurch on 16th March, 1936, the year he captained the British Team at the Berlin Olympics and took the Silver Medal in the 110 metres hurdles. He left Hornchurch in 1937, but returned in 1940 to command first 54 Squadron and then 41. In August, 1941, he commanded 608 Squadron at Montecorvino and, as a Group Captain, was Senior Air Officer in North Africa. He served in the RAF Engineering Branch after the war and retired on 23rd February, 1959. He was involved in a serious road accident, which impaired his mobility and died in 1970 aged 61.

FREEBORN, John Connell
John Freeborn joined 74 Squadron on 29th October, 1938, flying Gloster Gauntlets. He served with distinction in the Dunkirk operations and the Battle of Britain. After serving as an Instructor at Hawarden he became a Flight Commander with 602 (City of Glasgow) Squadron at Skeabrae. He went on to command 118 Squadron at Coltishall in 1943/4. He left the RAF as a Squadron Leader in 1946.

FREW, Matthew Brown
Matthew Frew was Station Commander at Hornchurch in 1937-38. He remained in the RAF in a variety of posts, retiring as Air Vice Marshal Sir Matthew Frew in 1948. He lived in Pretoria, South Africa, and died on 28th May, 1974, at the age of 79.

GRANDY, John
John Grandy joined 54 Squadron at Hornchurch on 29th August, 1932. In 1935 he was posted to Hendon, in 1940 commanded 249 Squadron and then the Training Wing at Debden. In 1942 he was Wing Commander Flying at Coltishall and Station Commander at Duxford, then going to the Middle East in 1943, before commanding a Wing of Dakotas in South East Asia Command. After the war he was Air Attaché in Brussels and later commanded Task Force 'Grapple', the nuclear tests in the Pacific. He went on to become Commander in Chief Germany, 1961-63, and Air Officer Commanding Bomber Command, 1963-65. John Grandy succeeded to the top post - Chief of the Air Staff - in 1967, holding the post four years. Marshal of the Royal Air Force Sir John Grandy was appointed Governor of Gibraltar and then Constable and Governor of Windsor Castle in 1978.

GRIBBLE, Dorian George

George Gribble joined 54 Squadron just before the war started. He destroyed two Me109s over Dunkirk: on 25th May he was shot up and made a forced landing on Dunkirk Beach, returning to England in one of the 'little ships'. He shot down six Me109s in the Battle of Britain, shared in several others and was one of the finest pilots in the Squadron. On 4th June, 1941, he suffered engine failure during combat, crashed into the North Sea and drowned. He was 21.

KINGCOMBE, Charles Brian Fabris

Brian Kingcombe joined 65 Squadron at Hornchurch on 30th July, 1938 and, after serving with the Squadron in the early days of the Dunkirk operation, he was posted to 92 Squadron at Northolt. After an outstanding record in the Battle of Britain, he led the Kenley Wing. In 1942 he led 244 Wing from Malta and, following the invasion of Italy, was promoted Group Captain. He remained in the RAF, serving post-war in Austria, Egypt and Italy, before he was invalided out on 26th January, 1954.

LEATHART, James Anthony

James Leathart, nick-named 'Prof' because of his academic nature, joined 54 Squadron on 27th November, 1937, flying Gladiators. He served with distinction during the Dunkirk operations and the Battle of Britain and piloted the Magister which retrieved S/Ldr F L White from Calais on 23rd May, 1940. He assumed command of the Squadron on 25th May and received the DSO from King George VI at Hornchurch on 28th June. After leaving Hornchurch he served at the Air Ministry and Flying Training Command before becoming CO of 406 (RCAF) Squadron at Acklington. Later he went to the Middle East as Wing Commander - Air Tactics and returned to England in July, 1943, preparing for the invasion of Europe. He landed on a French beach on D-Day with night fighting radar equipment. James Leathart had a series of appointments post-war, including HQ 12 Group, 1959-61, Air Ministry, 1961-62. He retired as an Air Commodore in October, 1962.

LEE, Arthur Stanley Gould.

Station Commander 1935-38. See also page ??.

MCMULLEN, Desmond Annesley Peter

Another pilot who joined 54 Squadron in September, 1939. Desmond McMullen destroyed a Me110 over Dunkirk with two Me109 'probables'. In the Battle of Britain he shot down 13 Luftwaffe aircraft. He had further successes with other squadrons, including 141 with its ill-fated Defiants, returning to Hornchurch as a Squadron Leader in June, 1942, with 64 Squadron. He then led 65 Squadron at Gravesend and 324 Wing in North Africa. He remained in the RAF post-war and retired as a Wing Commander in 1957. Desmond McMullen died on 1st July, 1985, at the age of 67.

MALAN, Adolph Gysbert

A South African, known to all as 'Sailor' because of earlier naval service, joined 74 Squadron at Hornchurch on 20th December, 1936, flying Hawker Demons. A superb pilot, he was a Flight Commander by 1937 and was another with a distinguished record in the Dunkirk operations and the Battle of Britain. He led the Biggin Hill Wing in 1941 and, in a period of three weeks, destroyed twelve Me109s. He went to the USA on a liaison visit and, on return, took command first at Sutton Bridge and then at Biggin Hill. On D-Day he escorted Albemarles, towing gliders full of troops. 'Sailor' Malan left the RAF in 1946 as a Group Captain. He died in South Africa on 17 September, 1963, aged 52.

MANNING, Edye Rolleston

Wing Commander E R Manning was Station Commander from 1930-3, retiring from the RAF in 1935. He was recalled at the outbreak of war and served in Malaya, Burma and India. He retired for the second time as an Air Commodore in 1945 and lived in Sydney, Australia. He died on 26 April, 1957, at the age of 68.

MUNGO-PARK, John Colin

John Mungo-Park joined 74 Squadron in September, 1939, and was another who distinguished himself over Dunkirk and in the Battle of Britain. He became a Flight Commander in September, 1940, and took command of the squadron six months later. On 27th June, 1941, during an offensive sweep over Europe, he was shot down and killed, and is buried in Belgium. He was 23 years old.

PARK, Keith Rodney

Arguably Hornchurch's most famous 'old boy', Keith Park commanded the station and also 111 Squadron, when it re-opened on 1st April, 1928. In an outstanding RAF career he went on to command 11 Group (which controlled Hornchurch) that bore the brunt of the burden in the Battle of Britain. He then commanded Air Headquarters Egypt and Malta, was Air Officer Commanding Middle East in 1944 and Allied Air Commander in Chief in South East Asia Command in 1945-46. As Air Chief Marshal Sir Keith Rodney Park he retired to his native New Zealand and died at Auckland on 5th February, 1975, aged 85.

PEARSON, Herbert McDonald

S/Ldr H M Pearson commanded 54 Squadron at Hornchurch 1938-1940, seeing the Squadron through from Gladiators to Spitfires. He continued in Fighter Command, seeing further service in France, Belgium and Germany. In post-war years he was Air Attaché in Peru, at the Air Ministry and Commanding Officer at Kai Tak, Hong Kong, in 1951-53. His last position was at HQ Allied Air Forces, Central Europe, 1953-55. He retired as an Air Commodore in 1955.

SLATTER, Leonard Horatio

S/Ldr L H Slatter commanded 111 Squadron and RAF Hornchurch, 1929-30, then flying Siskins. He had earlier commanded the RAF High Speed Flight and the Schneider Trophy Team that competed in Vienna in 1927. He flew solo to South Africa in 1929, a remarkable feat at that time. After leaving Hornchurch he was the Senior RAF Officer on the Aircraft Carrier HMS *Courageous* 1932-1935 and commanded the RAF in the Eritrea Campaign 1940-41. Leonard Slatter later commanded 15 Group and was Air Officer Commander in Chief Coastal Command 1945-48. As Air Chief Marshal Leonard Slatter he retired to Bedfordshire and died on 14th April, 1961, at the age of 66.

TREACY, 'Paddy' or 'Treacle'

Paddy Treacy joined 74 Squadron in 1936 and was a Flight Commander at the time of the Dunkirk evacuation. On 27th Slay, 1940, in company with the Hornchurch squadrons fighting over Dunkirk and Boulogne, he was shot down. He evaded capture and eventually made his way back to England, but was killed later in the war.

TUCK, Robert Roland Stanford

Stanford Tuck joined 65 Squadron on 5th August, 1936. His escapes from two collisions and other hazardous situations were such that his adventures were christened 'Tuck's luck'. He was one of the first pilots in the RAF to fly the Supermarine Spitfire and he too had a distinguished record over Dunkirk and in the Battle of Britain. He received the DFC from King George VI at Hornchurch on 28th June, 1940. He later commanded 257 Squadron at Debden and the Duxford Wing and was another of the pilots on liaison trips to the USA. He then commanded the Biggin Hill Wing. On 28th January, 1942, he was shot down by anti-aircraft fire and was in a prisoner of war camp until 1st February, 1945, when he escaped with Flt/Lt Z Kustrzynski: they made their way through Poland to Moscow, where the Ambassador arranged for their return by sea to Southampton. His biography *Fly for your life* was written by Larry Forester and was a best seller. Robert Stanford Tuck retired from the RAF in 1949 as a Wing Commander and became a mushroom farmer in Kent. He died on 5th May, 1987, aged 70.

WAY, Basil Hugh

P/O Basil Way, universally known as 'Wonky', because of his slim, tall and leaning stature, joined 54 Squadron in December, 1938, towards the end of the Gladiator regime. An excellent pilot he became a Flight Commander in Slay, 1940, and had several successes to his credit. On 25th July he shot down an Me109 - his eighth victory - but was, in turn, immediately set upon by a large formation of Me109s. He bravely fought back, but was hopelessly outgunned and was shot down into the Channel. 'Wonky' Way was 22 years old.

De Haviland Tiger Moth Training Aircraft

'ALLEGRO'
THE 'PHONEY WAR' AND THE DUNKIRK EVACUATION

With practice, training, procedures and tactics behind them, the Hornchurch squadrons were all geared up with the highest quality men and aircraft, waiting for the expected onslaught of the Luftwaffe. Eyes were constantly turned to the skies and all personnel were at a state of instant readiness. 1,500 airmen waited for the aerial shooting war to start in earnest. The Blenheims of the Auxiliary Air Force 600 (City of London) Squadron were activated for full time service and arrived at Hornchurch hours before the declaration of war. Primarily intended for night fighting, they changed base frequently between Hornchurch, Rochford, Manston and Northolt over the next year. Until December, 1939, the Squadron was commanded by Viscount Carlow, it was then taken over by Squadron Leader J Wells. It was regularly deployed over the Thames Estuary, experimenting with airborne Radar and attempting to counter the Heinkel 115s that were regularly dropping mines in the Estuary.

The actual sequence of events after the outbreak of war was, by contrast, something of an anti-climax. The sounding of air-raid sirens just minutes after the Prime Minister had finished his historic speech seemingly heralded the immediate start of the air war, but it was a false alarm caused by an unidentified unarmed aircraft returning across the Channel from France at just the wrong psychological moment. The months following - from 3rd September, 1939, to 10th May, 1940 - have gone down in RAF folklore and national history as 'The phoney war'. The bitter Norwegian campaign was fought out in April, 1940, and the war at sea went on relentlessly, but, as far as the United Kingdom was concerned, little of vital consequence happened to disturb the normal passage of a British winter, apart from routine flights by individual German aircraft, probing and testing out the defences and indulging in spasmodic attacks on naval units and in armed photographic reconnaissance.

Nuisance raids justified keeping Hornchurch squadrons in a high state of readiness and they indulged in regular daylight formation practice and gunnery.

Tragic accidents occurred in this high state of tension, the worst happening on the third day of war when 74 Squadron was 'scrambled' to intercept 'enemy raiders' over the inner Essex suburbs. The 'raiders' were, in fact, the Hurricanes of 56 Squadron up from North Weald, but they were being hotly pursued by 'friendly' anti-aircraft fire, lending credence to the suggestion that they were Luftwaffe aircraft. What became known as 'The Battle of Barking Creek' ensued. Flying Officer V Byrne and Pilot Officer J C Freeborn in their 74 Squadron Spitfires opened fire on the 56 Squadron Hurricanes and, in the resulting melée, two of the Hurricanes were shot down. The pilot of one - Pilot Officer Halton-Harrap - was killed and the other, Pilot Officer Rose, was injured.

A shocked 11 Group ordered an immediate investigation into the cause of the tragedy and, in the circumstances, it was inevitable that Byrne and Freeborn had to face a Court Martial. They were kept in suspense for six weeks during the period of enquiry and gathering of evidence, but when the Court Martial was finally held at RAF Hendon on 17th October, they were both acquitted. Eight months later Byrne was shot down over Dunkirk and spent the rest of hostilities as a prisoner of war.

A week later the first of many WAAFs arrived at Hornchurch to the barely concealed delight of the resident 'erks'. The immediate result was a marked improvement in language and a decline in the use of expletives when things went wrong in the vicinity of any of the WAAFS. There was also a noticeable improvement in neatly brushed and combed hair, clean collars and shining footwear. There were even sightings of nail files and scissors! Even Group Captain Bouchier showed the sunniest side of his nature to the WAAFS, especially when they were hauled before him for any misdemeanour; he was quite unable to dish out the recognised option of punishments that would have been the norm for an airman.

The same day as 'The Battle of Barking Creek' Flight Lieutenant G A Saunders got back to Hornchurch with his Spitfire damaged in two places, again from 'friendly' anti-aircraft fire, this time from Sheerness. The successful separation of friend from foe was still a major problem and the cause of many tragedies; it was to remain so, to a greater or lesser extent, for the duration of the war. Even on practice and training sorties and during uncontested operational sorties, casualties were suffered and, during the eight months of the 'phoney war' Hornchurch lost 4 Spitfires, 2 Blenheims and a Magister written off and four pilots killed. The war was certainly not all that phoney for the airfield and its occupants.

74 Squadron was frequently detached 'down the line to Southend' to RAF Rochford during September and October, 1939, but it was whilst the Squadron was at Hornchurch that it destroyed the first of the intermittent German raiders penetrating over England. On 20th November, 1939, Flying Officer W E Measures shot it down into the sea 15 miles off Southend and its two crew members were taken from their dinghy cold and wounded the following day. Fighter Command's first successes had been when two Heinkel 111s were shot down by the Spitfires of 602 (City of Glasgow) and 603 (City of Edinburgh) Squadrons when the Heinkels attacked units of the Home Fleet in the Firth of Forth on 16th October, 1939, but the Hornchurch Heinkel shot down by F/O Measures was the first success by the RAF over England.

In other fatal accidents Sergeant E J Cole perished after his Spitfire (K 9886) dived into the ground between Billericay and Basildon; Flying Officer A Vickers was killed in a night flying accident in a Blenheim; and Pilot Officer B Graham died in an accident flying the Station Flight Gloster Gladiator over at RAF Northolt.

Notable pilots who arrived as reinforcements in this period included Pilot Officers Cooper-Slipper and Colin Gray; the latter's arrival caused quite a stir at Hornchurch and the story, with embellishments, spread even further afield. Gray, a New Zealander, arrived in London in January, 1939, and, after completing his pilot training, was posted to Hornchurch on 20th November. He had the misfortune, whilst making a low approach, to cleanly whip off the aircraft's undercarriage on one of the newly constructed blast shelters ringing the airfield. The shelters reduced the landing area, which had caused Colin to make the low approach. He was being closely observed by the Air Officer Commanding 11 Group paying a visit to the airfield and the Station Commander, Group Captain C H Nicholas. As he belly landed in a great confusion of smoke, dust and tearing metal, Air Vice Marshal Keith Park was heard to observe that he "could have sworn that the pilot had his wheels down."

Stepping out of his battered Spitfire after his classic landing, the chastened pilot was allowed to clean up and get his breath back before being carpeted by a furious and embarrassed Station Commander who was all for promptly cutting his Hornchurch service short and posting him out to some remote unit. His presence was saved by his new boss, Squadron Leader H M Pearson, whose retained faith in Colin Gray was repaid in ample measure by outstanding war service, which secured him the Distinguished Flying Cross and a niche of honour as the highest scoring New Zealander to serve with the Royal Air Force during the war.

Almost one third of all the New Zealanders serving with the RAF were killed, including Colin Gray's twin brother, Kenneth, who is buried at Dyce, Aberdeen.

Two days after this dramatic arrival a Handley Page Hampden bomber almost suffered the same fate as the Hurricanes in 'the Battle of Barking Creek'. It was damaged by 'friendly' anti-aircraft fire and then by a 54 Squadron aircraft, before lowering its wheels and making a successful landing at Hornchurch, a much smaller airfield than most of those normally found in Bomber Command. The Hampden, nicknamed the Flying Panhandle, was rather similar in side elevation to the Dornier 17, nicknamed the Flying Pencil: both had remarkably slim fuselages.

On 15th November, 1939, RAF Manston, formerly a Training Command airfield, was transferred to Fighter Command and became the third airfield in the Hornchurch Sector, alongside Rochford and Hornchurch itself. It was one of the nearest airfields to mainland Europe and was destined to take an epic part in the Battle of Britain: it was the most battered of all Fighter Command airfields.

As autumn gave way to a long drawn-out winter, flying activity was reduced. There was some entertainment at the base every week, some of it excellent and some less good, but it was always well attended. A decoy airfield was laid out in fields five miles away, near the village of Bulphan, in an attempt to divert any future Luftwaffe interest away from the real thing. The decoys were complete with 'wood and string' aircraft that looked very realistic from the air and were constructed at the studios of the film industry. The decoys had little success during the war, however, and, as events proved, the Luftwaffe had no doubts at all as to where the real RAF Hornchurch was located

However, Group Captain Bouchier went along to inspect the new decoy on New Year's Day, 1940, and had a word or two of encouragement for the 18 men who had

In the opening phase of the battle for the Low Countries and France the brunt of air effort was borne by the two formations of the RAF actually stationed in France - the Air Component of the Field Force and the Advanced Air Striking Force - and by Bomber Command Blenheims, providing tactical support from bases in England.

Throughout the offensive the Luftwaffe enjoyed marked air superiority over the Low Countries. Their bombers raided 22 airfields in Holland, Belgium and France and the RAF suffered heavy losses in the process. Nazi parachutists captured bridges, communication centres and airfields, spreading alarm, dismay and confusion among the defenders; they followed the airborne raids with panzer divisions and heavily armed motorised troops in a skilful operation that spread-eagled and overwhelmed the outnumbered and disjointed Dutch and Belgian forces. Queen Wilhelmina and her Court sought refuge in London. The German army had brilliantly absorbed the new concept of mobility in warfare, abandoning the stagnation of the trenches. Nevertheless, the Dutch Army offered sterner opposition than the Germans had anticipated and, to counter this, an all-out assault was launched with a murderous air attack on Rotterdam that wiped out the centre of the city, killing nearly a thousand civilians: the following day the Dutch Army surrendered.

Pressure was put on the government to throw in the full weight of the RAF and more and more replacements were drawn from Fighter Command, but one of

Dowding's provisos remained secure - that which decreed that no Spitfire squadrons should be sacrificed in this way. Thus, RAF Hornchurch was not involved in the earliest days of the battle, but as agonized observers, it became quite clear to the airmen which way the conflict was going. It was realised that, following the battle for France, the battle for Britain would have to be fought and already more squadrons had been thrown in than prudence dictated, in a vain endeavour to postpone a French defeat. But within six days, Von Runstedt's panzers were across the Somme and the British Expeditionary Force was isolated from the remainder of France. At this point Dowding released the Spitfire squadrons to help in covering the withdrawal of the British troops as they fell back on the French coast.

'Stuffy' Dowding

Air Vice Marshal Keith Park

to maintain a presence at this bleak spot, lacking most of the facilities available at a regular base.

During the winter occasional enemy aircraft still flew towards the coast and one such raider became known as 'The Milk Train', as he arrived regularly just after dawn. The competition to shoot him down grew and, on 13th February, 1940, he was caught by a Flight of 54 Squadron led by 'Prof' Leathart. The Commander opened fire and the Dornier appeared fatally injured as it dived away into the prevailing mist, but the aircraft was not claimed as destroyed as it was not seen to hit the water. However, it had, in fact, crashed off the north Kent coast, confirmed when it became known that the Luftwaffe was enquiring for news of a missing Lieutenant-Colonel who disappeared at the same time and place with his crew. Further confirmation was provided when parts of the aircraft were picked up by the destroyer HMS *Brilliant*.

On 11th March a 600 Squadron Blenheim, detached to RAF Manston, crashed, killing an army passenger. Four days later the Hornchurch training Magister, being used by 54 Squadron, crashed at Upminster, killing Pilot Officer R E West and injuring Sergeant Rawes.

In April, 1940, during the period of the ill-fated Norwegian campaign, the Air Officer Commanding 11 Group, Air Marshal Keith Park, visited Hornchurch, sparking off rumours of postings, but nothing came of it.

In early May, 1940, Pilot Officer Stephenson and Sergeant Skinner wrecked Spitfires on successive days, the first at Canvey Island, the other at Rochford; the pilots escaped injury.

At Hornchurch Squadron Leader James Leathart took over command of 54 Squadron from Squadron Leader E A Douglas-Jones, who had commanded the force for only a short time before ill health caught up with him.

From 16th May the Hornchurch squad began operating over the Amiens, Lille, Étaples, Boulogne and Calais areas at every opportunity, ranging far and wide in search of the elusive enemy.

As the BEF fell back on Dunkirk the Hornchurch squadrons flew operation after operation

Winston Churchill visited Paris and saw that nothing short of a miracle could now save France; it was beyond remedy and the bottomless pit was absorbing more British aircraft. It was only the vision of Hugh Dowding that saved Fighter Command.

over the area, but at this distance they could not remain over the location for longer than an hour. 11 Group airfields were hard pressed to maintain constant daylight cover, even by refuelling and returning to the fray. This brought a bitter response from the hard pressed ground troops who asked, "Where is the RAF?" They could not know that the fighter squadrons were ceaselessly tearing into the Luftwaffe, mostly out of sight of the men on the beaches. How worse their fate would have been and how few would have been successfully evacuated had they not been there!

The full implication of what was happening was not lost on the Hornchurch squadrons. Returning from sorties they regularly reported the havoc that they could see below. The events at RAF Hornchurch in the 17 days between 21st May and 6th June can best be understood when chronicled on a day to day basis and, even then, it is not easy to capture the intensity of the atmosphere of the period. It was one of the most crowded and eventful fortnights in the history of the airfield.

21ST MAY

Johnny Allen of 54 Squadron was ordered to investigate a doubtful radar plot in the Channel. Doubtful it may have been, but it turned out to be 20 Junker 88s flying in formation. Regardless of the odds against him, Johnny Allen sailed into the attack and destroyed one of them. On the same day 74 Squadron was involved in a hectic dogfight over Dunkirk and claimed the destruction of six enemy aircraft - two of them shot down by 'Sailor' Malan - without loss.

22ND MAY

One aircraft was shot down by 74 Squadron over Calais. Flight Lieutenant G A Saunders of 65 Squadron had engine trouble on returning and finally it burst into flames; he made a forced landing with wheels up at North Foreland, between Broadstairs and Margate, leaping out of the aircraft in time to watch it burn out. Yet another identification error resulted in an already badly damaged Handley Page Hampden belonging to 144 Squadron at Hemswell and returning from Germany being held by searchlights and coned by 'friendly' aircraft fire. The pilot of the Hampden - who was the only crew member left in the aircraft, the rest having baled out over Germany - decided it was high time he did the same. He evacuated successfully and his bomber crashed half a mile from the airfield.

23RD MAY

The day started when 54 and 74 Squadrons crossed the Channel for a dawn patrol and were involved in dog-fights. 74 Squadron's Commander - Squadron Leader F L White - shot down a Heinkel, but received return fire from the gunner, which damaged his aircraft and compelled him to make a forced landing at Calais Marck airfield. At this time Boulogne had already fallen and Calais itself was surrounded and liable to be captured at any time. This did not deter 'Prof' Leathart, who had led 54 Squadron in that melée, from suggesting to the Station Commander and, from him, to the AOC of 11 Group, that an aircraft should be sent in a daring mission to retrieve White. The approval of 11 Group was forthcoming and James Leathart volunteered to fly the mission himself. Squadron Leader White could not, of course, be rescued by a single seater Spitfire and the only aircraft available at Hornchurch that was suitable for the task was a two seater Miles Master unarmed trainer. Leathart selected Alan Deere and Johnny Allen to escort him in Spitfires and, with a difference of 130 mph in their speeds, this in itself was not without difficulty. It was thought they might get away with it if just the three of them went over at low level and avoid attracting attention. It was hoped that the last thing the Luftwaffe would anticipate was the sight of a

Royal Air Force trainer in the midst of all the mayhem at the Channel ports. The intention was to land at Calais Marck, pick up Squadron Leader White and take off without stopping the engine, whilst the two Spitfires orbited above as protection.

The trip out went smoothly enough and the Master landed at Calais, leaving Alan Deere circling at low level and Johnny Allen orbiting at 8,000 feet. As the Master taxied to pick up its passenger, Johnny Allen from on high reported six Me109s making for the airfield. Almost immediately Alan Deere saw one of them hurtling towards the defenceless Master. There followed one of the most incredibly one-sided dog-fights ever witnessed between Spitfires and Me109s, in which the Spitfires shot down three of the marauding Messerschmitts and damaged the other three. The two Spitfires joined up again in mid-Channel and inspected each other for battle damage. Although Johnny Allen's aircraft had been badly shot up, he nursed it back to Hornchurch rather than go in to Manston. Shortly afterwards 'Prof' Leathart arrived back in the Master carrying a relieved Squadron Leader F L White, saved in the nick of time from spending the rest of the war a prisoner.

When notes were compared, it was revealed that the Master had just left the ground when the first Me109 opened fire. James Leathart promptly banged it back on terra firma and with German tanks a few hundred yards away evacuated himself and his passenger with great speed. He witnessed the destruction of the first Me109, which crashed a short distance away, and saw another dive into the sea. The third came down in flames. The dog-fight was all over in ten minutes and, as soon as it seemed prudent to do so, the Master, with two squadron leaders aboard took off for a second time and, with its wings almost caressing the waves, crossed the Channel, climbing over Dover just high enough to clear the white cliffs. Safely back in Hornchurch, a congratulatory signal was received from AVM Keith Park. Calais fell to the Germans on the night of 26th May.

A painting by Ken Summers called 'The Rescue Party', depicting the Miles Master and its escorting Spitfires retrieving Squadron Leader White, has pride of place in Air Commodore Leathart's Gloucestershire home.

As if this was not enough for a single day, 92 Squadron arrived at Hornchurch from Northolt under the command of the redoubtable Squadron Leader Roger Bushell, and with Flight Lieutenant Robert Stanford Tuck, now a Flight Commander. Roger Bushell was a South African barrister who had a practice in London. He was a champion skier and a considerable athlete and, although older than his squadron pilots, he invariably beat them when the order to scramble was received. He possessed an easy charm and an air of maturity and authority that made him highly respected.

In their first operation from Hornchurch this day, Pat Learmond was shot down in flames, but five enemy aircraft were downed. Stanford Tuck, who accounted for a Me109 on this sortie, observed the immense pall of smoke covering the Dunkirk beach area from burning oil tanks, and the long straggling columns of troops as the British

Expeditionary Force squeezed its way through choked narrow roads and lanes, down to the sea and the armada of little boats. The *Skylark*s that had previously given trips around the bay and a breath of sea air to thousands of holidaymakers at Burnham and Brighton, Frinton and Folkestone, Southend and Shoreham, Walton and Worthing were interspersed with larger Royal Navy ships that were too few in number to cope with the teeming thousands seeking rest and sanctuary and a safe return to their homeland.

Returning to Hornchurch the pilots of 92 Squadron stayed for a brief lunch and were off again at 1345 for their second operation of the day, with another pilot replacing Pat Learmond. In an even more ferocious dog-fight 92 Squadron claimed the destruction of another fifteen aircraft, but lost four of their own, including their leader, Squadron Leader Roger Bushell. After chasing a Me110 at low level he crashed and was seen to be waving a scarf, standing near his downed Spitfire. He survived to become a prisoner of war and was subsequently the inspiration behind the 'Great Escape' of RAF officers from Stalag Luft 3. Tragically, he was one of the fifty escapees murdered by the Gestapo after they had been re-captured. In addition to Roger Bushell, 92 Squadron lost Paul Klipsch; Flying Officer V Byrne, who became a prisoner of war; and Flight Sergeant K Wooder, who was seen going down in flames. Flight Lieutenant Stanford Tuck assumed command of 92 Squadron.

54 Squadron, also embroiled in the battles over Dunkirk and St Omer, shot down nine enemy aircraft without loss. It was an engagement that proved beyond doubt that the 'Fighting Area Attacks' which had been practised for years were now lost in antiquity. Those concentrating so hard on getting into the correct place for a set piece attack in the right formation ran the risk of being shot down themselves.

24TH MAY

54, 74 and 92 Squadrons were all in action and 18 enemy aircraft were claimed. Flying Officer Linley and Sergeant J Phillips of 54 Squadron were seen to crash-land on Dunkirk beach, but both were safe and waved to the squadron overhead: they both became prisoners of war. 92 Squadron lost Flying Officer Peter Casenove, who also came down close to the shore and was taken prisoner. 74 Squadron lost Flying Officer Hoare and Flying Officer Aubert, who had been shot down three days earlier, but returned to Hornchurch: he did not return this time.

Flight Lieutenant Brian Kingcombe - another pre-war regular at Hornchurch - arrived as a Flight Commander for the depleted 92 Squadron.

Tuck, who had destroyed five enemy aircraft in two days, suffered a thigh injury that was outside the scope of the airfield's Medical Centre. He was taken to the Casualty Department of Oldchurch Hospital, Romford, where, amidst muttering from some of the assembled patients awaiting attention, he was given priority. X-rays revealed a nut from the rudder pedal deeply embedded in his thigh; it must have shot up with a terrific force to penetrate so far. Enquiring about the nature of his injury, Tuck was told by the examining surgeon that 'a few inches higher and you would have had to remuster into the WAAFs'.

At the close of another remarkable day a signal was received from Air Chief Marshal Hugh Dowding which read, "By shooting down thirty-seven enemy aircraft today the four Spitfire squadrons at Hornchurch set a magnificent record that is especially creditable with such small losses. The Air Officer Commanding sends his sincere congratulations and hopes that most of the missing pilots will turn up again shortly. Immediately the critical military situation in France has passed, squadrons will be given a well earned rest."

25TH MAY

On its dawn patrol 92 Squadron shot down a Dornier 17 and then, after two very hectic days, moved out to RAF Duxford, swopping bases with 19 Squadron (the first ever squadron to receive the Spitfire in 1938), which arrived under the command of Squadron Leader G D Stephenson. On this day 54 Squadron claimed five enemy aircraft, but lost Sergeant E Buckland.

The Germans captured more of the coastline and surrounded the Belgian Army, as the British Expeditionary Force continued to fall back towards Dunkirk.

The attrition amongst the Hornchurch squadrons was now serious, as patrol followed patrol. By the end of the day, 54 was at its lowest ebb, temporarily reduced to twelve pilots and eight serviceable aircraft.

26TH MAY

On its first offensive patrol from Hornchurch 19 Squadron suffered the loss of its commander, Squadron Leader G D Stephenson, in what was a repeat of 92 Squadron's loss of Roger Bushell just three days earlier. Two other pilots suffered injuries. Another tragic loss was that of Flying Officer F H Welford - a Hornchurch regular from pre-war - who survived a furious dog-fight during which he destroyed a Me110, only to be lost due, it is thought, to 'friendly' anti-aircraft fire: for such a fine pilot to die in such a way was indeed a terrible waste. Pilot Officer K G Hart was also lost in this engagement, but later returned to England by ship.

54 Squadron lost George Gribble and Johnny Allen, but both turned up later that evening, Johnny wearing the uniform of a naval lieutenant given to him by the Royal Naval destroyer that fished him out of the drink and deposited him at Dover. Until these two turned up the Squadron had declined still further to ten pilots and five serviceable aircraft.

Squadron Leader Stephenson's replacement, Squadron Leader Philip Pinkham, survived in the job just three months before being killed over the Thames Estuary.

Nineteen enemy aircraft were claimed by Hornchurch squadrons.

27TH MAY

54 and 74 Squadrons both lost Flight Commanders; Flight Lieutenant Max Pearson of 54 and Flight Lieutenant W P 'Paddy' Treacy of 74.

Dunkirk was now like Dante's Inferno with flame and black smoke from the burning oil tanks, combined with low black clouds, to present a very sombre sight. It was into this pall of darkness that Max Pearson disappeared in pursuit of a Junkers 88 and was never seen or heard of again. Paddy Treacy, however, survived, evaded capture and was later heard of in Marseilles after the long journey to the French Mediterranean coast. He finally arrived back by devious routes many months later and told of three separate escapes from the Germans: he had first found a rowing boat near Dunkirk and pulled towards England, only for a German seaplane to land next to him; after his second escape he was recaptured by the German Army; and on his third attempt he made it. Sadly, he was killed in April, 1941, when his aircraft was involved in a collision with an inexperienced pilot.

A further nineteen aircraft were claimed this day and 222 Squadron arrived from Kirton in Lindsey to allow 74 Squadron to retire to Leconfield for rest and recuperation. Commanded by Squadron Leader H W Mermagen (later an Air Commodore), this Squadron had, as one of its Flight Commanders, the famed Douglas Bader, the legless pilot, who overcame his disability and was destined to become world famous later in the war. He was keen to get to grips with the Luftwaffe and was in combat the day after he arrived in Hornchurch. His eventful life, chronicled in *Reach for the sky* - and in a film - was indeed stranger than fiction.

28TH MAY

Dunkirk town was heavily bombed, adding to the belching black smoke and confusion. Three hundred and twenty-one sorties were flown by Fighter Command, and Alan Deere - now a Flight Commander in 54 Squadron - was amongst those shot down, together with Flight Lieutenant Heller of 616 Squadron operating out of Rochford.

54 Squadron had received orders to proceed to RAF Catterick for rest and recuperation, exchanging bases with 41 Squadron, and Alan Deere led the remnants of the Squadron, while 'Prof' Leathart remained to organise the move up to Yorkshire. On a cold, wet day the eight serviceable aircraft set out for the last patrol over Dunkirk before their move and Alan Deere closed in on a Dornier 17 looking for shipping targets. His first burst set the Dornier's port engine alight, but return fire from the gunner found his own engine and he was enveloped with the fine spray of glycol from a ruptured coolant system. He crash-landed on the beach at the water's edge, but struck his forehead a heavy blow, which knocked him out. With his face covered by a mixture of oil, blood and wet sand, he was challenged by a British soldier, who took him to a small town between Dunkirk and Ostend, where his wounds were skilfully dressed by a Belgian girl. He made his way to Dunkirk on foot, by bus, cycle and army truck, before securing his place - not without some difficulty - on a Royal Navy destroyer that deposited him at Dover. After taking a train from Dover to Charing Cross and then a District Line train to Elm Park, for all the world as if he were a tourist, Alan Deere explained his predicament to the ticket collector, who waved him through, and he turned up at RAF Hornchurch. The dirty bandage was

removed by the Station Medical Officer and the wound was cleaned up. The next day he flew to RAF Catterick to rejoin his colleagues in 54 Squadron.

In the week from 21st May, Hornchurch squadrons had accounted for 96 enemy aircraft for the loss of 26 of their own and 20 pilots.

41 Squadron, commanded by Squadron Leader H R L Hood, arrived from Catterick.

29TH MAY

Pilot Officer G Proudman, Flying Officer Walker and Flight Sergeant W H Franklin each shot down Me110s and a further two Me110s and one Heinkel 126 were also accounted for.

30TH MAY

Severe weather conditions restricted operations.

31ST MAY

The air battle over Dunkirk was resumed with fury, but in renewed attacks on shipping the Luftwaffe only succeeded in sinking one ship. Two enemy aircraft were claimed by the newly arrived 41 Squadron.

1ST JUNE

Determined efforts were maintained by the Luftwaffe to smash up the assembly of shipping off Dunkirk. 41 Squadron lost Pilot Officer W Stapleton, who became a prisoner of war, and Flying Officer Legard, whilst 222 Squadron lost Pilot Officer G Massey-Sharpe, Pilot Officer H E Falkus and Sergeant L J White. Sir Archibald Sinclair, the Secretary of State for Air, visited Hornchurch to witness the Sector control of operations over Dunkirk at first hand.

2ND JUNE

As the evacuation of troops from Dunkirk reached its climax, Hermann Goering ordered all-out air attacks on the beaches and on the assembly of little ships. The Luftwaffe attacked in such strength that they broke through Fighter Command's limited screen on several occasions to sink a number of transports and Royal Navy destroyers, although they lost 30 aircraft in the process. By evening, however, most of the rear-guard had been taken off.

3RD JUNE

The Royal Air Force continued to provide cover for the evacuation of French troops as the operation drew towards a close. Marshal of the Royal Air Force Lord Trenchard visited Hornchurch.

4TH JUNE

At 3.40 am the destroyer *Shikari* left Dunkirk. It was the last ship to participate in the evacuation and at dawn the Dunkirk beaches fell into German hands. 'Operation Dynamo' was finally completed.

When the final tally was made at the conclusion of 'Operation Dynamo' the grievous losses sustained by Fighter Command became self-evident. The Dunkirk operations alone cost the Royal Air Force 229 aircraft and 128 pilots, including several Flight Commanders and Squadron Leaders, from a total of 2,739 sorties flown in support of the operation. The aircraft loss equated to 8% of the sorties flown - an unacceptably high rate over the long term. The whole weight of air defence over the evacuation area had fallen on the few Fighter Command airfields that were within reasonable range and it necessitated their making hundreds of sorties each day.

Between 26th May and 4th June 310,000 Allied troops were brought back from the continent. They had no option but to leave behind their tanks, artillery and transport, but the military defeat was tempered by an outstandingly successful rescue operation.

The casualties suffered by the RAF's French-based aircraft were even greater. When the remnants were finally withdrawn 915 crew members and 730 aircraft had been lost - the crew members including 435 pilots (320 killed, 115 prisoners of war).

The loss of pilots from Hornchurch incurred over Dunkirk stood at 23 on 1st June, out of a Fighter Command total of 80 to that date (nearly 30%). Few, if any, of Fighter Command airfields could have suffered so heavily.

The total loss of aircraft in the battle for France and over Dunkirk - 959 - included 432 Hurricanes and Spitfires. The Luftwaffe lost a total of 1,284 aircraft in the same operations from all causes. It is not possible to say how many were destroyed by RAF fighters, but it would have been a substantial proportion: Hornchurch pilots claimed the destruction of 124 enemy aircraft.

Anxious to derive some useful pickings, Mussolini took Italy into the war when Britain and France were at their lowest ebb. Paris fell on 14th June; the French accepted German armistice terms a week later and all hostilities officially ended in France on 25th June.

As Hugh Dowding counted the cost he found that he could now muster only 1,094 pilots (362 short of his estimate of the minimum number necessary to defend the United Kingdom) and 466 serviceable aircraft, of which only 331 were Spitfires and Hurricanes. Rest, repair and recuperation were absolute necessities and it was fortunate that the RAF had ensured that the Luftwaffe too had taken such a mauling that it needed time to recover before resuming activities. Both Fighter and Bomber Commands had been seriously depleted and, in the brief lull that followed, strenuous efforts were made to restore the RAF's resources of pilots and aircraft.

The outstanding efforts of five of the principal Hornchurch pilots were recognised two days later on 27th June, 1940, when a special ceremonial parade was held for an Investiture by King George VI, accompanied by Air Chief Marshal Hugh Dowding, Air Marshal Nichol and Air Marshal W C Fielden.

On the hard standing apron between two of the hangars a square was formed with three sides drawn from non-commissioned officers, airmen and WAAFS, the fourth side by other station officers. Inside the square was a table and in one corner of the square stood the five officers who were to be decorated, trying their best not to look

King George V presenting the Distinguished Flying Cross to Flight Lieutenant Alan Deere at RAF Hornchurch, 27 June, 1940 (*Imperial War Museum*)

A Messerschmitt 109

too self conscious. The identity of the distinguished visitor was a close secret and many airmen working away from the area in their various sections were unaware of what was taking place. Even some of the airmen forming the square had little idea who the visitor might be.

Along the tarmac purred an elegant car from which the King alighted. He spoke first to Group Captain C A Bouchier, the Station Commander, and then other 'non-recipient' officers. The King then took his place at the table and an officer stepped forward with a list in his hand and read out the names of the officers who were to be decorated, one at a time. As each came to the table, he read out the citation detailing the events that had led to the awards to -

Squadron Leader J A Leathart 54 Squadron   Distinguished Service Order
Flight Lieutenant R R S Tuck 65 Squadron   Distinguished Flying Cross
Flight Lieutenant A G Malan 74 Squadron   Distinguished Flying Cross
Flight Lieutenant A C Deere   54 Squadron   Distinguished Flying Cross
Pilot Officer J L Allen   54 Squadron   Distinguished Flying Cross

As the Investiture drew to a close Group Captain Bouchier called for 'Three Cheers for His Majesty the King' and the three cheers dutifully rang out around the station. Although the proceedings were ceremonial, they were kept deliberately brief, as the station remained operational. The King and his escorting party took lunch in the Officers' Mess at 1 pm and drove away from Hornchurch an hour later.

In his autobiography *Nine lives*, Alan Deere wrote, "For me, it was a memorable occasion. As a New Zealander brought up to admire the Mother Country and respect the King as her head, it was the honour of a lifetime - an ultimate milestone of my flying ambitions - the Distinguished Flying Cross presented by the King, in the field of action."

###

The fight went on and in the so-called lull 'Sailor' Malan chalked up another 'first' for the airfield when he brought down a Heinkel 111 in flames over Chelmsford - the first enemy aircraft to be shot down by a fighter over England at night in World War II.

In the early days of July Hainault Farm - the same 1914-18 field that was then a neighbour to Suttons Farm - was re-opened as an Emergency Landing Ground and remained in that role until the adjacent RAF Fairlop was opened.

The satellite airfield at Manston was used each day as a 'forward' field by Flights or Squadrons of Hornchurch aircraft. In the lead up to 10th July a Spitfire flown by Sergeant White (74 Squadron) was struck by lightning and crashed between Margate and Broadstairs, Flying Officer Dowding shot down a Junkers 88 and, in further fierce engagements, 65 Squadron lost four pilots, including the Commanding Officer Squadron Leader D Cooke, and 54 Squadron lost two. In fact, it was anything but a lull so far as Hornchurch was concerned and the air operations between Dunkirk and the Battle of Britain merged one into the other without any really perceptible interval.

On convoy duty, Flight Sergeant Franklin pursued a Me109 across the Channel, almost to the French coast before shooting it down into the sea; returning to the convoy, he encountered another Me109 and destroyed that also. Sergeant Mould forced an aircraft down at Elham, Kent and the German pilot survived as a prisoner. Flight Sergeant Phillips also shot down a Me109: the NCO pilots at Hornchurch were achieving great success.

As a defence against invasion, particularly an airborne assault on the airfield, the whole perimeter was surrounded by barbed wire and guarded night and day by a strong contingent of Glasgow Highlanders, Royal Engineers, armoured cars and searchlights designed to illuminate airborne forces dropping in darkness.

Such was the position at Hornchurch as the Battle of Britain dawned.

Three cheers for the King. P/O Johnny Allen, F/L R R Stanford-Tuck, F/L Alan C Deere, S/L J A Leathart (*Imperial War Museum*)

'CRESCENDO'
THE BATTLE OF BRITAIN

At the start of the Battle of Britain the Hornchurch Sector was the most important of the seven Sector Stations in No. 11 Group, covering the vital south-east of England. The other Sector Stations - Biggin Hill, Debden, Kenley, Northolt, North Weald and Tangmere - controlled 15 squadrons of Hurricanes, 4 of Blenheims and only three of Spitfires between them. Hornchurch was the only station in the Royal Air Force then to be equipped exclusively with three squadrons of Spitfires, the airfield holding 50 out of the total of 300 on the strength of RAF Fighter Command.

Both sides were licking their wounds after the battle for France and air operations over Dunkirk, the Royal Air Force making intense efforts to restore the fighter squadrons to normality.

On 10th July, 1940, Sergeant E A Mould and Pilot Officer J C Freeborn of 74 Squadron were both damaged in combat, but landed uninjured at Manston: the squadron damaged two Me109s in reply. The Hornchurch squadrons all used Rochford and Manston as forward airfields and for emergency landings and, on occasions, remained on detachment to one or other of these bases for considerable periods.

In the opening days of the Battle of Britain the Luftwaffe tended to concentrate on coastal shipping, especially the convoys entering the Dover Straits under naval and RAF protection. Dog-fights off Dover, Deal, Ramsgate and Margate occurred virtually every day. It was not long, however, before the Führer opened the scope of the Battle by demanding that Fighter Command of the RAF should be annihilated as a necessary prerequisite for the launching of German invasion forces against England.

The first confirmed victory to Hornchurch in the Battle was on 12th July, when 74 Squadron destroyed a Heinkel 111 off Margate in a combined effort; the five crewmen of the Heinkel were lost. On the following day, Colin Gray chased a Me109 across the Channel before shooting it down near Calais; the German pilot, Lieutenant Lange dying in this incident. Other early victories were obtained by 'Sailor' Malan of 74 and 'Prof' Leathart of 54 Squadron.

The RAF was very fond of awarding nicknames to its principal characters and, in addition to 'Sailor' and 'Prof', Hornchurch also had, at one time or another, 'Al' Deere, 'Wonky' Way, 'Treacle' Treacy, 'Broody' Benson, 'Butch' Baker, 'Ras' Berry, 'Pip' Cardell, Eric 'Sawn Off' Lock, 'Bubble' Waterston and 'Tannoy' Read. It even spread to the higher echelons with the Commander of 603 Squadron as 'Uncle' George Denholm, the Hornchurch Station Commander 'Boy' Bouchier and, among the hallowed ground of the top brass were 'Boom' Trenchard, 'Stuffy' Dowding and 'Bomber' Harris. These were personal nicknames and not to be confused with literally thousands of 'Jocks', 'Taffys' 'Paddys', 'Scousers' and 'Geordies', according to birthplace.

Presentation of 8 Spitfires by the East India Fund, Hornchurch, 15 July, 1940 (*Imperial War Museum*)

54 Squadron pilots relaxing, July, 1940. F/O J Allen, P/O E Coleman, P/O G Gribble, P/O A Campbell (*Imperial War Museum*)

All Smiths were 'Smudgers' and Millers were 'Dusty'. Add the lot together and it is not surprising that nicknames usually outnumbered Christian names and few were addressed formally as 'George' or 'Bill'.

On Monday, 15th July, another special ceremony was staged when 65 Squadron was presented with eight new Spitfires that had been subscribed for by the 'East India Fund' - residents of eastern India. The handing over of the aircraft was attended by AVM Keith Park (Air Officer Commanding 11 Group) and Group Captain C A Bouchier, representing the Royal Air Force, Captain Balfour, the Under Secretary of State for Air, representing the Government, and Sir Edmund and Lady Benthall, Sir Alexander Murray and Mr Rowan Hodge, representing the East India Fund. The Spitfires were assembled in line abreast on the tarmac with pilots in the cockpits, ground crews standing to attention at the side and the Merlin engines purring over, presumably ready to disperse if any enemy formations appeared in the vicinity. In the event, nothing occurred to disturb the ceremonial presentation, which concluded with a fly-past of the new aircraft. 65 Squadron's Commanding Officer, Squadron Leader Henry Sawyer, had only been in the job a week, taking over from S/Ldr D Cooke. Following the ceremony his command was known as 65 (East India) Squadron.

Day by day the Battle ebbed and flowed and Flying Officer John Kemp of 54 Squadron twice had narrow escapes. On the first, his engine failed when he was over the sea, 15 miles from Clacton, he baled out and was fished out of the sea by a Royal Navy destroyer. On the second occasion, his aircraft was shot up in combat with Me109s off Dover and he made a forced landing at Lympne.

It would not be feasible to chronicle and analyze every Hornchurch success and casualty, but mention must be made of the first two deaths in the Battle, which, by their nature and because of the individuals involved, cast a gloom over the station.

On Wednesday, 24th July, the boyish John Laurence Allen was up from the forward station at Rochford on convoy patrol duty. Known to all and sundry as 'Johnny', he was a veteran of the Gloster Gladiator days at Hornchurch, having been there since 1938 and spending three months on Gladiators before transferring to Spitfires. Johnny Allen was involved in combat with Me109s over the sea off Margate. In the general melée his engine was hit in a burst of fire and cut out. Although losing height, he had enough airspeed to glide the aircraft towards the coast. At the Sector Control Room reception over the R/T was poor and crackly, but Ronald Adam, the Sector Controller, heard him say in his slow and easy drawl, and without any sign of panic, "My engine has been hit - I am trying to land."

He was apparently trying to make for Foreness Point - an oasis of open land between the built up areas of Margate and Broadstairs - when the Merlin picked up again and Johnny - making a quick decision - started to make a turn with the intention of pressing on the extra five miles to make a normal wheels down landing at Manston. At this point, however, the engine cut out again at a critical moment and, with his airspeed too low in the turn, the aircraft stalled, giving him no chance to bale out. It crashed to earth near the Old Church Inn in Cliftonville and burnt out. The nature of the tragedy was compounded by the fact that, if the engine had not re-started and prompted him to turn for Manston, he would, in all probability, have made a successful wheels up landing at Foreness Point, a stretch of land which, due to its geographical position, was almost an Emergency Landing Ground in itself.

And so died a gallant airman who had destroyed eight enemy aircraft and participated in other audacious exercises before he was, at last, struck down himself. Johnny Allen's dog was a well-known character, who used to sit on the lawn of the Officers' Mess at Hornchurch and gaze at the returning Spitfires, licking his lips in joyous anticipation of greeting his master's return. Johnny did not come back that night, but the dog maintained his lonely vigil until the onset of darkness. It was a very sad day, not only for Johnny Allen's family, but for 54 Squadron, RAF Hornchurch and his many friends in the RAF. He was 24 years old and lies buried in Margate Cemetery, close to where he fell.

Five enemy aircraft were claimed by 54 Squadron that day.

The second of the casualties to hit Hornchurch particularly hard occurred the following day, 25th July. 'Wonky' Way, who now commanded a Flight of 54 Squadron, was on convoy patrol in the Dover - Deal area, when the convoy was attacked by Junkers 87s. These aircraft - widely known as 'Stukas', an abbreviation of Sturzkampflugzeug (dive bombers) - achieved an almost legendary reputation in the Polish and French campaigns. The aircraft gave its crew good visibility and they frequently hit their targets in accurate dive bombing attacks.

The many successes of the Junkers 87s blinded the Luftwaffe to its weaknesses, the most obvious of which was that it was very vulnerable to forward firing fighters and its successful operation necessitated complete control of the skies: such control was managed in the earlier campaigns, but it could not be repeated over the United Kingdom unless and until the Luftwaffe gained the same measure of superiority it had enjoyed since September, 1939.

'Wonky' Way soon shot one of them into the sea, but was seen by the protective screen of Me109s flying above, who immediately dived to seek retribution. Over the R/T George Gribble shouted urgent warnings, "Watch out Blue One - 109s coming from above - hundreds of them", and then, even more urgently, "Break, Wonky, break." The warnings were either not heard or could not be acted upon or were too late and 'B' Flight's Commander went into the Channel amidst a hail of bullets.

A native of Hinton St George, near Crewkerne, Somerset, Basil Way joined the RAF in 1937 and arrived in Hornchurch in time to spend three months on Gloster Gladiators before converting to Spitfires. So died another gallant airman. Like Johnny Allen the previous day, he was not out-thought by a superior flier, but outgunned by sheer weight of numbers. Wonky Way's body was eventually washed ashore on an enemy occupied Belgian beach and he is buried at Oostdunkerke Communal Cemetery. He was only 22 years old and held the Groves Memorial Prize as the best all round cadet in his graduation year at RAF Cranwell (1938).

Of the seventeen pilots who were with 54 Squadron when the Dunkirk operations started, only five now remained with the Squadron. The loss of these two seasoned pre-war regulars, in successive days, was a savage blow. That evening, 54 was withdrawn to Catterick and replaced by 41 Squadron from that base. Many squadrons were now down to half strength after Dunkirk and the costly convoy patrols. They had to be pulled out for rest and re-formation, but sadly, the replacement squadrons, who in most cases lacked the combat experience of the squadrons they relieved, sometimes suffered even greater casualties.

At the same time as Basil Way was downed, the mass formation of Me109s also got Flying Officer Douglas Turley-George (54 Squadron), but, although his Spitfire was in such a state that it had to be written off, he managed to crash-land it near Dover and stepped out of it unhurt. In the same combat there was an unusual incident when Flight Sergeant William Franklin (65 Squadron) was attacked from behind by a Me109 whilst he was in a dive. Franklin managed to pull out of the high speed dive, but the Messerschmitt found it impossible so to do and crashed into the sea.

On a lighter side, the notorious 'Pilot Officer Percy Prune' was created at Hornchurch by Bill Hooper at this time. Percy was a fictitious character, but his counterpart was present in almost every squadron and he became widely known throughout the RAF. Bill Hooper says that the idea for Percy Prune originated when a 54 Squadron pilot stepped out badly shaken after a particularly hair-raising encounter with Luftwaffe fighters over Kent in July, 1940. He was consoled with a cigarette by a fellow airman, who said, "Not to worry, Mac, you are privileged to be fighting with the gallant Fifty Four." The shaken pilot replied, "Oh, aye - and I often wonder where the other fifty-three are!" Later that day a cartoon appeared in 54's Flight Hut showing an egg headed, mushroom nosed Spitfire pilot, surrounded by hordes of Me109s. It was captioned, 'Where are the other fifty-three?'.

The character of Pilot Officer Percy Prune spread throughout the Allied Air Forces. He was used by 'Prof' Leathart in his *Notes for fighter pilots* and in a book, *Forget me nots for fighters*, issued to every pilot in Fighter Command. Thousands laughed at the situations that Percy dug himself into that were seen in many magazines. They not only spelt out the salutary lessons that could be learned from Prune's mistakes, but introduced badly needed humour into the desperate battles of 1940.

On the last day of July it was learned that Flight Lieutenant A G 'Sailor' Malan (74 Squadron) had been awarded a Bar to his Distinguished Flying Cross, that Pilot Officer Dorian George Gribble (54 Squadron) and Pilot Officer John Freeborn (74 Squadron)

Ground crew scanning the skies, RAF Hornchurch, 1940 (*Imperial War Museum*)

41 Squadron

German pilots at a French base

had been awarded Distinguished Flying Crosses and that Flight Sergeant William Franklin had a Bar to his Distinguished Flying Medal.

Sadly, Pilot Officer Harold Gunn and Sergeant Frederick Eley were lost: Gunn was shot down off Folkestone, whilst Eley came down in flames near Folkestone Pier.

August opened with the loss of Squadron Leader Henry Sawyer, the Commanding Officer of 65 Squadron, who had held the job for just one month. On 2nd August he crashed shortly after taking off from the forward airfield at Rochford, for a night patrol to investigate a possible intrusion by enemy night bombers. There was a thick haze over Rochford when he took off, but there was clear sky above it. He opted for a steep climb to get through the mist quickly, but he stalled at a thousand feet and came straight down again. His Spitfire burned out. Another pre-war regular Sawyer had entered the RAF College at Cranwell in 1933, but was only 25 when he died. He lived at St John's Wood and had a baby boy only two months old.

At this time a young man who was to have outstanding success in the Battle of Britain joined 41 Squadron. Although it had been raging for over a month before he achieved his first success, he went on to be the highest scoring RAF pilot in the Battle. The little-known Pilot Officer Eric Stanley Lock, who for some reason soon acquired the nickname 'Sawn Off', destroyed a Me110 on 15th August and went on to be credited with the destruction of 22 enemy aircraft in the Battle. He was awarded the Distinguished Flying Cross and a Bar during the month of October, 1940 - a just recognition of a successful pilot.

The Hornchurch squadrons were making extensive use of Manston and Rochford, which were ideally situated for the many combats that were taking place over the sea. On 8th August 'Sailor' Malan took over command of 74 Squadron from Squadron Leader F L White (who had been retrieved from Calais), who was posted to Headquarters of Fighter Command at Bentley Priory. The same day 65 Squadron lost Sergeant David Kirton and Flight Sergeant Norman Taylor, up from Manston in combat with Me109s. 'Hornchurch's Own', 54 Squadron, returned to the fold from Catterick and 41 Squadron returned to their home base.

A highly popular event was the arrival of the Girls from the Windmill Theatre, London, chaperoned and directed by Sheila Van Damm. The poses, acts and dances displayed by the beautiful and scantily clad girls proved to be just the fleeting and pleasurable tonic that was needed as a diversion from the devastation of war. The airmen raised the rafters with their applause and cheering and left the smiling girls in no doubt that in baring all, they had made a valuable contribution to the war effort. The reception they were accorded ensured that it would not be the last visit the girls made to Hornchurch.

Over the ensuing days, 13th and 14th August, successive attacks were made on the

Hornchurch 'forward' field at Manston. Three enemy aircraft were brought down, but Pilot Officer Felix Gregory (65 Squadron) was lost when he baled out too low. His body was found seven miles away from Manston at Eastry, between Sandwich and Deal, with the parachute only partly deployed. On one occasion 65 Squadron was caught in the act of taking off. A hangar was blown up and only one pilot, Flight Lieutenant Jeffery Quill, Vickers Chief Test Pilot on attachment to test the Spitfire in operating conditions, managed to get airborne in the wake of the Me109s and Me110s. Manston was pitted with a hundred craters and was almost taken apart piece by piece.

Hermann Goering was convinced that Manston and Eastchurch airfields had been destroyed and that 65 Squadron was a 'write off'. 54 Squadron continued to operate out of Manston despite the shambles and the almost continuous bombing that marooned the ground staff in air raid shelters for considerable periods. Some of the airfields attacked - Eastchurch, Worthy Down and Upavon, among them - had little relevance to the Battle of Britain and did not usually house fighter squadrons. it just so happened that at the time of the attack 266 Squadron had temporarily deployed to Eastchurch and one of their Spitfires was burned out.

54 Squadron had just about had enough of Manston and they did not need telling twice when they were ordered to return to Hornchurch. Manston suffered seven major and several smaller attacks and had reached the stage where it was not possible to operate because of bomb craters and delayed action bombs strewn around. One small bonus the crews enjoyed was when a bomb brought down an avalanche of tasty Victoria plums in an adjacent orchard.

Back at Hornchurch the squadrons had a short time to savour their escape from the shambles of Manston, but it would not last long, for Hornchurch in its turn was marked for punishment.

74 Squadron left for rest and recuperation at RAF Wittering and this was the last Hornchurch saw of 74 - one of the three pre-war regular squadrons at the base. 'Sailor'

The success achieved by the Radar Stations scattered along the south-east coastline, giving advance warning of the assembly of the Luftwaffe over the Pas de Calais and their subsequent route to England, had sunk through to the enemy and the Radar Stations, together with coastal airfields, were heavily attacked on the day after the Windmill visit. By noon they had successfully knocked out many of the Radar Stations in concentrated dive bombing attacks, but, although they had severed communications and power, the actual towers were intact. By mid-afternoon all except Ventnor, Isle of Wight, were in operation again, some with the aid of stand-by generators. Ventnor was out of action for three weeks. The Luftwaffe could be forgiven for thinking they had taken them all out, as their dive bombers certainly did a lot of damage, both at the Towers and at Fighter Command airfields.

On 16th August the Ventnor Radar Station was given another good working over by dive bombers who succeeded in negating the frantic efforts that had been made to restore the facility. In ten days of frenetic fighting Fighter Command had shot down 360 enemy aircraft for the loss of 183 of their own. But it was in the loss of pilots that the RAF faced the greatest danger. 154 pilots had been killed or put out of action in those ten days, a rate of attrition that could not be made good by the recruits from the Flying Training Schools.

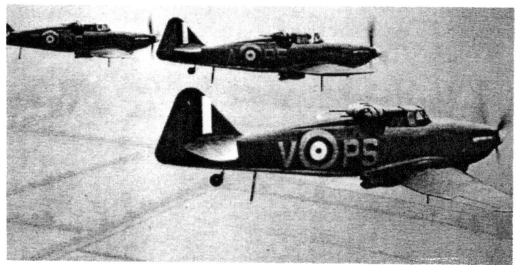

264 Squadron Boulton Paul Defiants

S/L P A Hunter with pilots of 264 Squadron at Hornchurch, August, 1940

Malan was somewhat surprised at the order to proceed to Wittering, but his pilots were in need of a breather. It had achieved success against the Luftwaffe, but its own strength was also inevitably sapped in the cauldron of combat.

54 Squadron was down to nine aircraft and, as they scrambled yet again, 'Prof' Leathart climbed them towards Dover with the intention of taking on the Me109s escorting bombers over the Channel. The Luftwaffe fighters were on this occasion, surprised by the attack from height and two of them were destroyed in 54's first attack. 'Al' Deere, however, got involved in another of his adventures: he chased another Me109 across to the French coast, but met many more Me109s over Calais Marck, who promptly chased him back home at sea level. In the process they riddled his fuselage, instrument panel, canopy and oil tank, although he was miraculously untouched. With the white cliffs of Dover a welcoming sight, the Me109s decided it was their turn to beat it for home. Deere, in his shattered aircraft, had no option but to bale out at Ashford, but his parachute snagged with the aircraft and he was too close to the ground for comfort when he finally broke free. In the process he gave his wrist an almighty thump against the tail plane and he landed quite close to where his Spitfire exploded on impact.

By a stroke of good fortune he was picked up by a passing RAF Ambulance returning to Kenley. He dozed off in the ambulance and awoke to find that the crew had missed the turn off to Kenley and turned up at the famous Burns Unit at East Grinstead where Sir Archibald McIndoe remoulded the burnt faces of so many RAF aircrews, who collectively became known as 'Guinea Pigs'. With no news of his fate back at Hornchurch, his parents in Wanganui, New Zealand, were notified that he was 'Missing', but the following day he turned up as large as life, with a plastered wrist. X-rays revealed no break, but Sir Archibald telephoned Group Captain Bouchier reporting his presence and suggesting that he should stay a few days as he was exhausted. The Station Commander concurred, but when Sir Archibald returned to the ward in which Al Deere had been placed, it was only to find that 'the bird had flown'.

At this stage of the Battle RAF Hornchurch witnessed one of the twists and turns of fate - the saga of the ill-fated Boulton Paul Defiants. 264 Squadron had received them in December, 1939, and arrived at Hornchurch from Kirton in Lindsey on 22nd August, 1940. Apart from the Blenheim night fighters they were the first break in the pattern of Spitfire squadrons that had rotated through the station.

The Boulton Paul Defiant was the first RAF fighter with a four gun turret and a two man crew - Pilot and Air Gunner. It introduced a new concept where there was no forward firing through the wings, as with the Spitfires and Hurricanes, and all the firing was done from the rear cockpit, primarily by flying alongside the target and raking the side of its fuselage and cockpit. Alternatively it could fire at enemy aircraft attacking from the rear. The squadron first took them into action over Dunkirk and they were very successful in early engagements. They were similar in silhouette to the Hurricane and Luftwaffe fighters coming in from behind were staggered to receive rearward fire from the four gun turret, but the element of surprise did not last for long.

Once the Germans had cottoned on to its armament the Defiant's time as a day fighter was to be brief. It had no answer to single seater fighters, firing through the wings, making head on attacks - a tactic that the Me109s duly concentrated on, whenever they appeared. Another discouraging factor was that, although the Defiant packed a Rolls Royce Merlin engine, the drag of the turret and its weight reduced its maximum speed to 303 mph, well behind that of the single seat fighters.

The only other squadron of Defiants in the Royal Air Force (141 Squadron) had already been shattered whilst operating out of Hawkinge and, in its one and only day-time encounter, lost six of a formation of nine aircraft in one combat with Me109s over the Channel. The remaining three might well have suffered the same fate, but for the arrival on the scene of the Hurricanes of 111 Squadron from Croydon. The Germans lost one Me109 to the Hurricanes and its pilot was rescued from the sea. This happened on 19th July and the Defiant Squadron was immediately taken out of the firing line, the remnants withdrawing to Turnhouse.

In these circumstances it is perhaps surprising that the Defiants of 264 Squadron were pitched into the front line a month later, although, at this stage in the Battle, there was probably little option. It was a tragic story as the Defiants operated for a week out of Hornchurch, Rochford and Manston. Gallantly as they fought to get at the Luftwaffe bombers they were quite incapable of engaging the Me109s. In this brief period the Squadron lost 14 pilots and gunners killed, including the Commanding Officer, Squadron Leader P A Hunter, who was flying his last sortie before handing over command to Squadron Leader G D Garvin. Others were injured: the air gunners had a very difficult task trying to bale out from the narrow confines of the turret and, if the electrical system failed, escape was impossible.

On 24th August three Defiants up from Manston were lost over Herne Bay with the loss of all pilots and gunners. Another, flying out of Hornchurch, was shot down just after take-off; the pilot, Pilot Officer R S Gaskell, baled out, but the Gunner, Sergeant W Machin, died of his wounds. Two days later two Defiants were lost from Hornchurch, but they had succeeded in getting at the Dornier 17s and had their greatest success in the Battle of Britain by shooting down six of them. Sergeants Edward Thorn and Frederick Barker had both won the Distinguished Flying Medal for the destruction of seven aircraft over Dunkirk and they received Bars to the award

On 20th August Winston Churchill was inspired to include in one of his speeches a phrase that has gone down to history: "Never in the field of human conflict was so much owed by so many to so few." The 'Few' has remained the collective noun for the Battle of Britain pilots in the fifty years since then and will forever remain so. To many airmen the content of the Prime Minister's speech was the first real indication that they had of the seriousness of the aerial battle being fought and the price that would be paid in the unthinkable event of defeat. Their courage, already amply demonstrated, was now laced with grim determination.

for their action in shooting down two Dornier 17s this day. A Me109, in turn, set their Defiant on fire, but, before crash landing, they shot it down and both escaped with slight injuries.

On 28th August, the last day that they were used in day fighting, the Defiants lost two aircraft from Hornchurch and another from Rochford. In this action the Defiants tried to get at Heinkel bombers over Canterbury, but once again they were pounced on by Me109s from above. One of the Heinkels was destroyed and another damaged, but 264's losses included the aircraft piloted by their new Commanding Officer, Squadron Leader G D Garvin: the CO baled out and survived, but his Gunner, who also managed to bale out, was killed when he struck the tailplane: Flight Lieutenant R C V Ash was probably the highest-ranking Gunner to be killed in the Battle. They had been unlucky enough to encounter 111 Gruppe of Jagdegschivader 51, led by the German ace, Adolph Galland, who knew all about the Defiant. In a few days of hectic fighting the Squadron had lost five pilots and nine gunners dead and twelve aircraft destroyed or written off.

The remains of 264 Squadron - just three serviceable aircraft - returned to Hornchurch and the three crews still operational wanted to scramble yet again. The finding of F/L Ash's body dead in his parachute had sparked rumours that he was shot while descending and feelings ran high until the truth was ascertained. What was left of the Squadron returned to Kirton that night, but, even then, their torment was not yet over. A week later, in the comparative peace of Lincolnshire, another Defiant was lost in a take-off accident at night and Flying Officer D H O'Malley and Air Gunner Sergeant L A Rasmussen were both killed: O'Malley had been a survivor from the devastation at Hornchurch. 264 never saw service as a day fighter squadron again, but at the end of October, 1940, they returned to Rochford as a night fighter squadron.

Later in the war, the night fighting Defiants with specially trained crews, emerged as a most useful weapon.

Meanwhile, on 26th August, six Spitfires of 65 Squadron, led by Flight Lieutenant Gerald Saunders, met thirty Dornier 17s, escorted by one hundred Me109s. 54 Squadron was summoned to assist, but until their arrival the odds were six to one hundred and thirty. Amazingly, as 65 tore in to the formation, the Messerschmidts formed a defensive circle, content to leave the bombers to work out their own salvation. Saunders shared in the destruction of one of the Dorniers.

The Senior Medical Officer from Hornchurch was visiting Rochford and was standing by the Control Tower when an obviously damaged Dornier made a good landing not far away; the aircraft finished its landing run and stopped both engines. In the front cockpit the badly wounded pilot slumped over the controls and the Medical Officer managed to extricate him and lie him down on the grass. Turning his attention to the tail turret from the outside, he was horrified to see the Gunner behind guns that were pointed at the Medical Officer. One close up look, however, was enough to ascertain that he was quite dead.

####

At the end of August the comparative quiet that Hornchurch had enjoyed while Manston was being pasted came to an end and the airfield was subjected to fourteen bombing attacks between 24th August and the end of 1940.

In the first, communications were cut and almost a hundred bomb craters had to be filled by a large posse of airmen and civilian workers. The most serious raid was a week later, 31st August, when two attacks were made on the same day. The first, at lunch time, was by four Me110s acting in the fighter bomber rôle, and the second, at 1800, was by thirty Dornier 17s, dropping a mix of high explosive and incendiary bombs. Damage was considerable, with six Spitfires destroyed and damage to the landing ground and hangars. Despite this, the Station never became non-operational.

During the first raid three Spitfires of 54 Squadron were in the act of taking off when they were caught in the blasts of a cluster of bombs. All the aircraft were destroyed, but, amazingly, all three pilots survived. Sergeant Jack Davis had just cleared the boundary fence and the blast blew his aircraft to the other side of the River Ingrebourne: his wrecked aircraft was seen from the airfield, but the pilot stepped out unhurt and, finding no gap in the boundary fence, he had to walk two miles the long way round, carrying his parachute. He entered through the main gate and walked down to the Squadron Dispersal Hut to report his presence. Flight Lieutenant Alan Deere had his port wing blown off and the rest of his aircraft careered along upside down, before it came to a halt leaving him suspended in his harness straps. Pilot Officer Eric Edsall finished the right way up, but his legs were badly injured and he could not walk. Seeing Alan Deere's plight, he dragged himself over on his hands and knees to find his Spitfire steeped in overpowering petrol fumes. He managed to wrench off the inverted cockpit door and helped to free Deere, who had facial injuries caused by stones and dirt, from his harness. it was as well that the Spitfire had a side door (unlike the Hurricane) otherwise, instead of pulling him out underneath, the Spitfire would have had to be craned off Alan Deere. One spark and they would both have been engulfed in flame from the carpet of petrol and oil that the inverted Spitfire had vomited. Edsall propped himself on Deere's shoulders for support and the pair of them staggered through the nearby hangar to the Station Sick Quarters. All three were ready to resume operations the following morning.

In the second attack many of the bombs fell harmlessly, but two Spitfires were destroyed on the ground and one airman was killed. Sergeant John Norwell of 54 Squadron described his day's experiences to a wide audience on BBC Radio.

When the dust had settled it was established that 60 bombs had fallen in a line through 54's Dispersal Area and on into the Elm Park housing complex. Casualties occurred in the domestic quarters and Ronald Adam, the Sector Controller, heard urgent voices outside the Operations Room, shouting for stretcher bearers. It was as well that the rest of 54 Squadron had been airborne when the attack occurred, otherwise there would have been heavier casualties as it was the only 54 fatality was that of the Squadron canary.

Downed Me109s were scattered over a wide area around Hornchurch, including Shoeburyness Beach, Jenkins Farm at Navestock, Bridge Road, Rainham, and Whalebone Lane, Chadwell Heath.

The YMCA Van struggled on to serve Hornchurch airmen throughout all the difficulties. It was rather like a super quality roadside coffee stall, manned by volunteers and it regularly toured the roads, hangars and perimeter track, stopping intermittently at established halts to dispense tea, coffee, buns, slices of apple tart, cigarettes and chocolate to eagerly waiting airmen. Never were their efforts appreciated more than on 31st August, 1940. It was quite a day.

As August drew to a close, with Hornchurch still in the thick of the Battle, 54 Squadron was now the only one of the original permanent three still at the airfield. 65 was at Turnhouse and 74 was at Kirton in Lindsey. On 3rd September the valiant 54 Squadron again moved up to Catterick for rest and recuperation. As they left their score stood at 85 enemy aircraft destroyed with a further eighty probables or damaged: seventy of these victories had been achieved in the previous 18 days.

One of the replacement squadrons arriving at Hornchurch at the end of August was 603 (City of Edinburgh) Squadron - an Auxiliary Air Force squadron commanded by Squadron Leader 'Uncle' George Denholm. It was destined to spend more time at the airfield during the Battle of Britain than any other except 41 Squadron. It was also the Squadron that suffered the highest number of casualties at the base. Group Captain Bouchier, the Station Commander wrote of the arrival of 603 in the following terms -

> It was my great good fortune in 1940 to command RAF Hornchurch and 603 Squadron came in on 27th August, 1940. I shall never forget their arrival. Could this really be a Squadron? The Commanding Officer had his little 'side hat' perched on the back of his head and meandered towards me with bent shoulders and his hands in his pockets, followed by the motleyest looking collection of unmilitary looking men I had ever seen. I was not impressed. Suddenly I remembered. It's an Auxiliary Squadron. Ah! I thought, that explains it, but what had I done to deserve this? How wrong I was. Somehow I feel that 603 will forgive these first impressions. No squadron was ever regarded more highly. No squadron ever went to war with such grace, so little fuss and more determination.

The Squadron included Richard Hillary, the author of the classic book *The Last Enemy*, one of the finest accounts ever written of war in the air and the human emotions it generated. He arrived with his great friend, Peter Pease, to whom he devoted a chapter on his own in the book. Hillary was shocked to find that, instead of holding one Flight of one squadron at 'Readiness', Hornchurch would have four complete squadrons at 'Readiness' at this period when the Luftwaffe was making determined efforts to wipe out Fighter Command, its aircraft and its airfields.

Aircraft often returned just long enough to enable ground staff to refuel and replenish them and load more belts of ammunition before they took off again. The ground crews worked wonders. Squadrons were coming back as individual aircraft, landing at odd intervals one after the other. Often there was a 'phone call from a pilot to say that he had landed somewhere else, even in a farmer's field.

There is no doubt that the arrival of 603 Squadron was a most valuable addition to the Hornchurch armoury and their record was second to none.

Hillary was there when the airfield was bombed on 31st August. Despite all the craters aircraft did not have to land at alternative airfields, safely negotiating the obstacles to reach their dispersals. Station personnel were conscious of being members of a community that had shared peril and come through it. The crew of a Heinkel 111 that crashed at Ockendon were brought into Hornchurch and were obviously surprised to see that their efforts had not reduced the station to chaos.

At this time a controversy blew up in the RAF about the tactics that should be employed in dealing with the Luftwaffe. A change was suggested by 12 Group's Air Vice-Marshal Trafford Leigh-Mallory to a system that became known as the 'Big Wing Theory'. The idea was to concentrate fire power in threatened areas into a 'Big Wing' or mass formation of three, four or five squadrons. Squadron Leader Douglas Bader was a leading exponent of the idea and he sold it to AVM Leigh-Mallory.

The policy adopted by Air Chief Marshal Hugh Dowding at Fighter Command HQ and Air Vice-Marshal Keith Park at HQ 11 Group was to involve Spitfires in squadron strength to take on the Me109 escorts and Hurricanes in squadron strength for the bombers. It meant a very tough and exacting rôle for the Hornchurch Spitfires; even though, in practice, these tactics were never more than broad principles.

The 'Big Wing' theory was not new to the RAF. Park had used it in 1940, but he did not consider it suitable for the Battle of Britain, where he required speed in assembly and flexibility at squadron strength to deal with a constantly fluctuating situation. He could not afford to assemble squadrons into Wings with the limited resources at his disposal. Dowding supported Park in this respect.

It is interesting to note that the Luftwaffe faced similar problems when it met the combined onslaughts of the Royal Air Force and United States Army Air Force from 1943 onwards. The two air battles - over Britain and Germany - were not identical, but it may be significant that the Germans, after experimenting with large formations, reverted to relying on small numbers operating independently, as the situation required.

11 Group could never know whether an attack was for real or a decoy to lure all available fighters into the air to leave room for another raid when they were back on the ground refuelling and rearming. In the event, 11 Group continued with their

tactics while 12 Group continued to assemble four, five or, on one occasion, seven squadrons into a 'Big Wing' Two squadrons were frequently found by 11 Group to be an ideal number to control.

###

Two days after Richard Hillary arrived he shot down a Me109 and was then shot down himself, making a forced landing in a field near Lympne. He was impressed when he saw an ambulance enter the gate into the field, only to find that the corporal and two orderlies hared off in the opposite direction, to where his friend, Colin Pinckney, was suspended in his parachute snagged round a tree, with his legs dangling in the air, slightly burned, but quite cheerful. They had landed almost in the back garden of an Army Brigade cocktail party and Hillary managed to negotiate his way through a number of double whiskeys proffered to him for 'his nerves'. The Brigadier then put Hillary up for the night as he was so pie-eyed that he answered all questions with a glazed stare.

Hillary claimed two more Me109s on 2nd September, including one that he chased across the Channel, and another on the 3rd. However, on this occasion he was shot down in flames over Margate and, although he managed to bale out, he was grievously burned. He had flown without gloves and with his goggles up on his forehead. After being fished out by Margate Lifeboat he was treated for three months before going to East Grinstead where he underwent surgery by Sir Archibald McIndoe to become a 'Guinea Pig'. Over many months the scars on his face were slowly and painfully repaired. He returned to active duty, but was killed when taking off in a Blenheim on 8th January, 1943.

The Last Enemy is, of course, death; and in his book Hillary claims that, while he was under anaesthetic, he saw his best friend Peter Pease killed. Two days later he had a letter from Colin Pinckney which a nurse read to him; it was very short, hoping that he was feeling better and saying that Peter was dead. The son of Sir Richard and Lady Pease of Richmond, Yorkshire was shot down in combat over Kent and crashed near Maidstone. *The Last Enemy* hauntingly chronicles the tragedy of the many talented young men who died with such gallantry in that blazing summer of 1940.

###

Back at Hornchurch, 41 Squadron experienced its own disaster when the Commanding Officer, Squadron Leader Hilary Hood, and one of his Flight Commanders, Flight Lieutenant John Webster, collided in mid-air during an attack on Dornier 17s over the Thames Estuary and both were killed. Following the accident Webster baled out, but was dead when he was found. His Spitfire crashed in flames at Bovills Farm, North Benfleet. Squadron Leader Hood's aircraft was thought to have disintegrated over nearby Wickford, but no trace of his body was ever found. Both were holders of the Distinguished Flying Cross, John Webster having received his just six days earlier.

It was a grievous blow to 41 Squadron, compounded by the fact that the loss of these two fine pilots had not happened through enemy action. Three days later

222 Squadron ground crew on a Spitfire, September, 1940

222 and 603 Squadrons at Hornchurch in 1940: note St George's Hospital chimney in the background

Squadron Leader Robert Lister arrived from Hawarden to assume command of the Squadron, but after only two weeks he was seriously injured and control passed to Squadron Leader Donald Finlay, the erstwhile Commander of 54 Squadron, whose service at Hornchurch dated back to the time of his 1936 Olympics honour. In the closing months of 1940 he shot down three enemy aircraft and shared in another.

On 7th September, 1940, the Luftwaffe amazingly switched its attacks from Fighter Command's Sector Stations to London. It was a change that caused heavy casualties to the already hard-pressed Londoners, but at the same time it gave a measure of relief to the damaged airfields and their resident squadrons. Hermann Goering heralded his personal command of this operation by appearing at Calais to gaze across the Channel to the distant, but visible, White Cliffs of Dover.

At 1616 nearly one thousand aircraft, 348 bombers escorted by 617 fighters, crossed the coast between Deal and North Foreland. They advanced on a wide front up the River Thames and their bombs cascaded down on London's Docks and East End residential streets from Beckton to Tower Bridge. They were the opening shots in a long, tortuous and horrifying ordeal for the sheltering Cockneys. Ferocious air battles were fought out by RAF squadrons from airfields as far apart as Middle Wallop, Hampshire, and Martlesham Heath, Suffolk, in an attempt to stem the tide. Great fires were started in incendiary attacks and burning warehouses in the London Docks complex blazed until they collapsed. At 1745 the Luftwaffe armada, the largest military air strike at that time, turned for home, scattered, but still an integral whole.

A second attack started at 2010 with further incendiaries intensifying the out of control fires that stretched from Bermondsey to Woolwich, and this continued until 5 the following morning. 450 people were killed and two thousand injured in the London area, many of them by falling structures. Post-war records showed that the Germans lost 37 aircraft, compared with the RAF's 24. Hornchurch lost five aircraft in the melée and another two were damaged, but, importantly, all the pilots survived. Hornchurch flew 92 sorties and claimed six enemy aircraft destroyed. Sadly Sergeants A F Saunders and J W White lost their lives in a Blenheim of 600 Squadron during a training flight, coming to earth at nearby Rainham.

Damage to London was very severe and it led the Luftwaffe to believe that Fighter Command's defences had, at last, been overcome by this massive raid. In fact, the respite given to the airfield by the change of tactics allowed them to restore communications, repair damage to buildings and services and deal with delayed action bombs. The defences became stronger than ever, a fact that the Luftwaffe found to its cost when it tried to repeat the opening success.

When they made a further mass raid the following week they were fought to a standstill and turned for home while still short of London. Hornchurch destroyed eleven raiders for the loss of three Spitfires and one pilot. One Me109 crashed to earth at Rainham Road, Hornchurch, close to the base.

15th September was another 'thousand aircraft' day and a record total of 185 enemy aircraft were claimed - one of the RAF's biggest 'over claims', as post-war research reduced the figure to 56. The RAF lost 26 aircraft itself.

Damage to London this time was much reduced and the German War Diary conceded that 'The enemy air force is still by no means defeated. On the contrary, it shows increasing activity'.

Hornchurch lost Peter Pease of 603 Squadron and Pilot Officer Gerald Langley, who crashed at Bulphan. Manston lost Pilot Officer F W Cale and Sergeant F B Hawley of 266 Squadron, Rochford losing Pilot Officers J T Johnson and M Rozwadowski of 151 Squadron. P/O Cale baled out into the River Medway, but was dead when found; his aircraft crashed on the banks of the river.

15th September was always referred to as 'The Longest Day' and is now recognised each year as Battle of Britain Day.

####

Amidst all the casualties at Hornchurch a few stand out as examples of particular sadness. Two occurred at the end of September.

On 27th Pilot Officer Philip 'Pip' Cardell of 603 Squadron destroyed a Me109 over the Channel, but was wounded in the process. He attempted to make it to a coastal field, but had to bale out at low level just a quarter of a mile off the coast at Folkestone and his parachute failed to deploy properly. His friend, Pilot Officer Peter Dexter, noticed movement and tried to attract the people along the sea front to his friend's plight by flying low and waggling his wings. There was no reaction, so he crash-landed his Spitfire on the beach and commandeered a boat, but 'Pip' Cardell was dead when he was reached. The Diarist of the Hornchurch Operations Record Book - now at the Public Record Office - commented, "It is to be regretted that the apathy of the occupants of the beach at Folkestone should have caused the death of a most valuable pilot."

The second was on 29th September, when Flight Lieutenant Harold MacDonald of 603 Squadron was shot down by a Me109 over Gillingham. He was the elder of two brothers with 603 and his younger brother, Pilot Officer Donald MacDonald, had failed to return from operations over Dover a month earlier. They came from Murrayfield, Edinburgh, and were 28 and 22 years old respectively.

####

In October activity continued at high level and ten pilots were lost during the month. The Luftwaffe daylight attacks ceased, but the nightly battering of London continued with an average of 500 civilian casualties (200 killed, 300 injured) each night. The East End and the City were savaged: Londoners could only take it resolutely and fight the fires with ARP (Air Raid Precautions) Stirrup Pumps until the Auxiliary Fire Service arrived. The night fighter force was still in its infancy and, although the heavy anti-aircraft guns installed at Barking Park and other open spaces made a lot of noise and gave some comfort, they had little real success. In local cinemas a notice would flash on the screen indicating that an air raid warning had been sounded. Older people would leave the cinema, while the teenagers simply cuddled up a little more tightly, until the explosions and noise got too close, when there would be hasty evacuation.

In October three Battle of Britain pilots who are buried in the military section of St Andrews Church, Hornchurch, met their ends. Pilot Officer John Broadhurst from Crayford, Kent, with four Me109s to his credit, baled out on the 7th, but fell dead; his aircraft crashed at Salehurst on the Kent-Sussex border. The other two were shot down on the same day, 27th; Pilot Officer Robin Dewey (603 Squadron) from Portsmouth crashed into a tree near Canterbury and Flying Officer Claude Goldsmith was shot down at Maidstone, dying the following day.

Perhaps the most poignant Hornchurch loss was that of 23 year old Sergeant Philip Lloyd of 41 Squadron, who was born not far away at Loughton. He worked for Chigwell Urban District Council and flew with the RAF Volunteer Reserve from Stapleford Tawney at weekends. On 24th August, 1940, he married his childhood sweetheart in the Church of the Holy Innocents at High Beech in Epping Forest, but they were soon parted when he was posted to 41 Squadron, then at Catterick. On 3rd September, 41 Squadron returned to Hornchurch and on 15th October he was shot into the sea. His body was washed ashore near Herne Bay twelve days later and he was laid to rest in the grounds of the little church at High Beech where he had been married two months earlier.

On 15th October the Sector Operations Room was moved from the airfield to the YMCA's Lambourne Hall, Western Road, Romford. The accommodation was far more spacious and less likely to suffer direct attack. The Controllers remained at Romford for the rest of the time that Hornchurch Sector existed.

During October Hitler postponed 'Operation Sealion' - the invasion of the United Kingdom - until the next spring. Despite all its efforts the Luftwaffe had failed to break Fighter Command and the Germans could not maintain concentrations of troops, arms and stores at the Channel ports indefinitely, in the face of Bomber Command attacks. Reconnaissance missions confirmed that they were being dispersed. In reality, the planned invasion was off for good. The greatest threat to its freedom the United Kingdom had ever known had been averted and the people of Britain survived. It had been secured by the courage and professionalism of 'The Few', as honourable a band of men who have ever been assembled. They inevitably lived for the moment, had riotous parties and sang silly songs to alleviate the numbing tension, but once inside the cockpits they were deadly serious and aware of what was at stake.

The last pilot to die from Hornchurch before the Battle of Britain is officially deemed to have closed (31st October, 1940) was Pilot Officer Hilary Edridge of 222 Squadron who, on 30th October, attempted a crash-landing at Langwood Farm,

Ewhurst, Kent, and died of his injuries.   Only two weeks earlier he had made a successful crash landing nearer the base at Tillingham Hall, West Horndon.

As the Battle drew to a close RAF Rochford was re-named RAF Southend.   It became a self accounting unit, rather than a satellite but, on most occasions, its resident squadrons were still controlled from the RAF Hornchurch Control Room at Romford.   The famous Wing Commander Basil Embry, whose escape from capture after he was shot down in a Blenheim bomber over France and his subsequent return to his base at RAF Wattisham in Suffolk is a legend, was appointed as Station Commander at RAF Southend.

Despite the victorious conclusion of this momentous chapter in the history of the Royal Air Force the architects of that victory did not receive the recognition due to them from official circles.   On the contrary, it was considered that the time was ripe for a change.

Air Chief Marshal Sir Hugh Dowding, the AOC in C of Fighter Command was replaced and sent on a mission to the USA. He retired from the RAF in 1942 without becoming Chief of the Air Staff or attaining the rank of Marshal. Rarely has a man who achieved so much for his country received so little honour and glory in return.

He was never subservient and probably ruffled a few feathers during his career, but he saved Fighter Command from disappearing into the bottomless pit during the battle for France and his Battle of Britain strategy is considered by most to have caused the maximum disruption to the Luftwaffe while carefully nursing his own resources. 'Stuffy' Dowding died at Tunbridge Wells on 15th February, 1970, at the age of 87.

He was replaced at Bentley Priory by Air Chief Marshal Sir William Sholto-Douglas.

####

Of the 2,945 who comprised 'The Few' 1,353 did not survive the war, but while attention inevitably concentrates on them, due to the nature of the Battle, the long arduous hours of work put in by the ground staff in maintaining and servicing the aircraft and repairing combat damage must not be forgotten. Fitters and mechanics at Hornchurch and elsewhere frequently worked on through the night after working all day to keep the greatest possible number of aircraft operational.   Other RAF ground staff took their part in keeping the services of the airfield functioning with a host of back-up duties: even those performing the most menial tasks were essential.

The ground staff men were the unsung and largely anonymous heroes of the Battle and, even though they have never received the plaudits accorded to the aircrews, they also faced death and disablement as the Luftwaffe hurled its fire at the airfields.   Amidst all the chaos of repairing damaged aircraft and receiving aerial bombardment the ground staff fought with might and main to keep things going and it says much for their proficiency, determination and discipline that they succeeded in so doing.   The backbone of the sections that kept the fighters flying were the products of Lord Trenchard's School of Technical Training at RAF Halton, Buckinghamshire.   All Hornchurch squadrons had their fair sprinkling of 'Halton Brats', as they were affectionately known.

####

Although 31st October was the official end of the Battle of Britain, it was as arbitrary a date as 10th July was for its opening. Airmen died in the ferocious combat with the Luftwaffe in defence of the country at a time when its back was to the wall for the whole of 1940, intensifying with the Dunkirk operations in May and continuing, albeit on a diminishing scale, after 31st October. The arbitrary dates have caused a great deal of misunderstanding. Hornchurch lost seven pilots in the early days of July, 1940, before 'The Battle' was decreed to have started. They ranged from a Squadron Leader to Sergeants, who died over and around Dover, Deal, and Margate in precisely the same 'convoy protection' duties that predominated after the 10th. Earlier, Pilot Officer W Stapleton went down over Dunkirk and spent no less than five years as a prisoner of war. All these pilots served in the same role in the most critical year in the nation's history. How much better it would have been if 'Year 1940' had been used as a benchmark to identify 'The Few': wherever the boundaries are set there will always be somebody unlucky to fall the wrong side of it, but there was little flying activity on 31st December, 1939, in the middle of the 'Phoney War' and little more in January, 1941, in the middle of a hard winter. So there would have been few hard cases, and few would argue that all those dying in aerial combat over and around the United Kingdom in 1940 should receive the same treatment.

On 2nd November a Luftwaffe Heinkel 111 went into a screaming dive over the airfield and finished up crashing into the centre of Hornchurch 'Village', as the Operations Book referred to it.

The Windmill Theatre girls made a second visit to the camp, receiving just as rapturous a reception as they did at the first show: encores were demanded again and again. At this time Winston Churchill's 'Never in the field of human conflict' speech was on everybody's lips and one airman, with a dreamy smile on his face, was heard to paraphrase the famous quotation "Never has so much been bared, by so few, for so many". They certainly took the gloom off an autumn evening!

On 17th November Eric 'Sawn Off' Lock shot down two Me109s, but suffered injuries to his right arm and both legs and had to make a forced landing on the heath at Martlesham, Suffolk. Although he came to earth only a couple of miles from a 12 Group RAF Station, he sat injured and motionless in his cockpit before being rescued by two soldiers who got him out and carried him to the airfield in a makeshift stretcher made up of service greatcoats with rifles stuffed through the arms.

Four days later Sergeant Eric Plant collided with a Heinkel 111 over Kent. He managed to bale out, but was dead when found.

A new twist was added to the air war on 23rd November when the Italian Air Force (*Regia Aeronautica*) made the first of two attacks from German bases in France. They fought with honour, but were hopelessly inexperienced and out-classed, as they lost seven Fiats to the guns of 603 Squadron, who did not suffer any losses.

In the run up to Christmas, 1940, veterans at Hornchurch were saddened to hear of the loss of Pilot Officer William Franklin on 12th December. A pre-war Sergeant Pilot with 65 Squadron, he was one of the most successful pilots, destroying eight aircraft over Dunkirk and a further eight in the Battle of Britain up to the time that 65 Squadron left Hornchurch. He was awarded a Distinguished Flying Medal on 9th July, 1940, a Bar to it on 13th August and was commissioned to Pilot Officer in September. He was lost from RAF Tangmere after chasing an enemy bomber in dense cloud.

At this time Group Captain Bouchier was posted away after an heroic and successful year as Station Commander at Hornchurch and was replaced by Group Captain Harry Broadhurst, a 35-year-old former Royal Artillery officer who transferred to the Royal Air Force in 1926. Harry Broadhurst had wide experience at fighter stations and had commanded 111 Squadron and 1 Squadron operationally since the war started. He took over at a vital time and was to reign supreme for the next eighteen months. During this time the station slowly turned from desperate defence to a more offensive role and it made sweeps over enemy occupied Europe and provided escorts to bombers in the same task.

In his book *We Rendezvous at Ten* that Ronald Adam wrote during the war, the principal characters at Hornchurch were all given fictitious names to comply with war-time censorship, but it is not difficult to translate them into their real names: Group Captain Broadhurst was re-named Group Captain Faversham in the book.

Ronald Adam reports that, as he went towards the house where his room was, he heard the snort of the Group Captain's pigs as he passed his house. "Pigs," the Group Captain had said one evening in the Mess, "why don't we keep pigs? There's enough swill from the Mess to feed a score of them." The response was a heavy silence. "I'll show you," the Group Captain said, "I'll get a pig myself. I'll show you."

As 1940 drew to a close the war in the air was slowly turning and, on Christmas Eve, the new Air Officer Commanding 11 Group, Air Vice Marshal Trafford Leigh-Mallory, presided over a conference of senior officers that was arranged to draw up the plans, the operations, the tactics that were to be introduced to Fighter Command to face a new challenge in 1941.

The final initiative of 1940 went to the Luftwaffe, who made an all-out incendiary raid on the night of 29th December that caused widespread devastation and turned large areas of the City into a desert of rubble. Famous buildings either destroyed or heavily damaged included the Guildhall, eight Christopher Wren churches (although St Paul's Cathedral miraculously stood intact in the centre of a blazing area) and Trinity House. 100,000 incendiary bombs were dropped in a few hours.

The effect on Londoners from the time that the assault was switched from the airfields to urban areas is demonstrated by the following figures -

CIVILIAN CASUALTIES

	Killed	Injured	Total
July	258	321	579
August	438	637	1075
September	6,954	10,615	18,569
October	6,334	8,695	15,029

Some 1,400 children were numbered among the dead. November and December continued at the same rate as October. For Londoners it was a long, hard winter.

Sticky end for a Spitfire - Hornchurch, 1940

Hornchurch under attack, 31 August, 1940: note the outline of a Spitfire through smoke in the gap between bomb bursts

RAF HORNCHURCH
PILOTS LOST FROM THE OUTBREAK OF WAR
TO THE EVE OF THE BATTLE OF BRITAIN
(3rd September, 1939 - 9th July, 1940)

Date	Rank	Name	Sqn	Remarks
8 11 39	Sgt	Cole, E J	54	Night flying, Basildon
16 11 39	F/O	Vickers, A A	600	Blenheim: accident
25 11 39	P/O	Graham, B	65	Gladiator: RAF Northolt
15 3 40	P/O	West, R E	54	Magister: Upminster
11 5 40	P/O	McKenzie, J	54	In sea off Manston
15 5 40	P/O	Ross, D S [Canadian]	54	Thorndon Park Golf Course
23 5 40	P/O	Klipsch, P	92	Dunkirk
23 5 40	F/S	Wooder, K	92	Dunkirk
23 5 40	P/O	Learmond, P	92	Dunkirk
23 5 40	S/L	Bushell, R	92	PoW: killed later
23 5 40	F/O	Byrne, V	74	Ghent, PoW
23 5 40	F/O	Gillies, J	92	Dunkirk
24 5 40	F/O	Linley, T N	54	Dunkirk, PoW
24 5 40	Sgt	Phillips, J	54	Dunkirk, PoW
24 5 40	F/O	Casenove, P	92	Dunkirk, PoW
24 5 40	F/O	Hoare, D S	74	Calais, PoW
24 5 40	F/O	Aubert, R D	74	Calais
25 5 40	Sgt	Buckland, F	54	Dunkirk
26 5 40	F/O	Welford, F H	65	British AA fire suspected
26 5 40	S/L	Stephenson, G D	19	Dunkirk, PoW
26 5 40	Sgt	Irwin, C A	19	Dunkirk
27 5 40	F/L	Pearson, M C	54	Dunkirk
27 5 40	F/L	Treacy, W P	74	Evaded & returned to UK 1941. Killed in collision later
1 6 40	P/O	Massey-Sharpe, G	222	Dunkirk
1 6 40	P/O	Falkus, H E	222	Dunkirk, PoW
1 6 40	Sgt	White, L J	222	Dunkirk
1 6 40	P/O	Stapleton, W	41	Dunkirk, PoW
1 6 40	F/O	Legard, W E	41	Dunkirk
3 7 40	Sgt	White	74	Struck by lightning, Margate
7 7 40	F/O	Proudman, G	65	Dover
7 7 40	P/O	Brisbane, N J	65	Dover
7 7 40	Sgt	Hayes, P S	65	Dover
7 7 40	S/L	Cooke, D	65	Dover
9 7 40	P/O	Garton, C E	54	Channel
9 7 40	P/O	Evershed, A	54	Channel

		ANALYSIS BY SQUADRON	
Killed	25	54 Squadron	10
Prisoners of war	8	65	6
Prisoner of war (killed later)	1	92	6
Evaded capture (killed later)	1	74	5
		222	3
		41	2
		19	2
		600	1

'CHORUS'
SWEEPS AND ESCORTS

1941 opened with very bleak weather and a carpet of snow covered the airfield for much of January, making a fresh appearance with a new heavy fall just as soon as it was cleared. The prewar routine of Fighter Command stations operating grass fields had been to flatten the snow on the flight paths and, if it was heavy and continuous, to abandon flying for the time being. In wartime, hard labour with shovels and somewhat inefficient snow ploughs were the order of the day, but even they were helpless when faced with continuous blizzards.

The year started with three Spitfire squadrons in the sector: 41 Squadron (S/Ldr D O Finlay); 64 Squadron (S/Ldr A R MacDonnell); and 611 (West Lancashire) Squadron (S/Ldr E R Bitmead). One or other of the squadrons was usually at Rochford with the other two at Hornchurch. It was the turn of 611 to be at Rochford at the start of the year, but they were relieved by 64 Squadron at the end of January.

Squadron Leader Aeneas Ronald MacDonnell, the Commanding Officer of 64 Squadron, was the 22nd Chief of Glengarry and had earlier served at Hornchurch with 54 Squadron, flying Bulldogs and Gauntlets from 1934 to 1936.

The gloomy winter was relieved by the entertainment laid on which included two Ralph Reader Gang Shows and a station dance attended by Air Vice Marshal Trafford Leigh-Mallory, the new Air Officer Commanding 11 Group, and his wife.

The view from the London Transport District Line trains that airmen travelled regularly on from Elm Park or Hornchurch to London, progressively revealed increasing piles of rubble from houses and other buildings blasted open or flattened: the scene was one of desolation. At night only the dimmest of lights illuminated the carriages of the train, whose windows were heavily protected with webbing.

More airmen were now billeted over the far side of the camp in the 1914-18 area at Suttons Institute. The original WAAF accommodation there was much extended and eventually resulted in half the airmen being billeted there. The final remnants of Suttons Farm itself disappeared under additional aircraft dispersal pens (one of which is retained to this day

The London blitz continued every night that the Luftwaffe found it possible to get off the ground and the men of the Auxiliary Fire Service became national heroes, battling against bombs and fire. They suffered heavy casualties and, at times, were so long at the scenes of uncontrolled fires, that they had to rely on the voluntary services and good natured members of the public for food and sustenance. They often returned to their fire stations dirty, exhausted, hungry and soaking wet.

For millions of Londoners their nightly home was an Anderson Shelter (named after Sir John Anderson, the Home Secretary), dug in almost every back garden. They were cold, draughty, crowded and highly uncomfortable, but they saved many lives. Made of thick corrugated iron sheets, which were then piled high with earth; they were sited over a three foot hole and most of the occupants slept on wooden bunks at or below ground level. Entry was by means of a short wooden step ladder leading from a small hole at the front.

S/L Donald Finlay and pilots of 41 Squadron at RAF Hornchurch, February, 1941 (*Imperial War Museum*)

Ground crews at RAF Hornchurch take a tea break from a YMCA tea car in 1941 (*Imperial War Museum*)

in Hornchurch Country Park).

Group Captain Harry Broadhurst, the Station Commander, moved his Headquarters to the Suttons side of the base. The Hornchurch CO was described by Ronald Adam, the Sector Controller, as 'a man whose face was set in lines of great pugnacity - a man of few words and immediate decision. Suddenly, the lines in the face would readjust themselves into laughter and he would look twenty years old again. Then the wide mouth would snap down once more, the jaw would thrust forward and the dark eyes restlessly resume their watchfulness'.

There was a new atmosphere in the air as the airfield's emphasis and predominant rôle slowly switched from defence to attack, which encouraged the formation of Squadrons into Wings in order to take the war to the enemy. With Air Vice Marshal Trafford Leigh-Mallory now at the helm of No. 11 Group, it did not take long for this to come into effect and a new post of 'Wing Commander - Flying' was introduced at each of the Sector Stations from March, 1941, the holder of the post usually being the second senior man on the airfield, responsible only to the Station Commander and acting as Deputy to him in his absence. The new Commander in Chief of Fighter Command, Air Chief Marshal William Sholto-Douglas, was another more at home attacking than defending and, for the first time in the course of the war, Fighter Command was strong enough and in a position to contemplate such action.

A new language was in the air as code words were implemented to identify the various types of offensive operations. A CIRCUS operation was a bombing attack by a Light Bomber Squadron escorted by a strong force of fighters. The first was flown on 10th January. A Circus was really designed to get the Luftwaffe fighters off the ground and was, if anything, more geared to that than the damage that would be caused by bombing. A RAMROD operation was similar to a Circus, but the emphasis here was on the bombing operation, rather than in getting the enemy fighter squadrons into battle. A RHUBARB operation was a low level Fighter Ground Attack strafing operation over enemy territory. Other subtle variations were ROADSTEADS and RODEOS.

As the weather eased in February Hornchurch lost six pilots during the month, most of them on offensive sweeps across France. Four were Sergeant Pilots. Two from 41 Squadron (I McAdam and R A Angus) baled out over the Channel on 20th February and McAdam's parachute was seen to be in flames as he dropped into the sea: he was picked up dead. Angus baled out successfully, but he was not found. Both were shot down by the ace German pilot Werner Molders. McAdam had earlier accounted for a Me109 and a Dornier 17 and had survived a crash landing at Rayleigh.

For the citizens of London, still taking a nightly hammering, these operations came as welcome news demonstrating that their tormentors were at last getting back some of their own medicine.

The air defences against night attacks were still in their rudimentary stages and the 81 aircraft claimed over the course of the blitz was less than 1% of the sorties flown: only eight of these were claimed by night fighters. In fact, the actual total was found to be higher after the war, but it was still insignificant in relation to the numbers employed.

The first low level ground attack operation (RHUBARB) proved to be very expensive and the limited range of the Spitfires, combined with the higher efficiency of the Luftwaffe as they got used to a defensive rôle, meant increasingly heavy RAF losses.

On 23rd February 54 Squadron (Hornchurch's Own) again swapped airfields with 41 Squadron and arrived from Catterick - this time, however, without 'Al' Deere, who finally came to the end of a long and hair-raising period with the Squadron, his service going back to the Gloster Gladiator of 1938. In yet another flying adventure he had survived a collision with Sergeant Squires whilst the Squadron was at Catterick. 'Al' baled out after the accident, but his parachute did not deploy in time to avoid a very heavy fall. He finished up in a farm cess-pool and the liquid landing probably saved his life, although it left him with a badly injured back and he crawled out of the cesspool in agony and not exactly smelling of roses. A passing motorist was his salvation, helping him into the car and driving him back the 7 miles to RAF Catterick. Medical tests and X-rays showed that he had chipped his coccyx at the lower extremity of his spine. On recovering, he took up duties in the Operations Room of RAF Catterick as a Squadron Leader - a well deserved promotion if ever there was one.

'Al' Deere vividly described in his autobiography *Nine Lives* how he came to end his service with 54 Squadron. 'On 23rd February, 1941, 54 Squadron passed out of my life for the rest of the war. Amidst thick snow, I stood at the end of the runway [at Catterick] as the aircraft lifted into the air and disappeared in a southerly direction into a snow laden sky. With two fingers raised in Churchill's V-sign and his smiling face bidding me a fond farewell, George Gribble's aircraft passed by in a final salute. I was never to set eyes on him again.' It would be most surprising if 'Al' Deere, his heart full of the most profound memories of 54 Squadron, did not have tears streaming down his cheeks at that poignant moment. George Gribble was to dive into the Channel three months later.

There was an inevitable difference in operations and losses between 1940 and 1941. In the year of the Battle of Britain, the pilots were defending their hearth and home against the Nazi tyranny and every enemy aircraft downed was a plus in that process. Now, they had pushed the fighting back across the Channel to France and it meant that, when they had to bale out, they usually became prisoners of war, instead of dropping into the friendly fields of Essex, Kent, Surrey or Sussex. Similarly, if aircraft damage compelled them to make a forced landing, the aircraft and pilot were both lost, instead of living to fight another day. It was confirmation of the 1914-18 Western Front experience of air fighting that losses increased to a point where they were greater than the enemy's, once the arena moved over to his side of the trenches. The losses of pilots at Hornchurch were higher in each of the years 1941 and 1942, than they had been in the desperate days of 1940.

In early March came yet another visit by the girls of the Windmill Theatre. They were now becoming regular visitors and they were sensationally popular - quite the most popular of the visiting entertainments. Had they carried out all the requests for encores, they would still have been there twenty-four hours later.

With the Hornchurch Wing led by Wing Commander Andrew Farquhar or Group Captain Harry Broadhurst - both in their thirties - the activity at the airfield was humming at full speed again by the spring of 1941, mainly in offensive sweeps over France, although there were still occasional battles over Kent or above shipping convoys off Dover and Deal. Two of 611 Squadron's casualties at this time were Sergeant E J Kean, a young New Zealander buried in St Andrews churchyard, and Sergeant Thomas, killed in a flying accident at Dengie Flats, out on the Essex coast near RAF Bradwell.

Intermittently at Hornchurch a tremendous staccato rattle of heavy machine gun fire would startle local residents and any airmen who had recently arrived at the station. Spitfires lined up at the firing butts with their tails in the air so as to make the aircraft horizontal in a 'straight and level' firing position; as eight Brownings were tested and fired the whole station shook and the area in front of the aircraft would be strewn with cascades of cartridge clips pouring on to it.

On 19th April, 1941, London had an exceptionally heavy raid in which 2,300 civilians were killed. One complete family was wiped out in Brentwood Road, Hornchurch, not far from the base, their remains being interred in one grave at St Andrews, close to the Military Section of the cemetery where so many RAF men lie. The headstone is 'In loving memory of

George Gill Father	64 years
Adelaide May Mother	39 years
Joyce Rose Mary	11 years
George John Alfred	9 years
John William	7 years
Mary Winifred	6 years
Adelaide Doris	5 years
Edward Richard	3 years
Pamela May	1 year

Killed by enemy action 19th April, 1941. At rest.

Rarely, even in the annals of World War II, can such a large family as this have been so devastated.

There were two royal visits in May. Air Commandant HRH the Duchess of Gloucester, who inspected the WAAFS, and Air Commodore Prince Bernhard of the Netherlands, who was naturally interested in the Dutch pilots on the station.

Early in June, 1941, Wing Commander Joseph Kayll, who had slugged out Dunkirk and the Battle of Britain from RAF Kenley, became the second Wing Commander - Flying at Hornchurch, replacing Wing Commander Farquhar, who left to command 53 Operational Training Unit at RAF Heston - near today's Heathrow.

On 22nd June the Germans invaded the Soviet Union and opened the Second Front that they had always sworn to avoid. Initially, they reaped the benefits of surprise, but the perils of fighting on two fronts were slowly driven home, as resources were withdrawn from the occupied western countries.

George Gribble, one of the last of the prewar 54 Squadron veterans, was lost at this time. After destroying six enemy aircraft in the Battle of Britain, he had been awarded his Distinguished Flying Cross on 13 August, 1940. In an engagement with Me109s over the Channel he suffered an engine failure, he stalled and crashed into the sea: he was still only 21 years old.

The Germans retained a formidable fighter force to oppose the Royal Air Force, a force that included two units, Jagdgeschwader 2 (Richtofen) and Jagdgeschwader 26

(Selilageter), with 240 of the latest Focke Wulf 190s between them. Their presence was in evidence when Wing Commander Kayll was shot down over St Omer on 25th June, after only three weeks leading the Hornchurch Wing. He made a daring escape from captivity, but was recaptured three weeks later in a forest north of Frankfurt.

Back at the airfield, the Signals Section was temporarily evacuated to accommodation near the Sector Operations Room at Romford. The airfield's telephone system had grown to 89 numbered extensions at Hornchurch and a further 15 at Romford. The building of Bradwell Bay and Fairlop airfields was coming on well, the latter approaching completion. The WAAFs had taken over an ever increasing variety of tasks, including working in the Station workshops, Parachute section, Equipment section, Signals, Accounts, Motor Transport, the Station and Squadron Orderly Rooms and other offices and the Airmen's, Sergeants' and Officers' Messes: now, more than ever, they were an indispensable part of the overall team effort.

###

There now briefly passed across the Hornchurch scene another distinguished young airman: Flight Lieutenant Richard Barclay - known to all by his second name 'George' - joined 611 Squadron as a Flight Commander on 7th August. He was an officer of outstanding courage, charm and character. His father was Vicar of Cromer, Norfolk, from 1939 to 1946 and had been Vicar of Great Holland, Essex, during George's childhood. George Barclay had accounted for seven enemy aircraft during the Battle of Britain with 249 Squadron at Leconfield, Church Fenton, Boscombe Down and (from 1st September, 1940) RAF North Weald. He had been awarded the Distinguished Flying Cross.

On 20th September, 1941, after only six weeks at Hornchurch, he was attacked by Me109s during a sweep over St Omer and, with his engine damaged, he force-landed in France, evaded capture and made his way via Spain and, eventually, got a lift on a flying boat to Stranraer in Scotland. He was later posted to command a squadron in North Africa and travelled to Egypt by sea: an airman travelling with him was Flight Lieutenant Neil Cameron, later Marshal of the Royal Air Force Lord Cameron. After destroying a Junkers 87, George Barclay was himself shot down and killed: he is buried at El Alamein. He was a quietly devout, pipe-smoking young man, whose favourite hymn was

> Be still my soul, the Lord is on my side
>
> To guide the future, as he has the past

sung to the haunting tune of 'Finlandia'. He told his own story in his autobiography *Fighter Pilot*. The Reverend G A Barclay suffered the agony of losing another son, when George's elder brother was killed serving with the Norfolk Regiment in India.

An unusual rôle fell to the Hornchurch Wing on 19th August, when it joined Tangmere Wing to escort the Blenheims of No.18 Squadron at Manston on one of its regular Circus operations. One of the 18 Squadron Blenheims (No. R 3843 F-Freddy) was given a special box to drop by parachute near St Omer containing a replacement artificial leg for the renowned legless pilot, Douglas Bader, now a prisoner of war in hospital. Bader had damaged one of his 'tin legs' when he baled out over France.

The Luftwaffe offered a safe conduct for a small, unarmed aircraft to land in France with a spare leg and Group Captain Woodhall, the Station Commander at Tangmere, where Bader had been Wing Commander, volunteered to take the leg to St Omer. However, the Luftwaffe's offer was not accepted: it was hardly the time for acts of chivalry when they were pasting London and other cities. Instead the leg was dropped in the course of a normal bombing operation to Cosnay. Perhaps the replacement leg gave Douglas Bader a greater mobility than his captors had bargained for. He escaped once from a first floor window with the aid of bedding sheets knotted together and, even when re-captured, proved a difficult prisoner, finally finishing up in Colditz Castle.

Into Hornchurch on 7th August came the first Commonwealth Squadron - 403 (Canadian) Squadron - which was very active from the time it flew its first Circus. The squadron lost four pilots in the first few weeks, including Squadron Leader Morris, who went down during a bomber escort mission to Chocques. Lost in that same mission was an American pilot, Sergeant Charles McDonald, who was taken prisoner of war, but made an amazing escape from the compound. He eventually lost his life with the United States Air Force in the Korean War.

On 1st September Group Captain Broadhurst took a personal hand in declaring RAF Fairlop fit to open as an operational station by flying over from Hornchurch and making the first trial landings on each of the three runways in turn. It was ironic that Fairlop, the wartime built satellite, had three fine hard surfaced runways, whilst Hornchurch, the permanent prewar regular Sector airfield, had to struggle on with its grass flight paths. The Fairlop runways were to prove their usefulness time and again as the Hornchurch squadrons diverted there during the worst months of winter.

A further ten pilots were lost in September, 1941, including four in one Circus on the 27th. Included in these losses was Squadron Leader N Orton, who had commanded 54 Squadron for only two months.

Distinguished visitors included Air Commodore HRH the Duke of Kent, a serving member of the Royal Air Force who lost his life the next year; Mr Robert Ruskin, the Editor of the influential American magazine *Liberty*; and Mr Eugene Mayer, the proprietor of the *Washington Post*. His visit was followed by Lieutenant Commander Storehouse, the United States Naval Attaché in London, Captain Wentworth and three other naval officers. The United States was still neutral at this time.

With the formation of the Air Training Corps in 1941, visits from the active local 452 (Hornchurch) Squadron became a regular feature of life at the airfield and the enthusiastic teenagers chipped in willingly with whatever they were asked to do, as well as learning something about the service they planned to join as soon as they were old enough. The motto of the Air Training Corps was 'Venture-Adventure' and the young cadets certainly had their fair share of both in their weekend visits to the airfield and at their week-long annual camps each summer.

As autumn approached 607 and 615 Squadrons from Manston, flying Hawker Hurricanes in the ground attack rôle, participated in the destruction of an alcohol distillery at St Pol, but three escorting Spitfires were lost. 607 lost eleven pilots in one month, including their Commanding Officer, Squadron Leader G D Craig, over Étaples. Hornchurch itself lost another eight pilots in October, including Pilot Officer Roper-Bosch, a Dutchman serving with 611 Squadron, who was lost over St Omer during an Air Sea Rescue Mission, and Sergeant McLusky of 402 (Canadian) Squadron at Rochford, who was giving a lift to the Hornchurch Station Dental Officer: they were both killed in a Magister that crashed while they were on their way back from Friston, Sussex.

Group Captain Broadhurst was selected as a member of the Royal Air Force contingent to visit the United States of America in October and, until he returned to Hornchurch on 30th November, the station was run by Wing Commander F S Stapleton, the Wing Commander - Flying.

RAF Fairlop was officially opened as an operational airfield within the Hornchurch Sector on 12th November and 603 (City of Edinburgh) Squadron left Hornchurch for the last time, after a tempestuous fifteen months, to take up residence there. Fairlop also had its own niche in aviation history, having been occupied by 207 Training Depôt of the Royal Naval Air Service in 1918 and being considered as a possible site for London Airport in the 1930s. Notable Station Commanders at Fairlop in WWII included Colin Gray and William Crawford-Compton, before the latter became Wing Commander - Flying in the Hornchurch Sector. The difficulties in overseeing the building of new airfields at a distance had proved quite taxing and it was something of a relief when Bradwell Bay opened that same month.

At the end of November Air Chief Marshal William Sholto-Douglas made his first official visit to Hornchurch in his role as C-in-C of Fighter Command and saw for himself the change of emphasis that Rhubarbs and Ramrods had introduced. Another visitor was Crown Prince Paul of Greece.

It was the end of an era when 54 Squadron left in November for the last time, on posting to Castletown. 54 Squadron spent more time at Hornchurch throughout its life as an airfield than any other fighter squadron. It had been a regular mainstay for most of the time since 1930, with only periods at Catterick (on exchange with 41 Squadron) for rest and reformation and a few days at Martlesham Heath breaking up the twelve year sequence. It had Commanding Officers in that time and flew five different types of aircraft Siskins, Bulldogs, Gauntlets, Gladiators and Spitfires. Some one hundred and fifty to two hundred pilots were members of 54 Squadron at one time or another over that period. How fitting that it should still be a Fighter Squadron in Strike

Command of the Royal Air Force, based only two counties away from Hornchurch, flying Jaguars out of RAF Coltishall, Norfolk, although currently engaged in United Nations operations and based in Turkey.

###

313 (Czech) Squadron was the first foreign squadron to arrive, although there had been a scattering of individual Europeans in the British squadrons. Most of the Czechs who had flown in France before coming to England were single, but a few had wives and families in occupied Czechoslovakia.

At the end of 1941 the Hornchurch Wing now comprised 64 Squadron (S/Ldr B J Wicks); 313 (Czech) Squadron (S/Ldr K Mrazec); and 411 (Canadian) Squadron (S/Ldr P S Turner). The Czechs were at Southend, while Fairlop was temporarily without a squadron after 603 (City of Edinburgh) Squadron returned to Dyce. All the Commanding Officers were veterans of the Battle of Britain.

Essex had started World War II with five airfields; now there were seven and the county would end the war with 23, sixteen being at one time occupied by the United States Eighth and Ninth Air Forces.

Some 120 Hornchurch pilots were lost in 1941, about twenty more than in 1940. The year's loss was the equivalent of losing the complement of six Fighter Squadrons.

###

1942 opened with the customary restricted flying in mid-winter weather conditions, but this enabled the cosmopolitan Wing of British, Canadians and Czechs to shake down and teach each other the traditions, sports and pastimes inherent in each other's culture.

The Czechs produced several incidents at Hornchurch, mainly due to the fact that, try as they might, they could not always remember that the throttle had to be pushed in to increase speed and pulled out to reduce speed in British aircraft, the precise opposite of the Czechoslovak planes on which they had trained. This caused a few spectacular high speed landings, occasionally with undercarriages retracted, watched with trepidation by ground observers. That they overcame these and other difficulties and also got to grips with the language problem to become valued members of 11 Group, Fighter Command, will be to their eternal credit.

The Canadians' main problem was with navigation. The small, tightly packed island was in stark contrast to the vast open spaces of North America and they found that the railways, towns, rivers and other landmarks, so vital to navigation by eye, were just too close together in what was, to them, a jumbled confusion.

164 Squadron had already been through Dunkirk and the Battle of Britain from Kenley, Leconfield, Biggin Hill and Coltishall before first arriving at Hornchurch in November, 1940. Now, after a six months' sojourn in Scotland, at Turnhouse and Drem, they were back, but now amongst Czechs and Canadians. However, they met former friends when the Kenley Wing returned from operations in poor visibility to land at Hornchurch and had to remain overnight.

113

In mid-January Wing Commander R P Powell arrived as Wing Commander (Flying) to replace Wing Commander H L Dawson. A 25-year-old prewar regular with 111 Squadron, Robin Powell already had eight enemy aircraft and a Distinguished Flying Cross to his credit.

The customary mid-winter show given by the girls from the Windmill Theatre was received, if anything, by even greater acclamation than before. They arrived in the afternoon for tea and were entertained by a display of aerobatics by Flight Lieutenant Prévot, a Belgian serving with 64 Squadron. Six months later, as a Squadron Leader, Leon Prévot was lost over France, but evaded capture, made his way back to England and returned to Hornchurch in January, 1944.

Sheila Van Damm, the Windmill Theatre's director, recalled that she found a letter written by Group Captain Harry Broadhurst to her father from the Western Desert, in which he said, "I wonder if you have been at Hornchurch since I left there. They were grand days." She also recalled that, just after the girls started one of their shows, the squadron at 'Readiness' was alerted and left rapidly. Before the show ended some of them returned to their seats, but the poignancy of those that remained starkly empty were one of her most vivid memories.

Two Czech pilots (Sergeants Joseph Valenta and Blazej Konvalina) were killed in accidents at this time and are buried in St Andrews Church. News was received that Robert Stanford-Tuck, now Wing Commander (Flying) at Biggin Hill, had been shot down by anti-aircraft fire over France: he survived as a prisoner of war, but escaped in early 1945, making his way home via Moscow.

With bad weather continuing and the grass flight paths in a sorry state, 64 and 411 Squadrons went temporarily to Fairlop and 313 to Rochford until things improved. Nevertheless there was an attendance of four hundred for a special Church Parade with the hymns played by the 9th Battalion of the Royal Engineers.

###

12th February, 1942, was one of the sadder days in the history of Fighter Command, when the German battle cruisers *Scharnhorst* and *Gneisenau*, the heavy cruiser *Prinz Eugen* and an accompanying fleet of five destroyers and thirteen motor torpedo boats broke out from the port of Brest where they had been under regular surveillance by reconnaissance aircraft. Bomber Command had regularly attacked Brest for months, but had not inflicted any vital damage. The ships left harbour before first light and were scheduled to pass through the Straits of Dover in broad daylight. The fleet was spotted by Group Captain Victor Beamish, the Station Commander of Kenley, and Wing Commander Baird, who were immediately attacked by Me109s of the covering force, but sped for home, low over the waves to arrive back at Kenley at 11.10 am.

Their report sparked off feverish RAF and Royal Navy activity. At Manston, operating under the Hornchurch Sector control, Lieutenant Commander Eugene Esmonde, leading the six Fairey Swordfish biplanes of 825 Squadron, Fleet Air Arm, briefed his crews for a 12.15 take off. They had arrived from Lee-on-Solent a few days earlier. 11 Group was alerted to provide Spitfire escorts for the Swordfish, but, in the bad weather prevailing, there was a lack of crews at 'Readiness' and there was a delay. Notwithstanding this, at 12.15 the Swordfish Squadron left Manston and, in the event, 72 Squadron led by Squadron Leader Brian Kingeombe, showed up just as the Swordfish patrolled the coast to await an escort.

Irish Eugene Esmonde was prompted to go into the attack immediately, regardless of the size of his escort, while the German fleet was at its most vulnerable and accessible position, but was soon attacked by Me109s, although at first they misjudged the slow speed of the biplanes and mostly fired wide of the mark. At 12.50 the German fleet was sighted and the Gravesend Squadron, now reinforced, engaged the Me109s in a confusing series of dog-fights.

As the Swordfish approached the ships they flew into a curtain of anti-aircraft fire and were soon in tatters.   Esmonde's lead aircraft was hit and set alight, the flames being tackled by his Gunner, LAC W J Clinton with gloved hands.   Another shell ripped off the lower port wing, but still it flew on. FW 190s queued up to deliver the *coup de grâce*. With his Gunner and Observer already dead and Esmonde himself dying, he continued towards the *Scharnhorst* to fire his torpedoes in a final supreme act of bravery before diving into the Channel. The other five Swordfish met a similar end, the entire squadron being wiped out. Only three of a total of eighteen aircrew men were fished from the water.

In the event, the major ships that broke through in this exercise all came to a sticky end. *Scharnhorst* was sunk by the Royal Navy as she approached to attack a convoy bound for Russia and only 36 of her complement of 1,800 were saved. *Prinz Eugen* had her stern blown off by a British submarine and, post-war, was destroyed in a nuclear test. *Gneisenau* was badly damaged by RAF bombers whilst she was in dock and never fired her guns in anger again.

The sacrifice of the six antiquated biplanes and 15 Naval airmen was all in vain. The torpedoes missed their mark and the German fleet passed by the coastlines of Belgium and Holland to reach the sanctuary of Germany in the River Elbe, although *Scharnhorst* was damaged by mines along the way.

Esmonde had his Fleet Air Arm squadron up from Manston ten minutes before the Hornchurch Wing (411 and 64 Squadrons) had cleared Fairlop. The third squadron of the Wing (313 Czech Squadron) at Hornchurch was earmarked for Convoy Escort duty, but Group Captain Broadhurst and Wing Commander Powell took off as a pair at 12.42. Neither the squadrons or the pair saw the German battle fleet, the Swordfish, the Gravesend Squadron, or the rest of the Biggin Hill Wing. The Broadhurst pair did, however, get in a tangle with Me109s, apparently acting as back stop to the warships. 64 and 411 Squadrons crossed to France and mounted a combat patrol along the coast between Calais and Mardyck. They saw nothing and landed back at Fairlop at 2.15.

Eugene Esmonde was awarded a posthumous Victoria Cross. Two months after the action his body was washed ashore on a Kent beach and he was taken home to his native Tipperary for interment.

It was a serious shock to the pride of the Royal Air Force and the Royal Navy, who had been caught on the hop. Ronald Adam, the Sector Controller, never forgot the courage of the Swordfish crews and, when the time came two years later, for him to send a final message to Hornchurch Sector, he included the name of the Royal Navy's 'Esmonde' in the list of distinguished pilots that the Sector had controlled.

At the conclusion of this sad day, Flight Sergeant R N Langley of 287 Squadron based at Croydon crashed his Hurricane at Upminster, and is buried at St Andrews. Later in the month, a shell exploded in the Station Armoury and Aircraftman K Weston, working there, was killed.

March, 1942, saw the continuation of Rhubarbs and Ramrods over Étaples, Le Touquet, Ostend and other targets in north west Europe, with the Hornchurch Wing sometimes escorting the Bostons of 226 Squadron, based at Swanton Morley, Norfolk, and making a rendezvous with them over the Essex coast at Clacton.

All the squadron Spitfires were now Mark V bs and were equipped with two Hispano cannons and four Browning machine guns. They were capable of carrying one 500 lb or two 250 lb bombs and had a range of 470 miles, suitable for the longer sea crossing from Clacton to Ostend. Rolls Royce had uprated the power of the Merlin engine to 1,470 hp, so there was 40% more poke under the bonnet than the original 1030 hp Merlin of the Mark 1. The Hornchurch Wing had several successes with the Mark V bs against the Focke Wulf 190s on these missions. The Douglas Bostons were first shipped from U S A to England in the summer of 1941, but needed several modifications before being used as a supplement to the Blenheims in daylight raids. They were first used in this rôle on 12th February, 1942, and 226 Squadron was the only squadron at this time. The Hornchurch Wing escorted them to Ostend Power Station on 27th March, shooting down three Me109s and a FW 190, for the loss of Czech Pilot Officer Michalek. The ratio was not always so advantageous.

April saw the arrival of the famed Pilot Officer Donald Kingaby, to join 64 Squadron. As a Sergeant Pilot he had fought out the Battle of Britain with 92 Squadron at Biggin Hill from 25th September, 1940, but between then and his Hornchurch posting had destroyed 18 enemy aircraft. He was destined to achieve even greater heights as he became a Flight Commander with 122 Squadron at Hornchurch and then Wing Commander (Flying) in April, 1943. From Sergeant to Wing Commander in under two years was the just reward for a truly remarkable airman.

Sadly, it was learned that Eric Edsall, who had been bombed on Hornchurch runway in August, 1940, had been killed in Ceylon.

On 28th April Doktor Eduard Beneš, President of the Czechoslovak National Committee in London, recognised by the Allied Powers as the President of the Czech Republic, and Mrs Beneš visited and presented medals to their compatriots in 313 (Czech) Squadron.

1st May was something of a watershed in the history of the airfield when its faithful satellite at Southend (Rochford) was temporarily taken away from its control and placed in the North Weald Sector. Rochford and Hornchurch had shared a common travail and destiny throughout two and a half years of ferocious air fighting, frequently with their backs to the wall, and rotating the squadrons between one airfield and the other. Most of the Hornchurch pilots had spent at least a week or two down the at the 'forward field' adjoining the Liverpool Street to Southend line near Rochford Station, a railway so close that several pilots had finished uncomfortably close to spreading their Spitfires over the tracks. The Czechs, with their forward throttle difficulties, had a particularly interesting time.

This was also the day that Alan Deere commenced a third tour of duty on fighter operations and was sent to command 403 (Canadian) Squadron, which moved from North Weald to Rochford on the first day that it severed contact with Hornchurch. In his autobiography Deere recalled the memories that came back to him as he arrived back at Rochford - the many happy hours spent there in 1939 and 1940 with George Gribble, 'Wonky' Way, Johnny Allen and several other missing comrades of 54 (his first and most loved) Squadron.

Alan Deere worked his 'grand bunch of Canadians' until they returned to operations on 5th May. His old friend 'Mitzi' Darling was posted in as one of his Flight Commanders and, with accommodation always tight at Southend, he allowed him to share his room providing he 'did not play his infernal gramophone'. In its first four weeks 403 had a few victories and did not suffer any casualties, but on 2nd June it was jumped by thirty Focke Wulf 190s and, in a gritting dog-fight, lost six pilots, including two that came down in the Channel. 'Mitzi' Darling did not come back and Alan Deere thought that he saw him down in the sea. Air Sea Rescue launches rushed to the area, but he was never seen again.

The squadron moved to Martlesham Heath the following day to rest and recuperate and on 18th June it returned to Catterick. This was the airfield that had frequently changed squadrons with Hornchurch and Alan Deere received a welcome from the many friends still there, but it was a sad day compared with the days when 54 Squadron had flown in to 'this happy little station' to rest and reform, very tired but flushed with success.

The sweeps across France were still proving expensive and on 5th May the Hornchurch Wing lost six pilots in one day over Lille, including Czech Squadron Leader Frantisek Fajtl, the Commanding Officer of 122 Squadron. He evaded capture and returned to England where he was awarded the Distinguished Flying Cross before taking command of 313 (Czech) Squadron at RAF Ibsley, Hampshire. It was by no means all doom and gloom and destruction of enemy aircraft was still, on balance, claimed on a more than one for one basis. The Wing also escorted Blenheims,

A Spitfire undergoing a '30 hours inspection' by 9 ground crew airmen at Hornchurch (*Imperial War Museum*)

Brendan 'Paddy' Finucane, June, 1942 (*Imperial War Museum*)

Bostons and Stirlings on numerous daylight raids on railways, airfields and enemy shipping.

Another six aircrew were lost on 17th May over Boulogne, two each from 64, 122 and 313 Squadrons: the punch of the FW 190s, with four cannon and two machine guns was not an easy proposition for the Spitfire Vbs two cannon and four machine guns.

Station personnel were delighted with the footballing success of one of their Physical Training Instructors, Sergeant Leslie Smith, a native of Ealing who played professional football for Brentford, who reached the Semi-Final of the London War Cup (a regional substitute for the FA Cup) where they beat the mighty Arsenal and then, on 30th May, in front of a crowd of 72,000 at Wembley, beat Portsmouth 2-0 in the Final. Smith raised Hornchurch rafters by scoring both goals. A few pints were sunk at Hornchurch that night.

The Wing Commander (Flying) was now Robin Powell, who led the Wing with flair in the first half of 1942. On a sweep over France in June, however, he was severely injured and fractured his skull. After hospital treatment he was awarded a Bar to his Distinguished Flying Cross, but did not return to Hornchurch. Robin Powell remained in the RAF after the war and died in 1970.

His place was taken for a tragically brief spell by another legendary figure, Wing Commander Brendan 'Paddy' Finucane, who had served with 65 Squadron flying 52 sorties from Hornchurch, Rochford and Manston. By this time he had 32 enemy aircraft to his credit and, after two years of fierce combat, had risen from Pilot Officer to Wing Commander, being awarded the DSO and DFC three times and becoming a legend in his own lifetime. His exploits were known to millions through newspapers, firstly anonymously as 'An Irish Flight Lieutenant', until eventually his identity was revealed. It was said of him that he could supervise four different dog-fights at once and fight his own at the same time. He had been born in Dublin of an Irish father and an English mother and the family had moved to Richmond, Surrey, in 1937.

He had a unique 'Twenty One double' by accounting for 21 enemy aircraft before he was twenty-one years of age. In two years the only time he was injured was when he broke a small bone in his foot trying to leap a low wall in the blackout, but he then had a more serious leg injury in combat with FW 190s and was *hors de combat* for three weeks.

A large sweep was fixed for 15th July and Finucane led the Wing as they shot up railways, airfields and gun emplacements. On the sand dunes at Le Touquet there was a machine gun mounted on a tripod and the German gunners opened fire on the low flying leader as he passed overhead. By a freak of chance they ruptured his radiator. He was too low to bale out and now lacked the engine power to climb. He turned over the sea in a desperate attempt to get home in his stricken aircraft and, after ten miles, was seen by his squadron colleagues to be removing his helmet and harness.

313 (Czech) Squadron scrambling at Hornchurch, 1942

64 Squadron at 'Readiness', RAF Hornchurch, 1942

Grafton Underwood Tower after 1st USAAF
mission, 17 August, 1942

He was unhurt and talking right up to a final, 'This is it, chaps,' as he planed down into the Channel. He must have been knocked unconscious by the impact and gone down with the Spitfire. Rescue launches found no trace. Of all the Fighter Command heroes between 1939 and 1945 none was remembered with greater affection than the smiling 'Paddy' Finucane. Three thousand mourners crowded Westminster Cathedral for his Requiem Mass.

Two other young pilots, Sergeant James and Flight Sergeant Bray, both of 122 Squadron, were lost over Étaples in combat during the same mission, concluding an unhappy day for Hornchurch.

Two days after 'Paddy' Finucane was lost a cheeky Dornier 217 flew unconcernedly over the airfield and took the station by surprise, before going on a few miles to drop its bombs around the Ford Motor factory complex at Dagenham: its audacity paid off and it got away with it.

At the end of July, 1942, Hornchurch Wing lost eight pilots in one day, a new high. Two were from 154 Squadron, two from 340, the Free French Squadron, and four from 122. These three, together with 6 Squadron, now comprised the Hornchurch Wing, with 154 operating out of Fairlop. The Free French were commanded by Commandant B Duperier and included Captain René Mouchotte, who was awarded the Distinguished Flying Cross on 1 September. The eight losses had included Squadron Leader Leon Prévot, but the Belgian evaded capture.

A new landmark was achieved in August when the Hornchurch Wing acted as a close escort to the B-17 Flying Fortresses of the United States Eighth Air Force in their first raid on enemy occupied territory. Eighteen B-17s of the 97th Bomb Group, based at Polebrook and Grafton Underwood in Northamptonshire, commanded by Colonel Frank Armstrong, made history this day as the first of an ever increasingly mighty armada. General Ira Eaker, the Commanding General of the Eighth Bomber Command (and later Commanding General of the Eighth Air Force) was carried on this mission. Twelve of the Fortresses bombed the primary target at the Rouen/Sotteville Marshalling Yards, while the others flew a diversion. The aircraft had names like 'Baby Doll', 'Heidi Ho', 'Dixie Demo', and most had ornate pictures of girls in pin up poses on their nose.

All the top brass of the United States Eighth Air Force crowded the Control Tower at Grafton Underwood to await the return of the aircraft from this historic mission, including General Spaatz and Colonels Beirne Lay (co-author of the Hollywood classic *Twelve o'clock High*) and Fred Castle. There were no casualties amongst the bombers or the fighters, but the Americans were later to suffer severe losses as they penetrated into Germany with their daylight raids, before long range fighter escorts were available to escort them all the way to and from their targets. Of the 111 men who manned the twelve B-17s to Rouen, 31 were subsequently lost before completing their tour of duty.

Later in the month Hornchurch Wing escorted the Fortresses to the Potez aircraft works at Meaulte and, once again, all the aircraft returned, although three Fortresses were damaged and one crew member was killed. RAF fighter escorts developed a healthy respect for the somewhat trigger happy tail gunners of the Fortresses, who seemed happy enough to fire off at any aircraft that didn't resemble a Flying Fortress.

It is a matter of history that the 'Mighty Eighth' of the United States Air Force went on to mount a total of 986 missions, involving 314,000 sorties and lost 5,400 heavy bombers in the process. The courage of the airmen in these daylight raids has been chronicled in detail elsewhere and graphically portrayed in the films *Twelve o'clock High* and *Memphis Belle*. Their bravery and magnificent contribution to the Allied war effort in Europe should never be forgotten.

The short range of the fighter escorts meant that they had to turn back at a line running from Brussels through Lille, Beauvais and Rouen. Beyond that the Fortresses and Liberators were on their own and heavy losses were soon the order of the day. The difficulty was finally solved by fitting supplementary tanks to the P-51 Mustang fighter, which thereafter became one of the truly outstanding fighters of the war.

On the last day of August, 1942, Wing Commander Eric H Thomas took over as Wing Commander (Flying) from Wing Commander Petrus Hugo. Eric Thomas had served earlier at the field with 222 Squadron and at Rochford with 611 Squadron.

The furious level of fighting over France continued unabated in early September and four Free French pilots of 340 Squadron were lost on the 5th.

453 (RAAF) Squadron, formed at Sydney in 1941, arrived during the month, the first Australian squadron seen at the base.

On the entertainment front, a cabaret dance at Suttons, organised by the WAAFs attracted a good audience; ENSA concerts were arranged on alternate Friday and Saturday nights; and the Ralph Reader Gang Show appeared on two consecutive nights.

It was learned that Squadron Leader Bryan Wicks, who had commanded 64 Squadron for three months earlier in the year, had been lost flying from Malta: he was still only 22.

The Secretary of State for Air, Sir Archibald Sinclair, accompanied by Group Captain Sir Louis Gregg, flew in to Hornchurch and Fairlop, and had tea with Wing Commander Eric Thomas, deputising for the Station Commander.

An unusual visitor was His Excellency Senhor Monir de Arago, the Brazilian Ambassador, who presented two Spitfires to 64 Squadron on behalf of his people: the BBC was present for the occasion and the Ambassador spoke in both Portuguese and English; Paramount News filmed the presentation and included it in the newsreels distributed to the cinemas. Mr Kenellopoules, the Deputy Prime Minister of Greece, was another visitor.

As September, 1942, drew to a close, Hornchurch had lost 345 pilots, an average of three each week since the shooting war had started in earnest. It was the equivalent of losing a whole squadron every seven weeks.

With winter closing in again flying activity was once more reduced and it would be idle to speculate that winter did not come as some relief. 1942 had been the peak flying year in the history of RAF Hornchurch and it had lost 145 pilots during the year. Ramrods, Rhubarbs, Escorts and Sweeps were not inexpensive.

Like Kipling, Hornchurch had 'met with Triumph and Disaster and treated those two impostors just the same', but, as the year ended, there was a feeling in the air that Fighter Command was now 'over the hump', that much of the heartbreak was behind them, and that 1943 would herald the dawn of the race to final victory.

At Christmas, 1942, the Hornchurch Wing was 122 Squadron (S/Ldr Donald E Kingaby), 132 Squadron (S/Ldr Ian Ritchie), 453 Squadron (S/Ldr J R Ratten) and 350 Squadron (S/Ldr A L Boussa).

Another famous Hornchurch personality - Richard Hillary, author of *The Last Enemy* - died on 8th January, 1943, while he was converting to night fighters in Scotland. After spending 1941 recovering from grievous burns at the Queen Victoria Hospital, East Grinstead (the 'Guinea Pigs' Hospital), Hillary went on to a course to regain his cherished flying status. Achieving this, he then went to RAF Charter Hall, Stirling, to take a course on Blenheim night fighters. While circling a beacon at night he went into a spin and crashed to earth: his Navigator was also killed.

Other Allied airmen lost that month included Belgian Flight Sergeant L Flabimont of 350 Squadron, who went down over St Omer, and Warrant Officer S D Earwaker, a New Zealander who is buried at St Andrews.

Group Captain A G Adnams arrived from RAF Northolt as Station Commander and the training of No.4012 Anti-Aircraft Flight commenced in the large concrete Dome Trainer, next to the South End Road: it was an architectural feature that puzzled passing car drivers, even some with RAF associations, for several years after the airfield closed down. It was 60 feet in diameter and simulated a variety of aircraft approaches by different types of engine noise and other background sounds associated with attack by enemy aircraft. The 'accuracy' attained by the trainee gunners was measured and recorded.

Lieutenant Colonel F W Wouters, the Belgian Air Attaché in London, visited Hornchurch and spoke to pilots of the 350 (Belgian) Squadron, who had seen so much action in the Sector over the past four months. They were destined to be one of the last Fighter Squadrons to operate in the Sector in 1944.

A new East-West flightpath to supplement the existing North-South flightpath, was laid out extending across South End Road, now closed to the public. It necessitated the construction of a new Control Tower in a somewhat remote position adjacent to the perimeter track on the River Ingrebourne side of the airfield; the only position from which a Control Tower could maintain visual observation over both flightpaths.

64 Squadron, commanded by Squadron Leader William Crawford-Compton, who

later became Wing Commander (Flying), moved into Hornchurch in March after spending the winter months at Fairlop. It was the eighth time that 64 Squadron had served at Hornchurch and they took up their old dispersal areas on the River Ingrebourne side of the airfield.

On 24th March, 1943, yet another ally was lost when Flying Officer R Sanders Draper, a citizen of the United States, crashed near Suttons School in Suttons Lane, when his engine cut out at 200 feet shortly after take off. Sanders Draper had flown ten operations in the space of two weeks while at Fairlop. The school narrowly avoided by the American was re-named Sanders Draper School as a tribute to his courage. His grave, in St Andrews, is regularly tended and, some years ago, relatives from the United States paid their homage.

Three days after Sanders Draper was lost, 64 Squadron moved out to Ayr and were replaced by the Australians of 453 Squadron who moved in from Southend.

1st April, 1943, was the 25th Anniversary of the formation of the Royal Air Force and a happy and memorable day was held at the airfield. It started with a visit from the BBC, in the person of Gilbert Harding, accompanied by two engineers, for a radio broadcast from Hornchurch. Squadron Leader Don Kingaby, Flight Lieutenant Prest and Flying Officer Hull of 122 Squadron were all interviewed by Harding in a transmission that went out nationwide. Later on, three Spitfires took off, crossed the Thames and made an appearance at Biggin Hill, where each of them dropped an ornate chamber pot on a small parachute 'to remind our rivals at Biggin Hill of Hornchurch's long start over them'. This was amplified by the painting of three zeppelins on each chamber pot. During the day there was a ceremonial Colour Hoisting Parade involving 450 airmen and 300 WAAFs in best blue, and a happy commemorative day for the Service concluded with a dance at the NAAFI after a special dinner had been served with a free allocation of beer.

Wing Commander John Kilmartin, a veteran of the fighting in France and then the Battle of Britain from Tangmere, arrived as Wing Commander - Flying.

Distinguished visitors included Viscount Knollys, the Governor of Bermuda, accompanied by Admiral Harcourt. The Viscount presented a 'plane, 'Spitfire Billy', to Pilot Officer Bernard, a Bermudan pilot. Major Cerwell, the Spanish Air Attaché, and Colonel Mossberg, the Swedish Air Attaché, were among representatives of neutral nations entertained at the airfield.

Squadron Leader Don Kingaby was appointed Station Commander at Southend, but this appointment was short-lived, as he returned to Hornchurch to take up duties as one of no less than six different Wing Commanders - Flying, who led the Hornchurch Wing in 1943.

Enemy intrusions into British airspace were now becoming rarer, but on 8th May, 1943, Sergeant Williams of 122 Squadron destroyed a Ju88, which came to earth on the Pitsea Marshes.

The 'Wings for Victory Week' parade at nearby Dagenham was led by a strong contingent of airmen and WAAFs in spite of pouring rain. It was well received by the many townsfolk who braved the downpour and Group Captain Adnams took the salute and made a speech.

An airman who went on, in post-war years, to a distinguished career in politics in his own country was South African Flight Lieutenant Pat Lardner-Burke of 222 Squadron. He accounted for two Focke Wulf 190s and the Spitfire that he flew (MH 434) was flown in post-war Air Shows by Ray Hannah, who at one time commanded the 'Red Arrows'. Lardner-Burke became a senior politician in the controversial post-war governments of South Africa.

On 10th May Ronald Adam, at Hornchurch since November, 1939, was promoted to the post of Senior Sector Controller. Few people were more conscious of the history and traditions of RAF Hornchurch than Ronald Adam and he captured the atmosphere of the station with his creative pen in his two books *Readiness at Dawn* and *We Rendezvous at Ten*. He was always perturbed about the 'noises off' made by Biggin Hill, compared with the dignified silence observed by the other six Sector Stations in 11 Group; Hornchurch, North Weald, Debden, Northolt, Kenley and Tangmere. This dignified silence was soon to be put to the test.

Marshal of the Royal Air Force Viscount Trenchard, accompanied by Australian Members of Parliament, visited in order to meet the airmen of 453 (RAAF) Squadron. The Commonwealth theme had captured the public imagination and the event was filmed by Movietone News for cinema presentation.

On 15th May the Biggin Hill Sector claimed its 1,000th enemy aircraft destroyed since the start of the war, an honour that was shared by Squadron Leader Edward Charles, a Canadian, and Captain René Mouchotte, a Frenchman, who each accounted for a German FW90 at approximately the same time.

Biggin Hill had an Intelligence Officer who could never be accused of hiding Biggin Hill's light under a bushel, but on this occasion, the keen publicity man upped the hype to colossal proportions. Biggin Hill was besieged by press, radio newsreel men wanting interviews with Charles and Mouchotte and a beano to end all beanos was arranged to take place at the Grosvenor House Hotel in Park Lane, London, on the night of Wednesday, 9 June, from 9 pm to 3 am. Air Chief Marshals Sir Trafford Leigh Mallory and Sir Arthur Harris, the leader of Bomber Command, were invited, together with all the Biggin Hill Sector pilots from Gravesend, West Malling, Hawkinge and Lympne, as well as Biggin Hill itself (excepting the Squadron at 'Readiness') and a fair number of others from 11 Group.

The lavish catering was on a scale almost unknown in wartime Britain and included salmon flown down from Scotland and lobster, together with a free bar. Three RAF bands were hired to provide the music and 300 London taxi drivers took them home to Biggin Hill in the early hours. Rumour had it that even the Luftwaffe knew about the party.

The only problem was the cost of all this junketing - £2,500 (a figure that should be multiplied by 50 or so for today's values) and there was an accounting deficit of £1,000. Ronald Adam took up the story in *Royal Air Force News* -

> A month or two later the AOC of 11 Group arrived at Hornchurch to see the Station Commander and myself, as Mess President. The AOC had come on a special mission. One of the 'family' had got into grave financial difficulties and, of course, it behove the rest of the 'family' to help out. The Air Council had discovered that Biggin Hill had been soliciting subscriptions for their party and had been horrified. Biggin had been ordered to send back all the money. But the AOC pointed out that Biggin wasn't able to do so.

So Ronald Adam drew a cheque, as did the other Sectors of 11 Group. The Hornchurch cheque was for £600 and went a long way to helping Biggin out of this party that their publicity hounds had wanted to give. The donation was not particularly appreciated by officers that had not been invited and thought it had all rather got out of hand in wartime Britain.

Ronald Adam added that 'at Hornchurch we had most of their outstanding pilots well before they did. 'Sailor' Malan, Alan Deere, Donald Finlay, Colin Gray, Edward 'Hawkeye' Wells. We had them all and Hornchurch had a wonderful record, but did not publicise it or shout the odds as Biggin Hill did all the time'.

The seven Sectors of No. 11 Group all had magnificent records and each had suffered both triumph and tragedy. It is rather unfortunate that we still hear about 'the most famous fighter airfield in the world' and similar epithets, and very little about the silent majority at Hornchurch, Debden, North Weald, Tangmere, Kenley and Northolt. It is not easy to judge the yardstick on which these claims are made. In the Battle of Britain, the three individual airfields that lost most aircrew were Tangmere, Hornchurch and Middle Wallop, in that order. In the war as a whole Hornchurch lost 481 and Biggin Hill 453. For my money, each of the seven Sectors should be remembered for their superb contribution to the air defence of the country and, within this context, Biggin Hill has its own niche of honour.

###

With 'Wings for Victory' weeks proliferating in the neighbourhood, the station participated in the Romford, Hornchurch and Chigwell Row celebrations. The Station Chaplain, Squadron Leader R G Davies, conducted a drumhead service, the Lord Lieutenant of Essex, Colonel Sir Francis Whitmore, took the salute and airmen and WAAFs participating in the parade were usually led by the band of the Hornchurch Wing of the Air Training Corps.

During 1943 the daylight bombing raids carried out by the United States Eighth Air Force stepped up another gear, with over 300 Fortresses and Liberators being despatched on some days (to eventually reach 2,000 sent in one day at the end of 1944).

On 22nd June the Hornchurch Wing took part in the escort provided for 235 'heavies' on the first US 8th Air Force major attack on the Ruhr industrial complex, the primary target being marshalling yards at Huls. The Americans lost 16 bombers, many of them to anti-aircraft fire. Although RAF Fighter Command participated fully in escorting the Americans, they were now being increasingly escorted by American fighters in the U.K. for that specific purpose - 'Little Friends', as the bomber crews called them. The American fighters moved into some of the most famous permanent prewar Fighter Command airfields, including Debden, Duxford, Wattisham, Honington, Martlesham Heath and Horsham St Faith. It should be mentioned that they were also allocated many wartime built 'acres of mud' airfields, with few civilised comforts.

They came in with P-38 Lightnings, P-47 Thunderbolts and P-51 Mustangs, the British Fighter Command squadrons and the American Fighter Groups working closely alongside one another. The United States 4th Fighter Group, which had been at Debden for a year, was formed from the three RAF 'Eagle' Squadrons composed of American volunteers who had joined the RAF while the United States was still neutral. Their combat experience was sorely needed by their countrymen as they transferred from the RAF to the USAAF. At a rain-swept Debden they marched on to a Ceremonial Parade as Squadron Leaders, Flight Lieutenants and Flying Officers, RAF, and marched off as Majors, Captains and Lieutenants, USAAF: Air Chief Marshal Sir William Sholto-Douglas handed over the squadrons to Major General 'Tooey' Spaatz. They swapped their RAF blue uniforms for the olive drab uniforms of USAAF not without a little heartache and continued to fly Spitfires until April, 1943, with the RAF roundels on the aircraft wings and fuselage painted over with the US white star insignia. Whilst in the RAF the 'Eagle' Squadrons - 71, 121 and 133 - had lost 77 pilots, 44 of these being from Rochford, North Weald and Debden.

In the summer of 1943 Major Heinrich and Lieutenant Ellis of the USAAF were attached to Hornchurch on liaison duties and Major General William Kepner, the Commanding General of Eighth Fighter Command being set up at Bushey Hall, near Watford, visited Hornchurch to see at first hand the problems involved with high speed fighters escorting slow speed bombers and the associated difficulties of identification and the separation of friend from foe.

Wing Commander William Crawford-Compton became the fourth Wing Commander - Flying on 30th July, eight days after 239 Squadron lost four pilots in one day: a rare event at this stage of the war. Before the conflict Crawford-Compton had been a crew member in a ketch that had got no further from New Zealand than New Guinea attempting to reach England. Determined to join the RAF he continued his journey and got to England in 1939 to enlist as a basic 'erk' Aircraftsman 2nd Class. He led the Wing with great dash.

Wing Commander Crawford-Compton was awarded the US Silver Star for his services in escorting American bombers. He notched up a remarkable total of 519 sorties. He was also awarded the French Legion d'Honneur and Croix de Guerre with

Palm. He remained in the service after the war, becoming Air Attaché to Oslo. In 1967 he captained an RAF skiing team with most of the men being half his age. In the 1980s he became step-father to Duncan Goodhew, the British swimmer who won a Gold Medal at the 1980 Olympic Games. He died in 1988 at the age of 72.

He had met Alan Deere and Johnnie Johnson, who controlled the Biggin Hill and Tangmere Wings, one of their agenda items being the formation of 'Balbos', which were usually made up of 70 aircraft - and they were not successful. They had a high profile and were seen at a distance by enemy pilots, who simply gave them a wide berth. Occasionally a 'Balbo' would skirmish with FW 190s, but it was impossible to keep it together as a fighting unit. All three Wing Commanders agreed that 'Balbos' were too unwieldy and cumbersome in fast moving combats and they decided to leave it to 11 Group to decide what size formation was required for any specific purpose. Marshal Italo Balbo, Hornchurch's 1928 visitor, who had conceived mass formation flying became Governor General of the Italian colony of Libya, but was shot down and killed by 'friendly' anti-aircraft fire on 28th June, 1940.

On 14th August, 1943, the 'Spitfire Only' wartime status of Hornchurch (broken only by the brief, but tragic, spell of 264 Squadron with their Boulton Paul Defiants) was interrupted when 239 Squadron brought their North American Mustangs in from Fairlop to continue ground attack and reconnaissance missions, but they only stayed a few weeks and then gave up their Mustangs and moved to Ayr to train as a night fighter squadron.

From the third week in August the Hornchurch Squadrons joined in 'Operation Starkey' - a plan of deception to make the Germans think an invasion of the Calais area was imminent. it was designed to confuse them and make them halt further troop movements to Italy and the Soviet Union. Large scale attacks were made on enemy airfields in France, Belgium and Holland, getting so intense that it was not only the Germans who thought an invasion was imminent: many of the British thought so too.

The effect of the United States daylight offensive had an ever increasing effect on Hornchurch. On 6th September a B-17 Flying Fortress (No. 28582), piloted by Lieutenant Butler, from the 384th Bomb Group at Grafton Underwood, Northampton, landed desperately low on fuel after a raid on Stuttgart. It just made it, having insufficient fuel in its tanks for another circuit: another landed at Fairlop. The Fortresses were based at airfields with long hard-surfaced runways and it was a feat of airmanship to put one down safely at grassed Hornchurch.

Italy signed an Armistice on 3rd September, 1943, and became 'co-belligerent': the status of the Italian prisoners of war in Allied hands also changed and they became 'Co-operators', many of them undertaking useful duties at Hornchurch before returning home after the war.

Later in the month two Fortresses from the 385th Bomb Group based at Great Ashfield, Suffolk, collided over nearby East Horndon and crashed. The Station Services found only one survivor, Sergeant Adams, a tail gunner. He was in a state of shock and was brought back to the airfield to recover in the Officers' Mess. With vast fleets now assembling collisions were becoming an all too common occurrence when these large aircraft were flying close together in poor visibility.

Lieutenant C H Rennall of the 65th Fighter Wing, which had groups at Debden and Boxted in Essex, Steeple Morden in Cambridgeshire and Martlesham Heath and Wattisham in Suffolk and its Headquarters at the Dame Bradbury School in Saffron Walden, was now attached for liaison duties.

The nearest Flying Fortress Group was the 94th Bomb Group at Earls Colne. They suffered devastating losses in the course of nine missions between 29th May and 13th June, losing half their original aircraft and crews in that time. On their first mission they lost three out of 23 aircraft and a fourth landed at RAF Northolt with a dead crewman aboard: it was an ominous start.

On their ninth and last mission from Essex, to the submarine yards at Kiel, the Earls Colne aircraft were scheduled to return to their new base at Bury St Edmunds. As they neared the East Anglian coast on their return journey and with tension relaxed, the Fortresses were pounced on by Luftwaffe fighters and nine aircraft, each with a crew of ten, plunged into the North Sea. Such was the scale of losses in daylight raids before long range fighters were available.

Ten days after the Kiel disaster the Fortresses at Ridgewell, near Halstead, were being loaded with bombs when there was an explosion, blowing the aircraft to pieces and killing 22 aircraftsmen and a British civilian.

On 14th October a Fortress from the 96th Bomb Group at Snetterton Heath, Norfolk, sought sanctuary on the field with a large part of its tail shot away and a wounded crew member on board. It was returning from one of the most costly American raids on the ball bearing complex at Schweinfurt, in which 60 heavy bombers and 599 crewmen were lost and a further seven aircraft were written off after return. On the same day an American P-47 Thunderbolt from Metfield, Suffolk, crashed at nearby Herongate, the pilot being killed.

Later in the year seven American pilots from this Group arrived on detachment for talks on RAF operating procedures. This Fighter Group pioneered the dive bombing and ground attack techniques that were subsequently adopted by the US Eighth and Ninth Air Forces. One way or another, Hornchurch had quite a lot of contact with the Americans in 1943.

The cosmopolitan nature of Hornchurch was compounded on 18th October when 485 (New Zealand) Squadron arrived under the command of Squadron Leader M R Hume. It came with the reputation of being the top scoring squadron of 11 Group in recent times, while escorting the American heavies and, in one raid, destroying six Me109s in quick succession. It only stayed in Hornchurch a month, before moving north to Drem in Scotland for rest and recuperation.

The Duke of Gloucester presenting the Squadron Crest to 164 Squadron at RAF Hornchurch, 26 October, 1943

485 (New Zealand) Squadron in the Dispersal Hut at Hornchurch, November, 1943. Left to right: F/L Al Stead, FSgt Bill Strahan, FSgt Doug Clarke, F/O 'Chalky' White, F/O Tommy Tucker, F/O 'Red' Roberts

The Duke of Gloucester visited the station at the end of the month to present a new Squadron Badge to 164 Squadron's commander, Squadron Leader H A Russell. The badge depicted 'In front of a rising sun, a lion passant guidant' and bore the motto *Firmes volamos* (Firmly we fly): 164 Squadron was actually based at Fairlop, with a nine days detachment to Twinwood Farm, Bedfordshire (the airfield from which Glenn Miller made his final take-off), but it flew over to Hornchurch especially for the Royal presentation.

The same day that Air Defence of Great Britain came into being, each fighter airfield became a self-contained numbered unit, with Hornchurch becoming '135 Airfield' and Fairlop '136 Airfield'. It was not realised at the time, but, although the end was still some months away, the re-organisation was a straw in the wind signalling the end of Hornchurch as a fighter station.

That autumn the Hornchurch Wing, now comprising 129, 222 and 485 (New Zealand) Squadrons, were engaged on Ramrod missions with the B-26 Martin Marauders of the United States 9th Air Force (a Tactical Air Force created for softening up invasion targets and then providing close support for armies in the field, once they had been established on the continent). The Groups escorted by the Hornchurch Wing were operating from the Essex airfields at Andrews Field (near Braintree) and Great Dunmow. The Marauders, after a difficult start, proved to be one of the outstanding aircraft of the war and their percentage losses were considerably smaller than the loss rate of the Fortresses and Liberators.

Distinguished visitors included HRH Amir Abdullah Illah, the Regent of Iraq, an Honorary Air Commodore in the RAF; HRH the Amir Feisal and HRH the Amir Khalid of Saudi Arabia, dressed in their national costume; and HE Señor Don Guillermo de Blanck, the Cuban Minister to London, who presented two Spitfires to the RAF in a ceremony covered by the national press and newsreels.

An escort was provided for American 'heavies' on 1st December, 1943, when the Wing rendezvoused with Liberators and Fortresses returning from an industrial complex at Solingen. This mission was a 'first', as auxiliary fuel tanks were carried, enabling the Spitfires to penetrate deep into Germany. The Americans lost 24 aircraft on the raid, out of 229 despatched. The losses included a Liberator of the 389th Bomb Group from Hethel, Norfolk, that broke up over Manston, killing nine of its crew.

On 16th December Squadron Leader Ronald Adam, the Senior Section Controller, left Hornchurch on posting to the Headquarters of 11 Group as Senior Controller in the rank of Wing Commander. He had been at the base for four years and was almost part of the furniture. He loved the airfield, its history and traditions, and is perhaps best remembered for an incident that has featured in many radio and television re-enactments of the Battle of Britain.

He reported that Alan Deere was leading 54 Squadron in search of the enemy when his voice suddenly crackled over the air, "Christ Almighty! Tally ho! Whole bloody hordes of them!" Somehow it epitomised the whole atmosphere of the Battle.

Two days later Wing Commander P J Sampson was appointed as the final Wing Commander - Flying in the history of RAF Hornchurch.

As 1943 drew to a close the Hornchurch Wing comprised 129 Squadron [from 28th June, 1943] (S/Ldr C Haw), 222 Squadron [from 29th April, 1943, (S/Ldr G J Stonhill), 66 Squadron [from 8 November, 1943] (S/Ldr K T Lofts and 485 (NZ) Squadron [from 18th October, 1943] (S/Ldr A I R Hume), but 222 left for Woodvale on 30th December, being replaced by 350 (Belgian) Squadron returning for a second tour at Hornchurch.

1944 started with much of the 'mixture as before', providing escorts for the US Eighth and Ninth Air Forces, particularly the Marauders flying from nearby Essex bases.

The American presence in Essex increased to a formidable size, surpassed only by Norfolk and Suffolk. Ninth Air Force Bomber Command was based entirely in the county and a further 24 Eighth Air Force officers arrived at Hornchurch for training in liaison duties. Essex grew to 23 military airfields in the early part of 1944 (compared with the five at the outbreak of war with the final two opening at Birch and Boreham. The United States Army Air Force occupied 16 of them and the county peaked at 45,000 United States airmen and 15,000 Royal Air Force men, together with 800 aircraft. It was a most formidable force, the last reminder of which - Wethersfield - closed down in 1990.

Essex airfields in the spring of 1944 were Fairlop, Hornchurch, North Weald, Southend (Rochford), and Stapleford Tawney in the hands of the Royal Air Force; Boxted, Debden, Ridgewell and Wormingford run by the US Eighth Air Force; and Andrews Field (Great Saling), Birch, Boreham, Chipping Ongar, Earls Colne, Gosfield, Great Dunmow, Great Sampford (also RAF Regiment), Little Walden, Matching, Rivenhall and Stansted with the US Ninth Air Force. It seemed as though the whole county was poised for what everybody knew would be a return to the continent, but for Hornchurch it was not to be.

With the station at the peak of its powers and geared for the highly intensive operations that lay ahead the blow fell as it ceased to be one of the seven proud Sector airfields. On 18th February, 1944, the Sector Control Room closed down. Wing Commander Ronald Adam, now at Uxbridge, must have had a lump in his throat as he sent the signal to the airfield where he had spent four years of war -

This is the final order on Ops 'A' line to Hornchurch Sector.

Hornchurch Sector Operations Room, which had controlled Malan - Gray - Bader - Berry - Locke - Scott - Mungo Park - Tuck - Kingcombe - Wells - Gillam - Broadhurst - Freeborne - Stapleton - Denholm - Kingaby - Hugo - Esmonde - Stephen - Duncan-Smith - Scott Malden - Hesselyn - Beaumont - Walsh - Deere - Finucane - Gilroy - Compton - Stevens - Gribble - and many others who have contributed to the total of 906 enemy aircraft confirmed destroyed since the outbreak of war, will now cease to operate. Despite seven major daylight bombing attacks during the Battle of Britain and innumerable night bombings, Hornchurch Sector never allowed itself to become non-operational by reason of attack. Hornchurch Operations Room will now stand down and its personnel are released to their duties elsewhere. What of the future? Though the Sector no longer exists, its unique spirit of comradeship lives on.

No one could argue with the names included by Adam in his signal, but a few eyebrows could, perhaps, be raised at some apparent omissions. No 'Prof' Leathart or Johnny Allen, who participated in 54 Squadron's rescue at Calais Marck and were stalwarts at Dunkirk and in the Battle of Britain; no 'Wonky' Way or George Barclay; no Franklin, Kilmartin, Lovell or Pease. But then, had the signal listed everybody worthy of inclusion, it would have been a very long document indeed.

The Sector total of aircraft, including 'probables' stood at 1,345 and there were also 255 locomotives, 149 ships and 47 barges. These were just the items that could be counted. The damage inflicted on enemy occupied airfields, gun emplacements, troop concentrations and the like could not be measured statistically. Nor could the satisfaction and relief that the crews of Bomber Command and, later, bombers of the Eighth and Ninth Air Forces experienced, as their 'Little Friends' came up to keep them company.

It was the end of the story for the Hornchurch Sector Room, but not quite for the Hornchurch Squadrons that comprised the Wing. They continued to operate, under the control of the North Weald Sector, for a few weeks longer. Indeed, on 23rd February, Monsieur Pierlot, the Prime Minister of Belgium, visited the airfield and, at a ceremony held on a space in front of the old 'Watch Office', decorated six Belgian pilots of 350 Squadron, to commemorate the one hundredth Belgian victory. Two days later, the Belgians used Bradwell Bay as a 'Forward' Station for escorting the Essex based Martin Marauders to Hesdin, under North Weald control.

A close examination of the Hornchurch Operations Record Book (now at the Public Record Office) shows that the very last combat operation mounted by fighter squadrons from the airfield was on the last day of February, 1944, when the squadrons bade their final farewell to the Americans by escorting the Marauders to Hesdin, again under North Weald control.

Slowly, the squadrons faded away to pastures new. On 3rd March 66 Squadron departed to Llanbedr. Twelve days later '136 Airfield' and its aircraft left Fairlop, which was then temporarily reduced to a 'Care and Maintenance' status. The Belgians of 350 Squadron left to become part of the Second Tactical Air Force at RAF Hawkinge, close up to the forthcoming front line, on 10th March.

Finally, 222 Squadron left on 4th April, 1944, to spend a week at Southend (Rochford) before leaving for Selsey and the Second Tactical Air Force.

With the need for fighter squadrons to move forward into the Tactical Air Force and then (after D-Day) to the continent, it was perhaps obvious that fewer fighter squadrons would be needed in their traditional bases in the United Kingdom. The departure of aircraft from the 'wartime only' airfields such as Rochford, Fairlop and Stapleford Tawney could have been anticipated, but the abandonment of Hornchurch, a fighter airfield dating back to the standing patrols in combat with the Zeppelins in 1915 was something different and difficult to come to terms with.

Although air combat was now finished at the airfield it was not quite 'good-bye' for Spitfire squadrons. In April three squadrons, 80, 229 and 274, arrived back from Italy for re-fitting and reorganisation to prepare them for the Second Tactical Air Force. They were the very last operational Spitfire squadrons to use the airfield, and the day they finally departed, 18th May, 1944, was also the last day that an operational RAF Fighter Squadron was in residence. There was then to be a gap of six months, until 14th November, during which no RAF squadrons of any sort were based at the airfield.

The station which had slugged out the critical stage of the war to the point where victory was no longer in any doubt, was now strangely silent and devoid of the sweet purr of the Rolls Royce Merlin engine. But the usefulness of the site that Lord Trenchard had once said 'Suttons Farm or an aerodrome in the vicinity is a necessity for the defensive measures of England' had drawn to a close. It was not the end of Hornchurch as an RAF Station, but it was the end of it as an active fighter station and the end of a proud era.

Plans for the invasion of Europe were now being drawn up and a new alignment of fighter squadrons was a necessary feature. The Second Tactical Air Force was born, including fighters, mainly Spitfires and Typhoons, for the mobile defence of Allied forces after they had landed on the continent. Fighter Command was to supply most of the squadrons and it was planned to reduce Fighter Command to one third of its 1943 size. To complicate matters further, the much reduced Fighter Command reverted to the cumbersome title of 'Air Defence of Great Britain', which it had borne from 1925 to 1936. The Command remained under this name from 15th November, 1943, to 15th October, 1944, when it returned to its more favoured and much loved soubriquet of Fighter Command.

U S 8th Air Force P-51 Mustangs (*USAF*)

'DIMINUENDO'
THE CAPTAINS AND KINGS DEPART

In the period immediately following D-Day the comparative air of peace and calm that prevailed over Hornchurch was soon disturbed by the arrival of the first of Germany's much vaunted V-weapons - the V-1 pilotless plane or 'Doodlebug', as it was immediately christened. It was a campaign lasting over nine months from 12th June, 1944, to 29th March, 1945, and it affected Hornchurch considerably as it received direct hits itself, was involved in setting up a barrage balloon complex at Fairlop, and housed a huge Repair Unit which provided 'first aid' and, later, 'secondary' repairs to thousands of damaged houses in east and south London. The greatest impact of the campaign was felt by an already sadly battered capital and some 40% of those that got through and crashed to earth came down in the London boroughs. Most of the remainder fell on the counties of Kent, Sussex, Surrey and Essex.

Ten days after they started and after several near misses, RAF Hornchurch suffered an orthodox bombing attack and a direct hit from a V-1 on the same day. At 1.15 am five high explosive bombs were dropped, followed a few hours later by a V-1 crashing down on to the built up Technical Site. Several buildings were damaged and huge craters out on the field had to be filled in, rather reminiscent of 1940. The built up area of Hornchurch also suffered badly, ten civilians being killed in one incident when houses in Great Gardens Road, Squirrels Heath, were shattered by a Flying Bomb. Others that impacted nearby and where casualties were particularly heavy were Penerley Road, Rainham and David Drive, Harold Wood: at both incidents twelve civilians died.

As a matter of urgency RAF Hornchurch supervised the installation of No. 24 Balloon Centre at Fairlop, as part of the greatest concentration ever hoisted for the defence of London. Each balloon was 62 feet long, 25 feet across and held 19,000 cubic feet of gas. It was Balloon Command's finest hour of the war and they undoubtedly saved many lives. Their bonus was that any Flying Bomb that they destroyed was one that had eluded anti-aircraft guns and fighters and was all set to descend to earth in crowded streets. It was dangerous work, though, especially when the bomb exploded on striking a balloon cable and scattered debris in all directions. It was not unknown for a stricken Doodlebug to become snagged up in the cable without exploding and then spin on the cable all the way down to impact on the Balloon Site. The WAAF girls manning the balloon had to remain on the alert and be ready to 'take to the hills' or, at least, the nearest air raid shelter. The danger was constant whenever V-1s approached and it was a strain from which there was no relief: annihilation was possible at any time. Over 1,000 Balloon Sites were manned by WAAFS, with two NCOs and 12 airwomen to each site.

The V-1s were launched by large, sloped catapult ramps in enemy-occupied Europe. They had a speed of 370 mph, a range of 160 miles and carried a one ton warhead. The first to cross the British coast exploded at Swanscombe, Kent, but five minutes later one reached London to fall on a railway bridge at Grove Road, Bow, on the Liverpool Street - Romford - East Anglia line. The iron bridge itself, dating from 1871, stood up well to the impact, but most of the parapet brickwork collapsed and two of the four railway tracks were destroyed. Four people were killed and tenants in neighbouring East End streets at first thought that it was a conventional aircraft that had crashed. It was only as the V-1 campaign rapidly developed that the reason for sustained Bomber Command and United States Army Air Force attacks on the Pas de Calais coastline became apparent.

Many Doodlebugs that eluded coastal anti-aircraft batteries and fighter aircraft generally approached singly in a dead straight line from the south-east and continued on a north-west course. Just so long as the noise of the engine could be heard, it could reasonably be assumed that the doodlebug was still flying and, if this continued, would pass on out of harm's way. Streets would be almost bare as V-1s were heard, but each was programmed to give out at a given moment. As the engine died, the 'bug' would stall, drop nose down and dive straight to earth, where its warhead exploded on impact. On the ground people's ears became tuned to a fine pitch and, if they were outside, it enabled them to dart for cover, in a shelter for preference, but crouching in a shop doorway if nothing else was available. The few seconds that remained before a tremendous explosion confirmed its arrival, an explosion sufficient to demolish a whole housing block, were full of apprehension. No one could know

for sure where it would fall and the blast effect - worse than with ordinary high explosive bombs - occasionally tore the clothes off distant civilians.

Gradually the volume of attacks diminished and on 29th March the last V-1 to hit England fell to anti-aircraft fire to crash harmlessly at Sittingbourne, alongside the same main road where the first had exploded nine months before.

V-1 'Doodlebug' plunging to earth over central London, having eluded fighters, guns and balloons

Remains of a Barrage Balloon Site after a V-1 had swung down the cable and exploded

136

In subsequent Flying Bomb attacks on the airfield, stores and buildings were badly damaged and telephone lines were destroyed.

The air raid sirens heralded their coming on 402 occasions; 6,139 people were killed; and 17,239 were seriously injured. The worst incidents were at the Guards' Chapel in Wellington Barracks, Westminster, which was hit during a service and 119 members of the congregation died, and Lewisham High Street, when 51 people were killed in the shopping centre. Croydon, Wandsworth and Lewisham in south London were the worst hit boroughs, but, nearer to RAF Hornchurch, Barking, East Ham, llford, Dagenham, Leyton, Hornchurch and Romford all suffered the impact of between twenty and thirty of the missiles.

Throughout the V-1 campaign 6,725 Flying Bombs were logged approaching over the coast and, of these, 1,878 (28%) were destroyed by anti-aircraft fire; 1,846 (27%) were destroyed by RAF fighters; 231 (4%) struck Barrage Balloon cables; and 2,770 (41%) eluded all the defences and got through.

In July, 1944, as the Royal Air Force peaked with nearly 1.2 million personnel, 215 V-1s were seen from the Fairlop Control Tower, 19 of these crashing into their balloons. In August there were even more, but, apart from broken windows and some blast damage, RAF Fairlop itself remained fairly intact. The peak day of the onslaught was 3rd August, when 97 Doodlebugs crossed the Channel. No. 24 Balloon Centre stayed at Fairlop for over a year.

The V-1s also caused some casualties amongst the fighter squadrons. One tactic adopted was to fly alongside and disturb the gyroscopic equilibrium by tipping the wing over, thus causing it to crash into the green fields of Kent or Essex, instead of the heavily built up urban areas. This was hazardous work and cost many fighter aircraft. 486 (RNZAF) Squadron, based at Newchurch on the Romney Marshes, lost 17 aircraft and three pilots. As continental launching sites were liberated V-1s were launched either from ramps further up the coast or from Luftwaffe aircraft over the North Sea: the angle of approach to London thus shifted north of the Thames and Essex became even more heavily involved.

At RAF Hornchurch there were three direct hits by rockets on the site and many more nearby. The NAAFI buildings, Sergeants' and Airmen's Messes and a Rest Room were all virtually demolished, other buildings were damaged less severely and there were the customary craters in the field to be filled in.

The rocket attacks caused widespread damage to houses in the crowded east and south of London streets and No. 55 Repair Unit - one of the most remarkable 'non-flying' units ever established at Hornchurch - started to arrive shortly after the first attacks. It had been created to help the Ministry of Works in carrying out basic repairs. Under the command of Group Captain H W Evans the Unit comprised 2,000 men. 200 vehicles and a mass of stores and equipment. The airmen included a large number who had been accepted for aircrew training and who were not exactly thrilled by their change in occupation, but they buckled to with a will.

The area covered from Hornchurch was Deptford (commanded by W/O Kelly),

Lewisham (W/O Horner), Hackney (W/O Watson), Walthamstow (W/O Caley), Leyton (W/O Castle) and Wanstead and Woodford (W/O Bailey), but this was only a provisional organisational list and, in practice, the airmen were deployed to wherever the greatest need arose and this could include Barking, Dagenham and Stepney. The first location visited by the airmen was the Becontree Estate in Dagenham where a Doodlebug had fallen, but as their strength built up they attended at up to 600 houses in a single day, making emergency repairs to make them wind and water tight.

The Dagenham commitment, completed on 23rd July, 1944, resulted in a letter of thanks from the lady Mayor of the Borough and a gift of cigarettes for each of the participating airmen. Subsequently, letters poured in from grateful residents and the Civic Authorities in areas where the crews worked. One thankful East Ender wrote, "We were at a low ebb wondering where help would come from, when your boys arrived. They not only repaired the worst of our damage, but they lifted our spirits with their happy laughing disposition. God Bless them all."

Airmen working in Mile End Road, Bow, had several Doodlebugs fall nearby and AC1 McCool was taken to hospital with serious blast injuries: others were hit with flying debris. Still the work went on with daily forays: it was exhausting work and a system of time off for rest and recreation had to be instituted at the request of the Station Medical Officer. On 6th August, 1944, a V-1 flew low over the Officers' Mess and exploded on houses at the side of the railway at Elm Park. Station Rescue Services rushed to the scene and the ambulance took some of the casualties to hospital. LAC Johnson, working at Stepney, espied two young boys in distress and apparently drowning in the Grand Union Canal. He dived straight in and, after a struggle, managed to save one of the boys. He received an Award from the Royal Humane Society. LAC Kouratou, a Greek serving with the RAF, was killed when a Doodlebug exploded near to where he was working in Leyton: three of his workmates were seriously injured and sent to Whipps Cross Hospital.

Time and again, the airmen were asked where they came from and more letters were received by 'The Commanding Officer, RAF Hornchurch' in praise of 'his lads'. Often, high spirits would be dampened when another Doodlebug attack would ruin a week's hard work and put them back to square one, but they stuck at it and graduated to 'secondary repairs', as they caught up with the backlog of 'first aid' repairs. During August, 1944, 21 airmen were seriously injured enough to be detained in hospital, and one of them died.

On 1st September, 1944, Southend (Rochford) was closed and placed on a 'Care and Maintenance' basis under Hornchurch, but two weeks later a United States P-47 Thunderbolt was forced to make a crash landing there and finished up by hitting an unoccupied Nissen Hut, near the Liverpool Street - Southend railway line. The pilot was unhurt, but it is not known how the unoccupied airfield, with no crash, fire or medical services (apart from a small Care and Maintenance Party) dealt with the

The second of Hitler's 'secret weapons' was the V-2 rocket, against which there was no possible means of defence. The first was fired on 9th September, 1944, to land at Chiswick: the effect of a mighty explosion without any warning was staggering. The Germans had progressed with rocket propulsion faster than the Allies, although it was now too late to affect the outcome of the war.

The V-2 was a more terrifying weapon than the V-1 because it could not be heard in flight or be intercepted. It was a liquid oxygen and alcohol propelled rocket weighing 12 tons and carried a one ton warhead at the fantastic speed of 3,500 mph.

At their apogee over a hundred a month were fired and two that landed at New Cross and Smithfield killed or seriously injured 268 and 233 people respectively.

Poor battered Londoners were being pounded by yet another form of aerial warfare and the 1,115 rockets that hit the area destroyed a further 30,000 houses and damaged well over a million more. 2,855 people were killed and 6,268 seriously injured.

First aid repairs on V-1 damaged houses

A Miles Martinet, used at Hornchurch as 'target tugs' by the anti-aircraft co-operation squadrons between November, 1944, and June, 1945

incident or how the pilot felt, stepping out of his cockpit after such a harrowing experience, to find nobody on the airfield.

In November it was decided that 55 Repair Unit would have to be found another home as the airfield was wanted for Air Sea Rescue and Army Co-operation Squadrons and there just wasn't the room. A site was examined at 'RAF Regent's Park', which spread itself out over the Park, buildings in St John's Wood, Lord's Cricket Ground and the London Zoo. Although having the geographical advantage of being in central London, it was not really suitable and an alternative site at Ruskin Avenue, Kew, a temporary building constructed in the 1914-18 War as a Record Office, was preferred.

At St Paul's Church in Ripple Road, Barking, a rocket made a direct hit on the morning of Sunday, 14th January, 1945; the church was ruined and there was extensive damage to adjacent houses and shops; rescue dogs and searchlights helped to recover 8 dead and 109 injured. The same evening a rocket destroyed the Methodist Central Hall and blasted Marks & Spencers and the Town Hall, 14 people dying, and a third landed at the Town Quay. They were dropping every day in the vicinity at this time, but the last V-2 fell on 29th March, the same day as the last V-1 Doodlebug.

During the first week of December the 2,040 airmen of the Repair Unit packed bags and made their way across London in a series of convoys, bringing to an end a most hectic period of five months in the story of the airfield. The Unit lasted only two months in its new home; with rocket attacks decreasing, the need for the Royal Air Force to aid the Ministry of Works diminished. The airmen were all posted away and the Unit closed in February, 1945.

The six months during which Hornchurch had not awakened to the noise of aircraft engines now came to an end and, between November, 1944, and June, 1945, four different squadrons occupied the airfield for anti-aircraft co-operation and Air Sea Rescue duties. This included the calibration of predictors and anti-aircraft radar, used at the many gun sites, target towing and gunlaying. A wide variety of aircraft were used for these duties -

AVRO ANSON In RAF service from 1935, nicknamed 'Faithful Annie'. Used on reconnaissance, aircrew training, transport and, at Hornchurch, on radar calibration and anti-aircraft cooperation. Maximum speed 188 mph; two 350 hp Armstrong Siddeley Cheetah engines. Over 7,000 were built and it remained in service for 33 years, the last six retiring from RAF Bovingdon with a Farewell Formation Fly-past on 28th June, 1968.

BRISTOL BEAUFIGHTER In RAF service from 1940 as the first night fighter to make really effective use of the secret AI (Airborne Interception) radar during the Luftwaffe night bombing raids of 1940-1. Some were converted as Target Tugs. Maximum speed 333 mph; two 1,679 hp Bristol Hercules engines.

MILES MARTINET In RAF service from 1942 as the first purpose-designed Target Tug. Maximum speed 240 mph; one 870 hp Bristol Mercury engine.

AIRSPEED OXFORD In RAF service from 1937, nicknamed 'Ox-Bow'. Widely used for aircrew training, but adapted for Air Ambulance, communications and radar calibration roles. Maximum speed 188 mph; two 370 hp Armstrong Siddeley Cheetah engines.

HAWKER TEMPEST In RAF service from 1944. A development of the Typhoon and used for Fighter Ground Attack operations and, very successfully, for dealing with V-1 Doodlebugs; adapted and used at Hornchurch on Target Tug duties. Maximum speed 427 mph; one 2,180 hp Napier Sabre engine.

VICKERS WARWICK In RAF service from 1941, serving as a troop carrier with a capacity of 24, but also had bomber and air sea rescue variants. Maximum speed 260 mph; two 1,850 hp Pratt & Whitney engines. The Warwick was the largest aircraft seen in regular squadron service at Hornchurch.

There were also a few SPITFIRES and HURRICANES, not for fighter combat, but to simulate attacks on gunsites.

These aircraft were used variously by 116, 278, 287 and 567 Squadrons Hornchurch, 278 Squadron being on Air Sea Rescue duties, the others on anti-aircraft co-operation. There was also a detachment of Wellingtons from 765 Squadron, Fleet Air Arm, based at Lee on Solent, which remained from 14th November, 1944, to 14th June, 1945; its main task was, in close liaison with 567 Squadron, to record the efficiency of radar units. However, the Wellington detachment, commanded by Lieutenant (A) D H Coates, was also used for long range reconnaissance, the naval airmen including a number of experienced photographers. Naval uniforms became a familiar sight around Hornchurch and the RAF men noticed a difference in the service jargon and military traditions.

The Vickers Wellington had entered RAF service in 1938 and was the backbone of Bomber Command before 4-engined bombers came into service. In the first 1,000 bomber raid in 1942, over half the aircraft were Wellingtons. Variants were used for reconnaisance, crew training and, with a 48 feet magnetic hoop, for exploding magnetic mines. Over 11,000 were built. They had a top speed of 255 mph driven by two 1,000 hp Bristol Pegasus engines.

Even in non-combatant operations aircraft and pilots became casualties in accidents. 567 Squadron soon lost a Hurricane, the pilot being killed when he crashed near RAF Detling, and another, Flight Sergeant Williams, was killed near Biggin Hill after radioing that he was in trouble. 278 Squadron's Warwicks were capable of carrying an airborne lifeboat for Air Sea Rescue: they too soon lost an aircraft when Flight Sergeant Evans crashed near North Weald. He was seriously injured and his crew members were badly shaken.

Group Captain R J Clare was appointed as Station Commander to open the new transit camp (33 Personnel Disposal, Unit) and the first transients arrived on 14th December, 1944, entering and leaving at the rate of one hundred a day at the start. The outward stream comprised airmen *en route* as reinforcements or replacements to the Second Tactical Air Force by now firmly established on the continent and the much smaller inwards stream were airmen arriving back for special leave or posting to other United Kingdom bases.

One of the major headaches was to keep the transients occupied. They were only suspended in transit for a few days, in most cases, until arrangements for their next posting or onward movement were completed. They did not have any particular duties, apart from a Morning Parade and Roll Call, going for their meals and indulging in domestic 'bull' which, in the nature of things, rarely reached great heights. Awaiting their Movement Orders they had to be prevented from sinking into a stupor of boredom. Concerts, cinema shows and the NAAFI went a long way to making this time slip past a little more pleasantly and, although the Windmill girls would probably have blanched at the prospect of appearing at that time, there was a packed concert on Christmas Eve, 1944, when the renowned Henry Hall Orchestra played for the permanent staff and transients in the Station Cinema. The concert was broadcast nation-wide on BBC Radio.

As 1944 drew to a close the resident squadrons were 278 in the Air Sea Rescue role and 567 in the Anti-aircraft co-operation mode.

####

In January, 1945, the transients passing through doubled and 7,100 personnel were dealt with during the month. Accommodation was very overcrowded and every room that could be pressed into service to hold beds or bunks was used. The two squadrons continued to operate, although 567 Squadron detached individual aircraft to other south-east airfields as need arose. In February, 1945, the Air Sea Rescue Squadron moved on to RAF Thorney Island, Hampshire.

RAF Southend (Rochford) was re-opened and pressed into service as a Transit Camp, mainly for RAF Regiment personnel. The flow of personnel, which started as a trickle and graduated to a stream, had now reached a flood, compounded at the end of April when the first of the released prisoners of war arrived. They came back by land, sea and air, their faces reflecting their absolute delight at regaining their freedom and returning home.

RAF Dakotas, Stirlings and Halifaxes from 38 Group started a series of circular tours, taking out fuel for the Second Tactical Air Force and returning with a grand total of 27,277 British and Americans released from captivity. Bomber Command brought back 75,000 prisoners and, in addition, dropped food to the starving Dutch in and around their big cities in 'Operation Manna'.

With the original NAAFI, Airmen's and Sergeants' Messes all badly damaged by a V-2 rocket, alternative buildings had to be improvised to fulfil these functions until repairs and rebuilding could be effected. The combined effects of a permanently over-crowded airfield; damage caused by V-weapons; temporary structures and buildings being used for purposes other than that for which they were designed; the 'Barrack Room damages' caused by endless transients who, quite naturally, did not have a knowledge of or feeling for the traditions of the airfield; and, the loss of the tightly disciplined Fighter Command squadrons all began to give the airfield a worn out look in sharp contrast to the immaculate layout that prevailed between April, 1928, and March, 1944. It was an over used and somewhat abused airfield.

This was relieved to an extent from 8th March, 1945, when a contingent of Italians, formerly prisoners of war and now 'co-operators', were drafted in as a labour force to work at the base and help restore it to something like its earlier condition. The Italians did indeed 'co-operate' and worked well, often at the most menial tasks that had to be undertaken, working willingly and without complaint. Sweeping roads

142

and cleaning buildings inside and out was their lot for four months and they worked under an Italian Army Sergeant Major, responsible to an RAF Sergeant.

Unusual transients passing through the Personnel Disposal Centre at this time were 46 RAF police dogs - Alsatians - with their handlers and feeding and caring for them caused a few new headaches. The profusion of buildings did not include dog kennels and the dogs were first chained to uprights opposite Anson Administration Block. They were later removed to Defiant Block, where it was easier for the handlers to care for them and walk them. A goodly supply of horse meat and dog biscuits was rushed in and water bowls were improvised to keep them happy for the five days they rested at Hornchurch in transit.

The war was now in its final stages and there were now three Army Co-operation squadrons in residence - 567, which had been operating at Hornchurch for six months, 116 and 287 Squadrons, which arrived from Redhill. Martinets and Oxfords were the aircraft most often seen flying from the airfield.

Warrant Officer Dandridge in a 567 Squadron Vengeance had engine failure over the Thames Estuary and landed on a sandbank ten miles from Herne Bay. Dandridge was rescued, but his aircraft was submerged by the tide before it could be salvaged.

VE-Day, 9th May, 1945, was a great day for everybody in the United Kingdom, civilians and military alike, who had undergone five and a half wearying years of war. At Hornchurch it was celebrated in style, first at the base and, later in the evening by some, in London. Bonfires were lit to celebrate the ending of all blackout regulations in the remoter parts of the airfield and 567 Squadron made sure that all its detached aircraft came back to Hornchurch for a great combined squadron celebration. A Thanksgiving Church Service was followed by memorable parties and dances at which the odd celebratory 'Victory' pint or two were consumed.

There was still a war to be fought in the Far East, but for British airfields the shooting war was over and it was a moment to take time off and rejoice. For the happy servicemen, who lived it up, danced and made merry until the early hours of the morning, the Pacific seemed remote.

It would nevertheless have come as a surprise to most of them to have fore-knowledge that, out of the 1,100,000 men and women in the service of the Royal Air Force on this celebratory night, two-thirds would be released from it within a year. The RAF finished the war in Europe with 55,469 aircraft, of these 9,200 were in front line service.

The Hornchurch Sector of Fighter Command had lost 481 airmen in combat and others in accidents, training flights and in later Army Co-operation Squadrons. Those that made their final take-off from Hornchurch must have been uppermost in the minds of many at a further packed church service held on 13th May, followed by a large Victory Parade at which all squadrons and sectors were represented and when Group Captain R J Clare took the salute.

In addition to the losses at the base, the nearby civilians in Hornchurch had also suffered heavy casualties, some of them from bombs aimed at the airfield which missed their mark. There had been 143 killed, 370 seriously injured, 1,119 injured;

566 houses demolished, 864 houses badly damaged and 28,348 houses damaged. These figures come from orthodox bombing raids, V-1 Doodlebugs and V-2 rockets.

As the shouting and the tumult died life had to go on at the airfield and the daily routine had to adapt to the change from war to peace. As many of the erks were heard to say, "I expect all the bull will come back now."

238 visiting aircraft landed during May for refuelling and/or inspection and, with the squadrons still in residence, there was still plenty of flying going on to interest the 'plane spotters in the locality.

Neighbouring Essex airfields, built on a 'wartime only' basis started closing down; they had few of the basic facilities of the brick built permanent stations and were largely collections of Nissen huts, three T-2 hangars, a control tower and, in the winter, acres and acres of mud. Chipping Ongar (Willingale) and Hunsdon (just across the Hertfordshire border) closed immediately after VE-Day and were taken over as satellites of Hornchurch. Birch, Borcham, Gosfield, Great Sampford and Matching did not house any aircraft after May, 1945, although some were used by 'Other Departments' for administrative purposes.

The huge T-2 hangars erected on airfields housing American Combat Groups were built up in sections, rather on the 'Leggo' principle and, eventually, North Weald cast envious eyes on one of the T-2s at Chipping Ongar, far bigger than their 1920s vintage hangars and it was arranged that it should be transferred. It was all rather reminiscent of the RAF Disciplinary Sergeant who instructed a bunch of new recruits to 'Dismantle your beds in Hut 4, take them to Hut 5, and mantle them again.' The T-2 hangar at Chipping Ongar was dismantled and mantled again at North Weald, where it can be seen today quite close to the M11 motorway.

On 15th June the realities of life were confirmed when Hornchurch lost its cherished Fighter Command status and was transferred to Technical Training Command. Hornchurch had been in Fighter Command from the time it re-opened on 1st April, 1928: in that time the Air Officers Commanding had been

Air Marshal Sir John Salmond, KCB CMG CVO DSO	1 1 1925
Air Vice Marshal F Scarlett, CB DSO	26 5 1928
Air Vice Marshal Sir Edward Ellington, KCB CRIG CBE	1 1 1929
Air Marshal Sir Robert Brooke-Popham, KCB CAIG DSO AFC	17 1 1933
Air Marshal Sir John Steel, KCB KBE CMG	1 8 1935
Air Marshal Sir Hugh Dowding, KCB CMG	14 7 1936
Air Marshal William Sholto Douglas, CB MC DFC	25 11 1940
Air Marshal Trafford Leigh-Mallory, CB DSO	28 11 1942
Air Marshal Sir Roderic Hill, CB MC AFC	15 11 1943

Also on 15th June Hornchurch lost its anti-aircraft co-operation squadrons with 116 Squadron disbanding, 287 leaving for Bradwell Bay and 567 to Hawkinge. As Hornchurch went to Technical Training Command, Balloon Command was disbanded, its task nobly completed. The Fleet Air Arm Squadron 765 left Hornchurch for Manston, before returning to the Royal Naval Air Station at Lee-on-Solent. With no flying squadrons left on the airfield Flying Control, refuelling and emergency facilities were also withdrawn and all further landings, with the exception of emergencies, were prohibited.

On 9th July, however, a Coastal Command Avro Anson from 1693 Flight in Copenhagen made an emergency landing at 8 am. The aircraft, piloted by Flying Officer Gamlin and with Lady Bowhill on board as a passenger, was in trouble and had to get down quickly. The undercarriage sheared off as it made a heavy landing and it slithered along in clouds of dust. Nobody was hurt, but it was found that one of its two engines and the braking system were unserviceable.

On 15th September, 1945, five years from the day when the Battle of Britain was at its height, the Royal Air Force celebrated with a magnificent Fly Past over London, led by Group Captain Douglas Bader. Twenty fighter squadrons from bases all over the country assembled at North Weald seen off by Sir Hugh Dowding, but watched broodily by the silent grass flightpaths at Hornchurch, 13 miles to the south east, which had seen it all, but were not now represented and whose landing area was 'banned' to all aircraft.

They took off to fly low over the East End boroughs, the City, and the West End, before describing a great circle to return to Essex. Hard bitten Cockneys turned their eyes to the sky and some openly wept at the sight of this impressive tribute to those who had paid the supreme sacrifice and they recalled their own ordeal from the skies over the preceding years. The Fly Past was led by Group Captain Douglas Bader, the intrepid legless hero, who had been at Hornchurch for a short time with 242 Squadron during the Battle of Britain. The mass take-off at North Weald was watched by Sir Hugh Dowding, the Chief of Fighter Command during the desperate days: for him, and for many others, it was a moment of haunting nostalgia.

Sir Hugh Dowding and Group Captain Douglas Bader, 15 September, 1945

A Mustang and a Percival Proctor were amongst the aircraft that made emergency landings at the airfield. Hornchurch was also used as rehearsal quarters for Ralph Reader's RAF Gang Shows, with such future stars as Peter Sellers and Tony Hancock.

In October the satellite airfield at Fairlop was evacuated, this time for good. It had only been open four years.

'Demob Numbers' were now the main topic of conversation amongst airmen, the number allocated to each individual being assessed by age and length of service. It was the regulating factor for releasing the 'Duration of Present Emergency' airmen serving with the RAF. It was a difficult situation as the service rapidly reduced in size and the excessive shortage of airmen in some of the skilled trades caused difficulties as the service readjusted to a peacetime rôle with a force eventually less than one tenth its maximum wartime strength.

As 1945 ended the permanent staff at Hornchurch numbered 555 RAF and 212 WAAF, supplemented by transit personnel, but these were falling by the year end. In January, 1946, the Transit Camp, now known as No. 3 Personnel Disposal Centre, handled 500 airmen a day - less than the permanent staff.

Transients gradually slowed as the Forces of Occupation stabilised the continent and averages were down to 300 in April, 150 by June and only a trickle of 40 by August, 1946.

Fairlop was closed 'officially' in May, 1946, after having been abandoned for 8 months. The demise of 'wartime only' airfields at the end of hostilities was dramatic and the sudden quietness of an abandoned airfield was quite eerie. Silence prevailed where engine noises, tears and laughter had been predominant. Few have disappeared quite so completely as Fairlop and today there is no indication that it once housed fighter squadrons and was a site from which many RAF pilots made their last take-off. Horses and their riders from a nearby Riding School now roam over part of the site, next to the old LNER line at Fairlop, today part of London Transport's Central Line.

It might all have been very different. In 1945, only a year before it closed, Sir Patrick Abercrombie's *Greater London Plan* envisaged Fairlop as a possible second London Airport to Heathrow as post-war civilian traffic built up. Fairlop and Matching were two of the Essex airfields on the short list; Stansted, today London's Third Airport, was not even considered.

In the early part of 1947 there was a further run down at Hornchurch. The Aviation Candidates' Selection Board, established in 1946, dealt with 800 applicants between January and March, but the desperate fuel crisis that hit the country in the freezing conditions of that winter needed equally desperate remedies. Military organisations had to economise as well as civilian homes and offices and the Board closed down on 26th February. Applicants wishing to extend their service in the RAF continued to be dealt with for a short time, until the Unit closed at the end of March.

The Transit Camp, Army Co-operation aircraft, Royal Naval Squadron and the massive 55 Repair Unit had all disappeared. The fighter squadrons had been gone for three years and, with Fighter Command in the process of standardising on the Gloster Meteor and De Havilland Vampire jets, it was obvious it would never regain its Fighter Command status. Jets needed hard surfaced runways and non-urban surroundings and generally more space than was available at Hornchurch.

The Captains and the Kings had departed!

'MASTERCLASS'
AIRCREW SELECTION CENTRE

While Hornchurch slumbered in freezing hibernation during the wretched winter of 1946/7 its inactivity only lasted a few weeks. On 28th June Air Commodore D McFadyen (1902-68) was appointed Station Commander, the highest ranking officer to hold the post to this date.

The reason was the establishment of the Officers' Advanced Training School (OATS), which stayed for fifteen months before moving on to RAF Bircham Newton, Norfolk. It was one of five Units in residence at Hornchurch between 1946 and 1962, having allied themes of advanced training, selection and allocation. They were Aviation Candidates' Selection Board (1946-7), Officers' Advanced Training School (1947-8), Combined Selection Centre [known as the Aircrew Selection Centre after 1952] (1948-62), Personnel Selection & Interviewing School (1951-55) and Aircrew Allocation Centre (1958-9).

The purpose of these Units was to examine candidates for commissions and/or aircrew training and to assess their aptitude, intelligence, education, physical qualities and, if acceptable, their most suitable aircrew position. Interview Boards, comprising experienced senior officers, and Medical Boards were an integral part of the process. Although the percentage of applicants who passed varied over the years, it was not usual for more than half the candidates to fulfil all requirements necessary to qualify.

This was to be the primary post-war rôle of RAF Hornchurch, although several other miscellaneous flying and ground units did appear from time to time.

One unit sharing little of the fame and glory, but playing a vital part for nearly twenty years was the 6221 Bomb Disposal Flight, located at a remote area at Gerpins Lane, Upminster, now the London Borough of Havering's Corporation Tip. The site had been requisitioned in May, 1941, from the Walker Sand & Ballast Company and the personnel engaged in this dangerous task were fed and accommodated at Hornchurch, although a Nissen Hut was put on the site for the convenience of the airmen on duty. Army Bomb Disposal Units also used the 'Upminster Bomb Cemetery', as the facility quickly became known. In 1947 the Unit transferred from one part of the gravel pit to another and continued dealing with unexploded bombs up to 1959, when it was returned to the sand and ballast company.

In October, 1947, RAF Hornchurch was officially 'adopted' by the Hornchurch Urban District Council. One of the majestic Sunderland flying boats (DV 976) ditched into the River Thames nearby at this time and 4 crewmen died.

New Year's Day, 1948, saw the establishment of a Recruits' Advanced Drill Unit (RADU) with an advance party of one officer and 30 airmen, formed to provide RAF

Guards of Honour on Royal and State occasions, ceremonial parades, military funerals, lining the route at public displays and various other functions, including the Royal British Legion Festival of Remembrance and the Edinburgh Tattoo.

The RAF Depôt at Uxbridge had maintained a Drill Unit from the earliest days of the Royal Air Force until the start of World War II. The coming of RADU at Hornchurch was, in effect, a re-formation of that Unit, but at a new home. It only remained at Hornchurch during 1948, but in that year was on ceremonial duties many times. Its first official duty was to attend the Memorial Service at Westminster for Air Marshal Sir Arthur Coningham, who had been a Royal Flying Corps pilot in 1914-18, formed the First Tactical Air Force in North Africa in World War II and retired in 1947 as the Air Officer Commander in Chief of Flying Training Command. Other duties included lining the route in Hornchurch as King George VI and Queen Elizabeth drove through and providing a Guard of Honour at RAF Northolt for the arrival of the Shah of Persia and, later, at RAF Andover, where the Shah was accommodated overnight. Military honours were accorded for the burial of Aircraftman Greer at Wickford Parish Church and Flight Lieutenant Nee at RAF Leuchars. Their final duty at

Since then it has gone from strength to strength, entertaining crowds around the world with its immaculate Continuity Drill - a series of precision drill movements performed without any word of command. From 1st November, 1960, its name was changed to the Queen's Colour Squadron; current strength is 4 officers, one Warrant officer and 100 NCOs and airmen. It represents the RAF at major ceremonial occasions and the Unit is the custodian of the Queen's Colour for the Royal Air Force in the United Kingdom. It has to memorise over 300 separate movements which come directly out of the *RAF Drill Manual* and are not compiled specially to entertain.

Memories of 54 Squadron's long association with Hornchurch were revived when the squadron (then based at RAF Odiham, Hampshire) made the first Atlantic crossing by jet aircraft. Six De Havilland Vampires, led by Squadron Leader R W Oxspring, made a goodwill tour of Canada and the U S A.

Hornchurch was to provide a Guard of Honour, comprising two officers and 50 airmen, for the visit of the Air Member for Personnel, Air Marshal Sir Hugh Saunders, and, on the following day, Air Marshal J Whitworth-Jones. RADU, under the command of Squadron Leader J S Sallows, returned to its spiritual home at RAF Uxbridge on 8th October.

Regular flying returned to Hornchurch in May, 1948, with the formation of No. 86 Reserve Centre. It had a modest opening full-time establishment of three officers (including a Squadron Leader Commanding Officer) and twelve airmen. It was tasked with re-enlisting 300 ex-service pilots and 250 ex-service navigators into the Royal Air Force Volunteer Reserve. With the other Reserve Centres that were formed, it was hoped to preserve the flying competence of a proportion of the many thousands of recently demobilised aircrew members.

Negotiations to find an operator to run the Reserve Flying School resulted in the contract being awarded to Shorts of Rochester, Kent. No. 17 Reserve Flying School was formed on 1st July, with Tiger Moths, Avro Ansons, Airspeed Oxfords and De

Havilland Chipmunks. As these interesting aircraft flew into Hornchurch, the Tiger Moths in particular were reminiscent of the Hornchurch of fifteen years earlier and its biplane fighters.

The Reserve Flying Schools were rather similar to the prewar Elementary Flying Training Schools (EFTSs), where so many of the RAF's wartime complement learnt their craft. The main difference was that the EFTSs took in untrained aviation enthusiasts and taught them to fly, whereas the Reserve Flying School's rôle was more in the nature of providing refresher training for fully experienced, but recently demobilised, pilots and navigators. At Hornchurch the Tiger Moths and Chipmunks were used for pilots and the Ansons and Oxfords for navigational refresher courses. No. 17 Reserve Flying School started off with just two pupils on continuous and eighteen on non-continuous training.

On 2nd September, 1948, Ralph Reader again visited the station to make arrangements for the forthcoming British Legion Festival of Remembrance at the Royal Albert Hall. It was arranged that Hornchurch would provide 150 airmen, under the command of Squadron Leader J S Sallows.

The peacetime routine of the station was now back in full swing and with the Officers' Advanced Training School, Recruits' Advanced Drill Unit, 6221 Bomb Disposal Flight, 86 Reserve Centre and 17 Reserve Flying School all in residence 1948 was a busy year. At the end of the year the Officers' Advanced Training School moved out to RAF Bircham Newton and the Recruits' Advanced Drill Unit went to RAF Uxbridge, being replaced by the Combined Selection Centre, which transferred from RAF North Weald. The Combined Selection Centre, with subtle changes in its rôle and title was to remain at Hornchurch for 14 years, becoming the gateway for thousands of eager young men with an ambition to serve with the Royal Air Force. In its first complete month at Hornchurch the Centre dealt with

Outcome	Direct Entry	Serving Airmen	Re-Enlist	Glider Pilots	Entry Scheme	Total	%
Recommended airmen/aircrew	149	24	83	7	10	273	44.3
Recommended Commissions	26	3				29	4.7
Rejected by Interview Board	173	20	35	5	19	252	40.8
Rejected by Medical Board	32	4	8	2	1	47	7.6
Withdrew	7		9			16	2.6
Total	387	51	135	14	30	617	100

Group Captain F C Sturgis assumed command of the station from Air Commodore A McKee.

1949 was notable as a year of industrial unrest in the United Kingdom and military personnel were called upon to provide essential services on several occasions. A tented camp was established at Hornchurch and accommodation, food and transport services were laid on for airmen involved with the London Docks' strike. Hangars were pressed into service for storage of equipment and vehicles. Later that year similar facilities were provided, as servicemen worked at Littlebrook and Barking Power Stations during the Power Workers' strike.

The Air Training Corps, formed from the Air Defence Cadet Corps in 1941 to provide recruits for the Royal Air Force, was re-organised on an area basis and the 'West Essex Wing' was established at Hornchurch with a full time serving officer to serve as Adjutant.

The Combined Selection Centre now had a permanent staff of 51. About a hundred applicants were in residence at any one time and one particular applicant in August, 1949, was 2435575 Aircraftman Second Class Norman Tebbit, who passed through the Selection Centre to be commissioned as a Pilot Officer flying Gloster Meteor jets with 604 (County of Middlesex) Squadron, Royal Auxiliary Air Force, based at North Weald. This was during a short period when the Royal Air Force accepted a limited number of National Service airmen for pilot training.

Tebbit had a narrow escape getting out of a blazing Meteor which failed to take off from North Weald. In later years he became a Minister of State, successively at the Departments of Industry, Employment and Trade & Industry. He was Chancellor of the Duchy of Lancaster and Chairman of the Conservative Party from 1985 to 1987. His RAF life and times at Padgate, Hornchurch, South Cerney and North Weald were recalled in his autobiography *Upwardly Mobile*.

On 17th September, 1949, the airfield was 'At Home' and opened to the public on the ninth anniversary of the Battle of Britain. Admission was free on purchase of a one shilling programme and 20,000 people attended, watching a fly past that included the Tangmere Wing of Meteor jets and B-50 Super Fortresses of the United States Air Force.

NATO (The North Atlantic Treaty Organisation) was formed on 24th August, 1950, under General Dwight D Eisenhower. The RAF in Germany now had responsibility for the support of NATO troops and its Commander was none other than the erstwhile Hornchurch Station commander, Air Vice Marshal Sir Harry Broadhurst.

The complement of the station was now 550 officers and airmen, 12 WRAFs (the Women's Auxiliary Air Force having changed its name to Women's Royal Air Force on 1st February, 1949) and an average of 110 candidates passing through the Combined Selection Centre.

As the year drew to a close four officers and 165 airmen were allocated to power stations, mainly on fatigues that included loading the coal conveyors for the furnaces and removing ashes. It was heavy work and the participants were not sorry to return to their normal duties when the strike was over.

The 1950s were the peak years for Hornchurch in its post-war rôle. The Royal Air Force, with its planned supersonic fighters and the V-bomber force in the offing, demanded an exceptionally high standard of excellence for its aircrew officers, be they pilots, navigators, engineers or signallers, and the selection processes took the utmost pains to ensure that it got them.

The candidates who were interviewed and medically examined came from a variety of sources: some direct from school, university or civilian occupations, while a substantial number came from airmen already serving either on 'regular' or 'National Service' engagements. All were keen to fly and anxious to surmount this formidable first hurdle. It was not an easy task for the assessors either; they had to search for the right combination of keenness and dedication, ability and physical fitness.

By the 1950s Hornchurch, with its grass flightpaths for take off and landing and its 1920s style gabled hangars, was beginning to look a trifle old-fashioned, compared with the ongoing fighter airfields, which had been re-furbished to the latest standards. But it still had that indefinable atmosphere reflecting its history and the highest traditions of the Royal Air Force.

In 1950 the station was again called upon to provide domestic and transport facilities for service personnel involved with another London Docks' strike at the end of April.

There was a rare Tiger Moth incident when one of the aircraft from 17 Reserve Flying School (T 6173) suffered an engine failure. Luckily, it had enough airspeed to continue to glide and made a successful forced landing at Southend (Rochford).

RAF Hornchurch now qualified for the award of a Station Badge, which is customarily given to airfields and squadrons after 25 years service in the RAF. With its four years service in the Great War, Hornchurch completed its qualifying period in 1949. That November, the Chester Herald at the College of Arms, Mr J D Heaton-Armstrong was advised that the station wished to introduce on its badge the bull's head, associated from time immemorial with the town of Hornchurch, against a background of a portcullis, indicative of the defensive role played by the airfield in two world wars. The badge was duly commissioned and a photograph sent to King George VI for his approval. This photograph, duly signed 'George R' and 'J D Heaton-Armstrong - Chester Herald and Inspector of RAF Badges - College of Arms - December 1949' is now in the possession of the Public Record Office. The motto at the foot of the badge reads 'First things first'.

On 14th July, 1950, the Station Badge was presented to Group Captain F C Sturgis at a ceremonial parade by Air Vice Marshal B V Reynolds, the Air Officer Commanding 22 Group, Technical Training Command.

As a postscript to this story: the Station Badge found its way on to a demolition contractor's lorry, when the airfield buildings were demolished in the 1960s. It was fortunate that it was noticed by someone with a sense of history and contact was made with Glyn Richards, once Editor of the *Romford Recorder* and, at this time, the Public Relations Officer of the London Borough of Havering. Glyn immediately went to the

Avro Anson of No 17 Reserve Flying School at RAF Hornchurch, 1951

De Haviland Tiger Moth of No 17 Reserve Flying School

Gloster Gladiator

rescue of the Badge and ensured that it was renovated and placed on display in an honourable position, first at Langtons, an 18th century house in municipal hands, and later at Hornchurch Library.

The 'At Home' display on 16th September, 1950, attracted 23,000 spectators and the extensive programme included fly-pasts by Mosquitos, Vampires, Chipmunks, Lincolns, Tiger Moths of the resident Flying School, a Sunderland flying boat and York transport aircraft. The static display, submerged by small boys, included a Wellington,
Anson, Mosquito and, inevitably, a Spitfire, which took off and made its own fly-past.

The permanent staff was now increasing and comprised 764 RAF and 11 WRAF. With aircrew candidates in residence and the part-time weekenders there were now almost a thousand men and women at the base.

614 Gliding School was a newcomer. It was one of 27 gliding schools that the Air Training Corps had in Britain, from RAF Kinloss and Arbroath in the north to Old Sarum and Chivenor in the south. The school gave the first experience of flying to thousands of fresh faced youngsters from 14 to 18.

On 27th January, 1951 two Reserve Flying School Tiger Moths (N 6706 and N 6987) collided over Ockendon and crash landed nearby. They were both write offs, but the Pilots survived. Another Tiger Moth was written off when it hit an obstruction while taxiing in gusty conditions. The Tiger were now aggregating 1300 flying hours a month - over 40 flying hours daily - a very considerable number. Another 150 hours a month were flown in Ansons.

During 1951 there were two changes in command. Group Captain H L Parker took over from Group Captain F C Sturgis on 2nd April, but after only three months, he handed over to Group Captain J N Jefferson.

The new Station Church (The Church of St Michael and All Angels) was dedicated on 10th March, 1952, at a ceremonial service led by the Bishop of Chelmsford, the Right Reverend Faulkner Allison, assisted by the Chaplain in Chief of the Royal Air Force, Reverend J A Busley. The congregation, made up of airmen, their families and local dignitaries, sang hymns at the Dedication Ceremony, the service concluding with a choral rendering of the National Anthem.

On 1st April, 1952, the title of the Combined Selection Centre was changed to Aircrew Selection Centre to more accurately reflect its scope. It now recommended entry to the categories of pilot, navigator, signaller, engineer and (very few) gunner. The Centre was now twice as busy as it had been on arrival at Hornchurch in 1948. 15,000 candidates passed through in 1952, 7,000 being accepted. One hundred applicants were recommended for pilot training direct from National Service. In addition other candidates were aptitude tested and medically examined for Army pilots, University air squadrons, Royal Navy (Fleet Air Arm), Cranwell entry and Air Training Corps flying scholarships. The only aircrew position open to members of the

WRAF at this time was 'Loadmaster', but this too was to eventually change.

On 2nd May the Under Secretary of State for Air, George Ward, visited the airfield to be shown around the Aircrew Selection Centre and other sections of the base.

The annual 'At Home' for the commemoration of the Battle of Britain attracted the largest attendance in post-war years at 40,000. The Fly-past included a Solent flying boat and a Washington bomber. The Washington was the RAF's name for the American Boeing Super Fortress, which had a crew of ten (three more than the wartime Lancaster), including five gunners. Additional attractions were the WRAF Central Band and displays by the Air Training Corps and Police dogs. The mandatory Spitfire was included in the static aircraft display and pleasure flights, given by Olley Air Services of Croydon, proved very popular.

####

1953 was a disastrous year for the East Coast and RAF Hornchurch became heavily involved in a massive civilian relief programme that dominated national attention throughout February. The possibility of a flood disaster was well known and, in 1949, RAF chiefs had liaised with the Chief Civil Engineer of Essex when 'Operation Canute' was worked out in detail. In the event of a flooding disaster it provided for a force of 480 airmen, made up of 40 sections of 12 airmen from RAF Honington (11), RAF Hendon (5), RAF Ruislip (4), RAF Debden, RAF Felixstowe, RAF Hornchurch, RAF North Weald (all 3), RAF Martlesham Heath (2), RAF Duxford and RAF Kidbrooke (1 each). Each section comprised one officer, one NCO and 10 airmen, including a driver with a 3 ton vehicle. It was designed to meet a brief emergency of from two to five days and temporary restoration of the sea defences to counteract any subsequent break-through. This number proved to be totally inadequate when the crisis struck and many times this number were provided by the RAF, with additional assistance from the Army, the Royal Navy and the United States Air Force.

During the night of 31st January/1st February a freak combination of severe winter gales and high spring tides brought the angry seas cascading through the sea defences along the east coast from Yorkshire to the Thames Estuary, where they reached a peak culminating in the swamping of Canvey Island, Jaywick Sands (near Clacton) and Tilbury. 58 people were drowned on Canvey during that terrible night and most of the island was under deep water, with virtually all the bungalows and houses rendered uninhabitable. Little of Canvey is above normal sea level, let alone the freak high tide of 1st February. This then was the situation faced by the RAF when they reached the Island.

For some time it was not possible to discern from the mainland what exactly had happened to Canvey. Even on the Island the residents could only await first light to find out the extent of the disaster. Between midnight and 2 am they faced imminent death and took refuge The infirm died in their of shock and exposure as they struggled to reach the highest point of their homes. One mother and father used their final moments to push their baby daughter to safety in her pram, utilised as a boat; the baby was rescued, the parents drowned. Others were marooned up to their chins in icy water before collapsing into the flood.

Jacqmar
Ready-to-Wear
16 Grosvenor Street W.1

Evening Standard

MONDAY, FEBRUARY 2, 1953   Three-halfpence

Holland
Toffee
Best on Earth

100 BODIES FOUND ON CANVEY ISLAND

And this was the scene there to-day

23 women & children missing in plane

Evening Standard Reporter

Two British servicemen, their wives and 15 children, are in an airliner missing over the North Atlantic since early to-day.

The airliner, a four-engined York, with a crew of six, was taking the 33 passengers from Britain to Jamaica. It is owned by Skyways, of London, and is on charter to the War Office for flying troops and their families.

Monday, 2 February, 1953
Men of the Royal Air Force at work on Canvey Island

A Service Headquarters was set up at the *Red Cow*, quickly renamed the *King Canute*. The County Surveyor tried to meet a Water Board Engineer at the *Lobster Smack*, wading in parts and cycling in others: he finally gave up when the flood water topped his saddle and he was rescued by a RAF truck, returning to the *Red Cow* with his 'cycle slung in the back.

Six square miles were completely engulfed and the scale of suffering was appalling. Rescue services struggling to get through on the only road to and from the island, met refugees wading along in the opposite direction with young children on their shoulders. Many were frantic over the fate of dear ones who were trapped in water and unable to wade to safety.

A relief centre was set up at Benfleet Secondary School and Hornchurch, with the help of the Essex Regiment from Warley Barracks, managed to supply sufficient bedding to settle a thousand people in relative comfort. Other relief centres were set up at Rayleigh, Nevendon and Pitsea. Doctors were provided by the Aircrew Selection Centre from the Medical Boards always on hand for the examination of aircrew aspirants. They set up day nurseries at Whitehall Lane, Grays, and at Canvey, with 35 beds installed for sufferers to rest and recover and be medically examined before despatch, if necessary, to a permanent hospital. They treated a thousand patients during the emergency.

The RAF high wheeled ambulances were very useful in getting through the waters to collect the sick, the aged and the infirm as a matter of priority. Some needed persuasion to leave their homes. One 87-year-old lady was reported as 'Very obstinate - refuses to move': she reluctantly gave in after a long chat.

Even amid stark tragedy, however, humorous stories abounded. The airmen kept working all night on the sea wall, illuminated by searchlights, struggling to make an emergency wall, five sandbags thick. Two searchlight operators concluded an exhausting shift at daylight and clambered over the tailgate into their lorry and crashed out, fast asleep. They took no notice of the 'twin' lorry parked next door, but were awakened by a thunderous descent of shovels flung over the tailgate by a crew from the wall, mistaking the searchlight lorry for their own. No dictionary contains the descriptive epithets roared out by the unfortunate airmen buried under a heap of

It was not only people who were distressed. Animals were drowned or in difficulties and some of the marooned dogs were crazed with fear and hunger. One truck reported that a greyhound and a terrier had teamed up on an islet in the water and would sit up hopefully with wagging tails whenever they heard a truck. They were never disappointed; the well-known love affair between servicemen and dogs worked to the benefit of the canines. Cats were also treated with care and affection, but much of the Island's farmyard stock was tethered and many perished in the rising.

shovels. On another occasion, a volunteer cook, wading through floodwater to fill a kettle, walked into a hole and disappeared from view - kettle and all. His workmates were creased with laughter and had some difficulty composing themselves sufficiently to rescue him from his predicament.

Working parties coming off the wall were exhausted, cold and wet through. Large heating machines were supplied to assist in drying out houses, but one was earmarked for the working parties to line up and thaw out. Inevitably, the machine was soon named the 'Chestnut Roaster'.

The other location attended by Hornchurch was Tilbury, where there were 6,000 homeless. Only one person was drowned, as the waters did not rise so perilously high as at Canvey. The ancient, timbered *World's End* pub was the RAF Headquarters at Tilbury and they were relieved at night by naval crews from the School of Military Engineering at Chatham.

The United States Air Force from Wethersfield also assisted here and chipped in with 22 3-tonners, each with a driver, rations and equipment. They began evacuating people to rest centres and a Tilbury Police inspector said, "Nothing was too much trouble for the Americans. They took infinite pains to retrieve anything to make people happy, whether it was the cat, the canary or Dad's pension book!"

At the earliest opportunity the RAF took thousands of photo-reconnaissance pictures which were assembled to form a mosaic of the flood-damaged coastline, providing government engineers with their first overall view of the damage.

The British and American armed forces provided 15,000 men along the coast and the help was invaluable. Following the resolution of this disaster, a revised 'Operation King Canute' was drawn up with RAF Hornchurch, Chelmsford and Colchester as the key areas: it did not last long, however. In July, 1955, the Army had to take over the commitment due to the reduction in the size of the Royal Air Force.

On Coronation Day, 1953, most townships had their own ceremonial functions. At Hornchurch there was a march through the town, assembling at the airfield and including RAF representation.

Group Captain Jefferson handed over the reins to Group Captain E J Corbally and there was a change in the flying formations at Hornchurch. 17 Reserve Flying School was disbanded on 31st July and within another year the last of the other Flying Reserve Flying Schools had gone, the final seven closing on 20th June, 1954. They had served their purpose well in keeping demobilised fliers on a part time capacity, but by the 1950s the complexities and technological advancement of military aircraft had reached such a pitch that part time service in Chipmunks and Ansons was insufficient to keep a pilot or navigator up to date with the demands of operational flying.

To replace the Reserve Flying School, No. 1 Civil Anti-aircraft Co-operation Unit (CAACU) arrived, with two Beaufighters, two Oxfords and four Spitfires. The Spit had returned to Hornchurch!

With the cold war in Europe continuing and shooting wars in Kenya and Malaya, Air Observation Post (AOP) duty involving liaison with the Army, reached a post-war peak. To exercise anti-aircraft defences, five CAACUs were established at Hornchurch, Langham, Exeter, Llandow and Llanbedr; their role was, in essence, a repetition of the duties exercised by the Army Co-operation Squadrons at Hornchurch between November, 1944, and June, 1945, including the trailing of target drogues.

In October the station was again used for a week for the accommodation of service personnel during a tanker drivers' strike, 'Operation Tanker' succeeding in distributing considerable quantities of liquid fuel.

Sadly, there was a tragedy at the airfield when Aireraftsman W G Welch collapsed and died of a heart attack during a football match. He was buried, with his erstwhile colleagues providing full military honours, at St Andrews Church, where so many other RAF personnel lie.

The Secretary of State for Air, the Rt Hon Lord de l'Isle and Dudley VC, visited the airfield on 5th November.

By the end of 1953 the permanent staff was reduced to 430 airmen - and no WRAF. Pilots passing through the Aircrew Selection Centre now learnt their craft on the 555 hp 200 mph Hunting Provost. Cynics predicted that death and disaster would follow the doubling of engine power, but the improved manoeuvrability of the Provost and the pupil and instructor sitting side by side, instead of one behind the other, produced an improvement in the quality of pupils at the end of basic training.

1954 was notable for a succession of Station Commanders with Wing Commander A J Hicks taking over from Air Commodore Corbally and, in turn, being succeeded by Wing Commanders W G Devas and C A R Crews.

On 1st April, 1954, the last operational sortie by an RAF Spitfire was a photo-reconnaissance mission out of RAF Seletar, Singapore, flown by 81 Squadron. Strangely this squadron also flew the RAF's last operational mission in a Mosquito five years later. It was the end of the operational story of two of the RAF's most famous aircraft. 81 was the squadron that flew countless sorties from Hornchurch and Fairlop when the Wing was led successively by Wing Commanders Powell, Finucane and Hugo in the spring and summer of 1942. 81 was then commanded by Squadron Leader (later Air Commodore) Ronald Berry.

The airfield was now slowly reducing in permanent staff and was down to 394 in July, 1955, and 335 by the end of the year. Hornchurch's own last ever Spitfire sortie took place on 3rd December, 1955, when Spitfire TE 358 was flown out by Squadron Leader P F Hart of the Civil Anti-aircraft Co-operation Unit to the Maintenance Unit at RAF Kemble, Gloucestershire. Spitfires would still be seen at the airfield after this date, but only at Air Shows and not in resident flying units.

In the four years from April, 1951, to March, 1955, the Aircrew Selection Centre had dealt with an intake of over 43,000 candidates, made up -

Civilian and service applicants arriving at the RAF Aircrew Selection Centre at Hornchurch, 1960
A Spitfire at the Air Show, 1959

	ACCEPTED							REJECTED
Type of Candidate	Intake	Pilot	Navigator	Signaller	Engineer	Gunner	Total	
National Service	13818	2714	1617	944	295	394	5964	7854
Direct entry	14990	3392	1562	1225			6179	8811
Serving Airmen	4780	960	365	470	118	2	1915	2868
NS to regular	645	105	265	253	16	6	645	
Pre-assessment	8824	1857	662	939	110	78	3646	5178
TOTAL	43057	9028	4471	3831	539	480	18349	24708

The increasingly high standards demanded by the RAF during the 1950s are reflected in the fact that little over 40% of the candidates were accepted for aircrew positions. The numbers show that there must have been an average of 250 candidates resident at any one time.

On 10th February, 1956, a great airman from an earlier age, Marshal of the Royal Air Force Lord Trenchard (always known as Father of the Royal Air Force) died at the age of 83. He was the man who had said in 1923, in a Minute to the Chief of Air Staff, "It is decided that Suttons Farm or an aerodrome in the vicinity is a necessity for the defensive measure of England." How prophetic his words proved, less than two decades later.

By the end of 1956 the building being used for training courses had been named 'Battle of Britain House', but the strength of the permanent staff had declined still further to 309.

In 1957 Wing Commander H D U Denison took over as Station Commander from Wing Commander A N Jones. The reduction in the rank of Station Commander from the time of Air Commodore E J Corbally was in line with the departure from the station of the flying units and miscellaneous ground units with the consequent reduction in permanent staff strength.

Five airmen had to be placed in isolation at this time, when the Station Medical Officer encountered four cases of Rubella (German measles) and one case of normal measles. The isolation effectively kept the disease under control: a feared outbreak did

The V-Bomber Force came into being in 1955 with the Vickers Valiant, followed by the delta winged Avro Vulcan a year later, and the Handley Page Victor in 1957. Each of these bombers had a crew of 5 and they formed the backbone of Bomber Command. The awesome looking delta winged Vulcan had an amazing wing area of 3,554 square feet, but the Vulcan and the Victor were slightly longer and had greater wing spans. The 1991 Air Show at Southend included the only Vulcan still airworthy, giving its customary thrilling and noisy display. The longest range bombing operation in military history was under taken by a Vulcan against Argentinian positions in Port Stanley during the Falklands conflict, taking off from Ascension Island, 4,000 miles away.

The Air Officer Commanding in Chief of Bomber Command overseeing the V-Bomber Force was none other than Air Marshal Sir Harry Broadhurst, who had overall control for three years from January, 1956.

Ronald Adam (left), former fighter pilots and a Spitfire at
a re-union at RAF Hornchurch, 1959

'Sailor' Malan (right) visiting 74 Squadron at Coltishall,
17 June, 1959

not materialise.

At the end of 1958 contingents were sent to Remembrance Day Services at Westminster Cathedral, Romford and Hornchurch, but, with permanent staff down to 13 officers and 124 airmen at year's end, Hornchurch was once more beginning to look ominously empty.

Another significant reduction in the strength of the Reserve Forces associated with the RAF took place in 1957, when the Royal Auxiliary Air Force was disbanded on 10th March. With it went 20 Fighter Command squadrons, mostly equipped with the Vampire and Meteor.

In 1959 a detachment from Royal Air Force Balloon Unit, Cardington, Bedfordshire, arrived with a deflated balloon and all the necessary equipment to inflate and hoist it. Territorial Army paratroopers were lifted to enable them to keep up to date with their parachuting techniques and memories of World War II were revived for the local population when they saw the once so familiar barrage balloons hovering in the sky. The paratroopers dropping out of the baskets suspended beneath the balloons attracted a wide audience with fingers pointing to the sky up to five miles away.

At an Air Display during 1959 many of the wartime stalwarts returned to Hornchurch for a re-union and to make acquaintance again with a Spitfire. They included Sector Controller Ronald Adam (whose fame as an actor had spread and whose face was frequently seen on television), Robert Stanford Tuck, the former Commanding Officer of 65 Squadron, who had spent four years as a prisoner of war, Colin Gray, 'Ras' Berry, Tony Bartley and Norman Ryder. They grouped themselves lovingly around the Spitfire and many amateur snapshots were taken alongside the press photographs. It was just like old times, except that many of the ground staff chores were performed by the enthusiastic cadets from the local 452 (Hornchurch) Squadron of the Air Training Corps.

There was another reunion in June, 1959, when the renowned 'Sailor' Malan returned to England on a visit from his native South Africa. His emotional ties with the Royal Air Force in general and with 74 Squadron in particular were very strong. 74, his old Hornchurch squadron, was still a fighter squadron, based at RAF Coltishall near Norwich, flying Hawker Hunters. On 17 June he returned to his old squadron, flew in a Hunter and, at the end of the day, was regaled with a party on the Norfolk Broads. He was to live only four more years, dying in South Africa on 17 September, 1963, aged 52 years. Adolph Gysbert Malan was, by any standards, one of the more remarkable pilots to serve in the RAF. He destroyed 31 enemy aircraft, with another six 'probables', was awarded the Distinguished Service Order and Bar, Distinguished Flying Cross and Bar and both the Belgian and the French Croix de Guerre.

Later in the year Donald Finlay, now an Air Commodore, also returned to Hornchurch and led a contingent to Romford for the Remembrance Day Service.

Wing Commander B L Duckenfield led a similar contingent to St Andrew's, Hornchurch, and Flying Officer J A Colgreave a contingent to Westminster Abbey.

By February, 1960, the permanent staff strength was down still further to 125, as there was no longer the demand for aircrew in the same numbers as earlier years.

Hornchurch staged what was to be its last Air Show in 1960: it still attracted large crowds who enjoyed the static exhibits and the fly-past. By 1961 the purpose built buildings were under construction at RAF Biggin Hill to enable the Aircrew Selection Centre to move there. West Essex Wing of the Air Training Corps held their last Wing Parade at RAF Hornchurch before the Wing Headquarters moved to North Weald and the Gliding School to North Weald, Debden and Wethersfield.

On 9 April, 1962, the Aircrew Selection Centre, the last Unit left at Hornchurch, finished its 14 years' work at the airfield and moved to Biggin Hill, where it was re-named Officers' and Aircrew Selection Centre to reflect the wider scope of its work.

After forty-seven years the curtain finally came down on one of the most remarkable RAF stations of all time.

Air Commodore A G Dudgeon inspecting the last West Essex Wing Parade, 1961

The hangars at RAF Hornchurch shortly before dismantling in 1967
An astro-dome survived in South End Road long after the airfield closed

GOTTERDAMMERUNG
CLOSURE - DEMOLITION - REDEVELOPMENT

On the departure of the Aircrew Selection Centre to RAF Biggin Hill a small Holding Party was left at Hornchurch and, for three months, acted as caretakers to keep the airfield secure and ticking over until the buildings were handed over to their new owners.

This time Hornchurch was not granted any reprieve, as it had been after the Great War. There was no 'Care and Maintenance' period while a search was made for a new rôle. This time its closure was for good and, on 1st July, 1962, the Holding Party was disbanded and Royal Air Force Hornchurch irrevocably closed down.

The honour of being the last RAF serviceman to leave the airfield was given to Senior Aircraftman David Phillips, a member of the Holding Party. At a clearing in front of the Guard Room and in front of press reporters and cameras, he symbolically handed over the keys of the buildings (or, at any rate, a representative bunch of them) to Mr Ronald Thornton, representing Messrs Hilbery Chaplin, estate agents.

On 27th February, 1963, the Air Ministry put up for 'Sale by Auction' the considerable acreage comprising the former take off and landing area of the airfield, surrounded by the perimeter track. The auction was handled by Messrs Kemsley, Whiteley & Ferris of Romford and the field became the East London Quarry of the Hoveringham Gravel Company who, for the next decade, dug it all up and methodically extracted all the gravel.

Two thirds of RAF Hornchurch was now disposed of. The remaining site on the western side of South End Road comprised the Officers' Mess and Officers', Senior NCOSI and Other Ranks' Married Quarters. The Mess was sold off to become company offices. The Married Quarters were re-established as a domestic unit that stayed in Air Ministry hands for another decade as Married Quarters for personnel working at the Air Ministry and other RAF Establishments, mainly in central London.

When all the gravel had been extracted, the resulting hole in the ground was converted into a refuse tip and progressively filled in with rubbish. It was an undignified end to an airfield with such a distinguished history in the defence of the nation in two World Wars. In the airfield's built up area the demolition contractors moved in and, with crane jibs swinging their mighty concrete pendulums against the fabric of the structure, there was soon little left of the Operations Block, Airmen's and Sergeants' Messes, two storey Accommodation Blocks, Workshops, Tennis Courts, Armoury and Fuel Dump areas. RAF Hornchurch was reduced to debris and carted off in contractors' lorries.

No official policy has ever been laid down to prevent the utter destruction of abandoned military airfields. They form an integral part of the nation's heritage and history and, while they could not be preserved as museums, it is surely undesirable

Air Commodore Alan Deere (left) and Air Vice Marshal R I Jones explaining the Station Badge of RAF Hornchurch to a group of Mitchell School pupils, 2 December, 1968

that they should be 'crane walloped' down to the last two bricks standing on top of one another, without even the smallest item being retained with a suitable plaque to remind future generations of the historical significance of these places, as their exploits fade.

On 1st April, 1965, there was a municipal marriage between the Urban District of Hornchurch and the Borough of Romford. Until then both Councils had been part of the County of Essex; now they formed Havering, one of the 32 Boroughs in Greater London. It was now official that London's 'carpet of bricks' had spread on to the doorstep of the remnants of the airfield and was now threatening to run right over it.

Fortunately, however, in the re-development of the site after the destruction teams had finished their work, the Mitchell Junior School was erected on the area previously occupied *inter alia* by Station Head-quarters. The school was named after Reginald Joseph Mitchell [1895-1937] who was on the design staff of Supermarine Aviation at Southampton and designed the aircraft that won the Schneider Trophy in 1927, 1929 and 1932, for which he was awarded the CBE.

The Mitchell School opened as a Primary School for 5 to 11 year olds on 6th September, 1967, with its major intake being children from the RAF families still in the Married Quarters on the opposite side of South End Road. The school had actually been built in advance of the houses that were intended to provide its primary intake - the 'New Elm Park Housing Estate', built over the Technical and Domestic site of the old airfield, with its streets named after renowned fighter pilots, Station Commanders, First World War heroes, other airfields and aviation subjects generally.

The Supermarine Scapa and Stranraer flying boats and the Walrus amphibian (affectionately known as the 'Shagbat') were also designed by Mitchell, but it was the immortal Supermarine Spitfire that was the zenith of his creative life's work. The prototype Spitfire flew in 1936 and Mitchell knew that he had produced a wonderful aircraft. And so it proved. It was the only RAF aircraft to be in front line combat service as a fighter at both the start of the war in 1939 and at its conclusion in 1945.

Regrettably, Mitchell did not live to see the product of his genius go on to be one of the salvations of his country. He had a major operation for cancer in 1933, when he was only 38; he took a holiday in Austria to recover and became convinced that Germany was building up a mighty air force. He returned to work at Supermarine with an even greater dedication on his Spitfire project. Reginald Mitchell died on 11th June, 1937, at the early age of 42.

The official Opening Ceremony of the Mitchell School took place a year later, on Monday, 2nd December, 1968. At this ceremonial occasion a replica of the RAF Hornchurch badge was presented to the school by Air Vice Marshal R I Jones, CB AFC, the Air Officer Commanding 11 Group Fighter Command, representing the Royal Air Force. He was accompanied by Air Commodore Alan Deere, DSO OBE DFC, who had been so much a part of the Hornchurch story.

Local civic dignitaries included the Mayor of Havering, Alderman W A Sibley, JP; John Symons, the Town Clerk; David Wilcockson, the Chief Education Officer; Councillor Mrs Lydia Hutton of the Education Committee; T S Jarron, the Chairman of the School Managers; and Alan Thake, the Headmaster.

The uniform adopted for the school included a tie and blazer badge designed by

Alan Thake, bearing the RAF colours of light blue, dark blue and maroon, but in a different order. The School Badge incorporates a blue Spitfire against a background of a red shield with a white 'M' (for Mitchell) superimposed. As Alan Thake, an ex-RAF man himself, said at the time, "Men died ensuring a decent future for these children and we thought that it would be fitting to remember the Royal Air Force in this way."

Mr R A French, who succeeded Alan Thake as Headmaster in 1971, took the RAF theme a stage further and started a system of four Houses to foster a friendly competitive spirit amongst the schoolchildren. The Houses were named Broadhurst, after Air Chief Marshal Sir Harry Broadhurst, GCB KBE DSO AFC, Knight Grand Cross of Orange Nassau, Legion of Merit (US), Station Commander from December, 1940, to May, 1942; Deere, after Air Commodore Alan Christopher Deere, OBE DSO DFC* AFC DFC(US), Croix de Guerre, a pilot with 54 Squadron from September, 1938, to January, 1941; Tuck, after Wing Commander Robert Roland Stanford Tuck, DSO DFC* DFC(US), a pilot with 65 Squadron from 5th August, 1936, to 1st May, 1940; and Stephen, after Squadron Leader Harbourne Mackay Stephen, DSO DFC, a pilot with 74 Squadron from 10th April, 1940, to 11th January, 1941: after the war he was Managing Director of the *Daily Telegraph* and *Sunday Telegraph*.

Air Commodore Deere, Wing Commander Tuck and Squadron Leader Stephen visited the school to inaugurate the 'House' system in June, 1972, and were honoured by the school recorder band playing the 'March Past of the Royal Air Force' in front of a full school assembly. The House Trophy, presented by the four named airmen, is a fine silver cup engraved 'Spitfire Pilots' Trophy'.

The School Badge, presented at the Opening Ceremony, was originally mounted on the outside wall of the school, adjacent to the school entrance. Fears of deterioration led to the plaque being brought inside and placed in a prominent central position in the school assembly hall. During the war an eminent artist, Captain Cuthbert Orde, was commissioned to sketch individual fighter pilots who achieved distinction and each of the four men whose names form the school Houses were sketched in this way. These pictures, mounted on polished wooden shields, are placed two on either side of the Badge. There is also a specially designed scoreboard for House Points and there are pictures of a Spitfire in flight and of Reginald Mitchell on the school staircase, together with an early Spitfire propeller. Doctor Gordon Mitchell, Reginald's son, maintains a close contact with the school.

In the early 1970s Wing Commander P Collins, AFC, the Commanding Officer of 111 ('Treble One') Squadron at Wattisham, Suffolk, from August, 1970, to June, 1972, and Wing Commander R Horsfield, the Commanding Officer from June, 1972 to October, 1974, visited the school each year on Open Day. They presented the various awards and trophies won by individual pupils and by the Houses. 111 Squadron was, of course, the first squadron to inhabit RAF Hornchurch when it re-opened in 1928.

The tradition was broken when 111 Squadron left Suffolk for Lincolnshire and then Scotland in 1974. There were also visits by Sir Harry Broadhurst, the RAF Police Dog Demonstration Team and Wing Commander Stanford Tuck, who served on the Board of the school.

When first built in 1967 few could have anticipated the extent of the growth of the links between the school and the RAF, but it is pleasing that the story of RAF Hornchurch is perpetuated in this way. In 1979 a broadcast was made from the school on the occasion of the 39th anniversary of the Battle of Britain and in 1980 an exhibition was held there showing RAF Hornchurch photographs and memorabilia, interest being so great that it led to the formation of the Battle of Britain Memorial Fund, which, in turn, was to lead to the establishment of a permanent memorial in the school grounds, fronting South End Road.

On the airfield itself, the perimeter track deteriorated, but became a popular venue for learner drivers, who revelled in the opportunity to acquire driving proficiency without the hassle of thick traffic. Young motorcyclists also used it for practising 'wheelies' and cross country skills, off the public roads. The perimeter track was fairly quiet during weekdays, but came alive at week-ends and was, on occasion, almost as busy as the public road outside.

The hangars remained intact after the station buildings were demolished and were used by the Ford Motor Company for vehicle storage for a time, until the hangars too were pulled down. Another feature that remained long after the rest of the station had gone was the Dome Trainer, used for gunnery instruction, adjacent to South End Road. The reason may have been associated with the fact that the thick reinforced concrete domes were not that easy to demolish and cart away. Even the swinging cranes had their work cut out with the dome trainers and one or two survive at other derelict airfields to this day.

The only other remains left standing in the operational area were an old Spitfire dispersal site, complete with air raid shelter provided for the ground crews working on the aircraft, and a few pill boxes on the eastern side of the airfield put up as army defences in 1940, when invasion threatened.

The impressive ornate entrance gates guarding the airfield, close to the Guard Room, and a second set of gates, were removed after closure and transferred to RAF Kenley, another 11 Group fighter airfield. On the Main Gates an engraved brass plaque was fitted, which read

These gates and those on Whyteleaf Hill were originally at RAF Station
Hornchurch, Essex, famous in the first World War as a RFC aerodrome (Named
Suttons Farm) and also famous in the second World War as a Battle of Britain
station. Upon the closing of RAF Hornchurch in 1963 the gates were fittingly
transferred to RAF Station Kenley, also a famous Battle of Britain station.
'Lest we forget'

When RAF Kenley, in its turn, ceased to be an RAF station, one pair of gates was transferred to RAF Biggin Hill. Biggin Hill itself is now closed, but an RAF presence is maintained by the creation of an Enclave, the centrepiece of which will be the St George's Memorial Chapel. To add to the pathos of this permanent memorial to the airmen involved in the Battle of Britain, the two entrances to the enclave will be secured by the gates from RAF Hornchurch and RAF Biggin Hill. And so, two famous fighter airfields, friendly rivals for almost half a century, are unified by their respective gates. The gates at the Whyteleaf Hill entrance to the Officers' Mess at RAF Kenley were left in position when the base closed down, as the Mess was retained for officers working for the Ministry of Defence.

There is a strange, sad and eerie fascination about an airfield as it is allowed to die. Even when it is stripped of its hangars, control towers, technical sites and accommodation, there remains an indefinable atmosphere that can almost be felt. In the 1970s the operational area of the airfield had a tortured appearance as it was mined and then infilled with rubbish. It was an almost lunar landscape when seen on a dull and rainy day, the sad sight of what had been done to this historic field was almost impossible to believe.

During those years there were several scares for the local population in the adjacent housing estates, not to mention the diggers themselves, when a crop of thirty year old bombs were unearthed. They were relics, for the most part, of the heavy raids made on the airfield in July and August, 1940, particularly the raid of 31st August, when 30 Dorniers scattered a hundred bombs all over the airfield. Mining work had to stop immediately a new bomb was discovered. Local inhabitants had to be warned to keep windows open, take precautionary measures, and stay away from the area. Disposal Squads from the Royal Engineers had to be called in to de-fuse and dispose of the bombs; the RAF's own 'Bomb Cemetery' at Upminster was long gone. The nose cone of one of the bombs was given to the landlord of the *Good Intent* in 1976 as a potent reminder of the pub's wartime rôle.

Other more peaceful items of interest that were unearthed were Bronze Age, Iron Age and Roman artifacts and Stone Age tools, providing evidence of the ancient history of the site prior to its existence as the Manor of Suttons. By the late 70s the torture of the airfield had run its course and the landscape was bulldozed over and flattened to allow nature to progressively heal the scars and return the field to something like it was before, albeit with a raised level on some parts of the acreage.

The time was now ripe for the historical dignity of the old airfield to be restored and the Hornchurch Country Park was the outcome. The London Borough of Havering carried out an honourable and large scale landscaping from 1980 to create the Park, incorporating the remaining features of the airfield and providing a haven for wildlife, walkers, horse riders, anglers and bird watchers.

MEMORIALS

And so, what memorials exist to Royal Air Force Hornchurch? What are the items that recall its story in the air defence of Britain and what has transpired since its closure that enlarge in any way upon its history?

Firstly, a three year campaign for a Memorial Stone was launched in 1980 by Ted Exall of Elm Park, the co-founder, with D Purkiss of Gidea Park, of the RAF Hornchurch Memorial Fund. The Fund, set up to provide a permanent memorial, started when a former RAF pilot sent a donation to the *Romford Recorder*, following Ted Exall's exhibition at the Mitchell School in 1980. Wing Commander Stanford Tuck became a Patron of the Fund, Ted Harrison became Secretary and G Howgego of Upminster took on the post of Treasurer. The original target figure of £3,500 was raised by public subscription and a grant from the London Borough of Havering.

The great day for the unveiling of the Memorial on the edge of the airfield site was 5th July, 1983. A crowd of several hundred, including 20 former Spitfire pilots, assembled to see Air Chief Marshal Sir Harry Broadhurst now 75 years of age, unveil the Memorial, which had been draped with the Royal Air Force ensign. Also present were Air Vice Marshal William Hayr, the Air Officer Commanding 11 Group, representing the Royal Air Force, the Mayor of Havering, Mrs Winnie Whittingham, and Dr G Mitchell, the son of the Spitfire designer. Wing Commander Stanford Tuck suffering from cracked ribs, the result of a fall, was unable to be present.

Prayers were led by Canon Peter Peatfield, of St Andrew's Church, Hornchurch, a former RAF Honorary Chaplain. St Andrews had featured in so many happy and sad, ceremonial and memorial occasions in the life of the airfield.

Former Hornchurch aircrew members present included Squadron Leader Henryk Szczesny, who fought in the Battle of Britain with 74 Squadron and later led the Polish Wing from RAF Northolt; he collided with a Luftwaffe fighter in April, 1943, and spent two years as a prisoner of war. An extrovert character Henryk was in great demand for autographs, which he signed with a flourish 'Henry the Pole SZ - 74 Tiger Squadron'. He had remained in the Royal Air Force until 1965. Another was Flight Lieutenant Gerald Robinson, who was an Air Gunner with the ill fated Boulton Paul Defiants in August, 1940; he was fortunate to survive and his damaged plane made a forced landing at Manston on 24th August. Squadron Leader Ronald Stillwell, who, as a Sergeant Pilot, fought with 65 Squadron was also among the guests.

Many children from the Mitchell School were at the ceremony, as were Air Training Corps cadets from 452 (Hornchurch) and 1838 (Elm Park) Squadrons. Numerous former RAF and WAAFs added to the poignancy of the occasion. When the ceremony was over 150 invited guests repaired to the *Good Intent* for lunch and an exhibition of memorabilia of the wartime airfield was staged.

One slightly puzzling feature of the Memorial Stone is that it commemorates RAF Hornchurch 1928 - 1962, without mentioning the Great War airfield that was on the same site between 3rd October, 1915, and 31st December, 1919, and was the airfield most involved with dealing with the Zeppelin onslaught of 1916. A strange omission.

####

The Hornchurch Country Park is, in its way, another memorial, covering as it does the site of the former operational area of the airfield. One can discern the remaining features along the Eastern Pathway which starts at the main car park located on a former aircraft dispersal bay with its attendant air raid shelters. The car park is at the end of a road aptly named 'Squadrons Approach'. The Pathway follows the route of the old perimeter track and first passes a concrete circle, the base of a windsock. The sites of other aircraft dispersal bays can also be seen. Further along the walk are gun emplacements, turrets, pillboxes (decorated with the inevitable juvenile graffiti) and trenches which were a part of the defence system.

The Country Park is a haven for wildlife with trees, grassland, marshes, a lake and the River Ingrebourne; a Nature Reserve of special interest. The Park provides afternoons of Walks and Wildlife Competitions, programmes to witness the 'dawn chorus' at 5 o'clock and sponsored bird watches. Children are encouraged to plant wild flowers and the RAF Hornchurch Association provides guided airfield tours. Programmes have included a Mad Hatter's Tea Party, a mini safari and a picnic by Albyns Farm Lake, stocked with carp, roach, tench, perch and pike.

The Mitchell School is another form of memorial, as is the Sanders Draper School, commemorating the American Spitfire pilot, Flying Officer R Sanders Draper of 64 Squadron, who died on 24th March, 1943, after suffering engine failure and crashing on what are now the playing fields of the school. The squadron was commanded at that time by Squadron Leader William Crawford-Compton, later Wing Commander (Flying) at Hornchurch.

There is an impressive Military Section of the cemetery adjacent to St Andrew's Church. In wartime it was the general practice for the bodies of airmen who died in battle to be returned to their home town or village for burial whenever that was practicable. Sadly, many were shot down over the Channel and have no known grave. Their names are commemorated on the Royal Air Force Memorial at Runnymede, near Egham, Surrey. Many of the airmen buried at St Andrews were allied airmen from European and Commonwealth countries, who could not be returned to their homeland.

St Andrew's contains the graves of three pilots who died in the Battle of Britain, amongst the 37 RAF personnel buried there, who include four Czechs, three New Zealanders, a South African, a Canadian, an American and a WAAF. There are also 14 Army personnel, one Royal Marine, one Member of Trinity House and an ATS girl.

The list of RAF personnel buried at St Andrew's Military Cemetery is -

P/O Broadhurst, J W	7 Oct 40	Sgt Lambert, V G	21 Jun 42
P/O Dewey, R B	27 Oct 40	W/O Earwaker, S D	24 Jan 43 New Z
P/O Goldsmith, J W	28 Oct 40 S African	F/O Draper, R S	24 Mar 43 American
AC2 Dilloway, W L	23 Apr 41	AC2 Lendon, W	16 Jun 43
Sgt Kean, E J	17 May 41 New Z	F/S Holledge, N R	19 Jun 43
Sgt Stevens, J B	9 Jun 41	Sgt Fentiman, D V	22 Aug 43
Sgt Mack-Laing, F	17 Jul 41 New Z	Sgt Pack, L A	27 Sep 43
P/O Swarsbrick, E W	26 Aug 41	Sgt Copsey, L G	1 Dec 43
LAC Leggoe, R S	30 Aug 41	W/O Smith, T W	22 Dec 43
P/O Tucker, E J	13 Sep 41	Sgt Bailey, V G	9 Feb 44
AC2 Derry, K F	23 Sep 41	AC1 Amey, A	28 Apr 44
Sgt Valenta, J	11 Jan 42 Czech	LAC Holden, S	21 Jun 44
Sgt Kinvalina, B	22 Jan 42 Czech	Sgt Girling, C A	20 Jul 44
F/S Langley, R N	12 Feb 42 Canadian	Sgt Norman, D S	7 Dec 44
Sgt Bohnisch, F	23 Feb 42 Czech	ACW1 Barrett, J R	26 Jan 45 WAAF
F/S Braza, P	24 Apr 42 Czech	Cpl Harper, R J	3 May 45
LAC Cornell, G A	29 Apr 42	F/S Jones, C A	28 Aug 45
Sgt Craven, A H	5 May 42	F/L Helmore, T M	1 Jul 47
AC2 Byrne, F G	21 May 42		

This list includes RAF personnel at other airfields, who were brought back to their home town of Hornchurch for burial.

###

Yet another memorial to RAF Hornchurch still regularly flies the skies of the United Kingdom on parade in front of hundreds of thousands of spectators: the Battle of Britain Memorial Flight is now one of the most popular visitors to all the principal air shows and one of its star performers - Spitfire P-7350 - has a direct connection with Hornchurch. It is the only Spitfire still airworthy that actually fought in the Battle of Britain. It was issued to 266 Squadron (under the command of Squadron Leader Desmond Spencer) at Hornchurch on 9th September, 1940.

The Battle of Britain Memorial Flight was formed in 1957 and, since 1976, has been based at RAF Coningsby, Lincolnshire. It operates five Spitfires, two Hurricanes, and its flagship, the Lancaster bomber 'City of Lincoln'. The aircraft are crewed and maintained in peak condition by a dedicated group of volunteers whose skills and industry enable the Flight to thrill the crowds (and veterans to shed the odd tear or two) at some 150 air shows every year.

After delivery P-7350 was flown in the Battle of Britain by Sergeant Harry Cook (released from the RAF in 1946 as a Flight Lieutenant), Pilot Officer Edward Wells (retired on 15th June, 1960, as a Group Captain), Squadron Leader Patrick Jameson (assumed command from Desmond Spencer in mid-September, 1940; retired from the RAF on 6th August, 1960, as an Air Commodore and returned to New Zealand) and Pilot Officer Richard Trousdale (killed in flying accident (Mosquito) from RAF Pershore on 16th May, 1947). All except Cook were New Zealanders: Wells and Trousdale flew P-7350 several times.

After the Battle of Britain P-7350 went on to serve with 64, 603 and 616 Squadrons. The first two, at one time or another, featured in the Hornchurch Wing between November, 1940, and March, 1943, so it is reasonable to assume that P-7350 was rarely based away from the airfield between those dates. After surviving the war, P-7350 became the 'Gate Guardian' at RAF Colerne for 20 years from 1947. In 1967 it was completely renovated and restored to airworthy condition for a star part in the film *The Battle of Britain*, which in itself is a tribute to all Fighter Command airfields. Wing Commander Bob Stanford Tuck was a technical adviser in the shooting, with former foe, General Adolf Galland, the Luftwaffe ace.

Another Spitfire, MH-434, with which Flight Lieutenant Pat Lardner-Burke, DFC, shot down two FW 190s whilst flying with 222 Squadron at Hornchurch, was frequently flown in post-war years by Squadron Leader Ray Hannah, the first leader of the 'Red Arrows'. This aircraft also appeared in the films *The Battle of Britain* and *A bridge too far*, and was paraded at British and European air shows by Hannah. It then went to the Imperial War Museum at Duxford, where it continues to be flown, as well as becoming a star ground exhibit.

In the film are three Spitfires and one Hurricane from the Memorial Flight and many other aircraft gathered in from all over the world, including 31 Heinkel bombers and a Junkers 52 Transport from the Spanish Air Force. More than a hundred authentic WWII aircraft were brought together over a 3 year period and, when completed, it represented the 35th largest military air force in the world! The British aircraft were flown by current RAF pilots, who were trained to fly the aircraft of the 1940s, while the Heinkels and Junkers were flown by Spanish Air Force pilots. There were 800 applications from RAF personnel to fly the Spitfires and Hurricanes. The sight of Messerschmitts flying low over the Channel and zooming over the White Cliffs of Dover was, even in 1968, an eerie sight. Memories of 28 years earlier were re-awakened with a curiously sinking feeling in the pit of the stomach. As one pilot joked, "I thought they'd all been shot down years ago!"

One of the pre-war regular pilots flying with 222 Squadron from Hornchurch was Sergeant Ernest Scott from Mansfield, Nottinghamshire. Between July and September, 1940, he shot down 6 Luftwaffe aircraft before being killed in action on 27th September, falling to the German ace, Major Werner Molders. His Spitfire crashed into an orchard at Greenway Court, Hollingbourne, near Maidstone, Kent, and buried itself in the ground on impact. There Ernest Scott remained at rest for fifty years until December, 1990. His remains were then exhumed, still in his Spitfire, by the RAF's Airfield Salvage and Transportation Flight from Abingdon.

It was fitting that he should be conveyed to his final resting place, with full military honours, by a bearer, party from RAF Manston, an airfield in the Hornchurch Sector at the time he died. His funeral service, which attracted national media attention, was held in the village church at Manston, the burial service being conducted by the Reverend Robert Cole, the Officiating Chaplain at RAF Manston. The service was attended by Sergeant Scott's relatives, Royal Air Force personnel and members of the Aircrew Association. The interment took place at the Commonwealth War Graves Commission section of St John's Cemetery in Margate.

A final reminder locally of the airfield are the names of numerous roads on the housing estates that have been built in post-war years on both sides of South End Road. They are on sites that were either on the airfield itself or adjacent. Many of the streets are named after distinguished pilots who flew from RAF Suttons Farm and RAF Hornchurch in both world wars. Others are named after types of aircraft and of other Royal Air Force stations.

The list is

AIRMEN: Adnams Walk, Bader Way, Beaumont Crescent, Bennions Close, Berry Close, Bouchier Walk, Boulter Gardens, Broadhurst Way, Carbury Close, Cavendish Avenue & Crescent, Crawford-Compton Close, Dawson Drive, Deere Avenue, Denholm Close, Dewey Path, Edridge Close, Esmond Close, Finucane Gardens, Franklin Road, Freeborne Gardens, Gillam Way, Gilroy Close, Gray Gardens, Hayes Drive, Hesselyn Drive, Hugo Gardens, Kilmartin Way, Kingaby Gardens, Leathart Close, Locke Close, Lovell Walk, Malan Square, Mermagen Drive, Mungo Park Road, Pease Close, Robinson Close, Ryder Gardens, Sarre Avenue, Simpson Road, Scotney Walk, Sowrey Avenue, Stapleton Crescent, Stephen Avenue, Tempest Way, Tuck Road, Wells Gardens.

RAF AIRFIELDS: Aldergrove Walk, Bradwell Close, Coltishall Road, Debden Walk, Detling Close, Digby Walk, Duxford Close, Fairlop Close, Gosport Drive, Hawkinge Way, Kirton Close, Leconfield Walk, Manston Way, Martlesham Close, Northolt Way, Pembrey Way, Roborough Walk, Rochford Close, Stansted Close, Tangmere Crescent, West Malling Way, Wittering Walk.

OTHER RAF CONNECTIONS: Airfield Way, Astra Close, Blenheim Court, Squadrons Approach.

And scattered around all parts of the world are veteran airmen who look back over the mists of time from their native heath and remember RAF Hornchurch with great nostalgia and affection: Australians, Belgians, Canadians, Czechs, Dutch, New Zealanders, Poles and South Africans - as well as Britons - all served in Spitfire squadrons at the base.

Typical of them, perhaps, is the much decorated Jaroslav Hlado, a Czech who commanded 312 Squadron in 1944, who vividly recalls his much loved dog. Dogs were always a favourite with airmen; they became part of squadron life and were widely fussed over. The sadness over the loss of a Master who failed to return sometimes seemed even tougher on his dog than on his squadron companions, who knew the risks. Such a dog was 'Coopie', a loveable great bundle of chow. When his first owner died, he refused his food and hid himself away underneath the wooden floor of a dispersal hut, but he eventually emerged to choose Jaroslav Hlado as his new Master.

'Hlado' was a most difficult name for the English tongue to wrap itself around, so 'Coopie' became the Squadron's Call Sign instead. The chow became Hlado's loyal friend and a mascot to all the Czechs, despite his loud snoring'

When Hlado cycled from one part of the airfield to another, the huge bundle of dog managed to drape himself over handlebars and crossbar. He would enter the Mess Dining Hall and go to the kitchen to get his lunch. He lived for the squadron and, when a 'scramble' klaxon sounded its urgent wail, he would rush to sit by the exit door with his snout uppermost for the pilots to touch his nose for luck, as they sped by.

One morning the squadron returned to Hornchurch and there was 'Coopie Dog' in the centre of the Flight Path, moving slowly and looking very tired. Pilots were told to watch out for him; he had been in a terrible fight with his arch enemy, the 'B' Flight dog, thought to have been his rival in a love affair with another squadron dog. Both had to stay in the vet's for treatment. When the squadron left in preparation for D-Day, 'Coopie Dog' had to be left behind to live with the WAAFs on a Barrage Balloon Site. One day he rushed out to help the girls bring down their balloon and was killed.

Jaroslav Hlado never forgot 'Coopie'; he retained his name as the Squadron Call Sign until the end of the war and then took his memory back with him to Prague. Hlado was just one of the thousands of overseas airmen who descended on Hornchurch during the conflict.

###

It is to hoped that future historians will look back on the aerial conflict fought out over British and European skies as being an integral part of 'Their Finest Hour' and that a true and accurate balance will be struck on the participants - men, aircraft, airfields - of the conflict.

Certainly RAF Hornchurch has no need to bend the knee to anyone. Its record speaks for itself -

* In the First World War it destroyed three out of the five Zeppelins that were brought down over the British mainland.

 * It was the only fighter airfield that was involved with Victoria Cross Awards in both wars. Lieutenant William Leefe Robinson, for shooting down SL-11 on 3rd September, 1916, and Lieutenant Commander Eugene Esmonde, the Fleet Air Arm pilot, controlled from Hornchurch, who took his squadron into Manston in February, 1942, to take on the escaping German Battle Fleet.

* It housed the squadron that destroyed most Luftwaffe aircraft in the Battle of Britain: 54 Squadron commanded by Squadron Leader James Leathart.

* It housed the individual pilot who destroyed most Luftwaffe aircraft in the Battle of Britain: Eric Stanley 'Sawn Off' Locke of 41 Squadron.

* It was the first airfield in the Royal Air Force to be equipped with 3 Spitfire squadrons and the only airfield so equipped at the start of the Battle of Britain.

* The Hornchurch Sector lost 481 airmen in combat during World War II.

* In 'Non-Combatant' roles it housed the Aircrew Selection Centre during its busiest 14 years, dealing with up to 12,000 applicants a year.

* It came to the aid of the civil power in dramatic circumstances during the V-1 Doodlebug and V-2 Rocket attacks in 1944/5 and then again during the East Coast Floods of 1953.

In this book mention has been made of Ronald Adam's famous quotation, "We got on with the job without shouting the odds." It possibly sounds as if I am trying to make up for this silence now; maybe I am, but it is only in an attempt to put the

Prayers led by Canon 'Pete' Peatfield at the unveiling ceremony of the Memorial to the Fallen on the site of RAF Hornchurch, 5 July, 1983. Sir Harry Broadhurst is nearest the camera

history of the airfields that featured in the Battle of Britain and later encounters into a balanced and possibly more accurate historical perspective and help redress the marked imbalance in the state of public awareness.

The air war in Europe was not won by one airfield and not even by seven 11 Group Sector airfields. It was won by a combination of all Commands of the Royal Air Force, United States Army Air Force, Royal Navy (Fleet Air Arm) and all allied air forces fighting from some 720 airfields - most of them now windswept farms. These airmen, with their courage, spirit, humour and dedication steered this island through the air war at the most dangerous period of its history.

####

But back to Hornchurch.

It was conceived in 1915 to participate in the defence of the British Isles from the air. It had its great moments of glory and survived (apart from a short interval) from 1915 to 1962. When further use for it was exhausted it was left empty and derelict to die the death of a thousand cuts: it deserved a better end, but at least some of it has been converted into a Country Park.

It should be remembered and live on in the hearts and minds of all who knew it, as the place where different generations of fighter pilots made their own intensely personal *Per ardua ad astra* and, by dedication, overcame their difficulties and reached the stars. Even today it is not hard to stand in the Country Park, close one's eyes and, in the imagination, hear the purr of the Rolls Royce engines, as combat weary Spitfires, frequently damaged, returned to set down on the grass field.

It is nearly forty years since the last aircraft took off and the very last RAF truck rolled out of the main gate, but it retains the atmosphere of the high endeavour of the laughing young men who inhabited this spot and, by contrast, an aura of sadness associated with those who failed to return. For all the atmosphere that is heaped upon individual airfields they are inanimate objects and it is the flesh and blood of the airmen who served there who breathed life into them and endowed them with a soul.

It is perhaps inevitable that succeeding generations have short memories, but, when walking through the quietitude of Hornchurch Country Park or travelling by bus or car down Airfield Way, please spare a thought for those brave young men. Each of them, in making the supreme sacrifice, gave up their tomorrows in order that we should live in peace and enjoy our todays.

Look back and remember them as a rather special generation of airmen. For such they undoubtedly were.

REQUIESCAT IN PACE

SQUADRONS IN HORNCHURCH SECTOR
From 1928
(for First World War squadrons, see page??)

Squadron	From	Until	Aircraft	Commanding Officer	Remarks
19	25 May 40	5 Jun 40	Spitfire	G D Stephenson	Disbanded 1991
				P C Pinkham	
	16 Aug 42	20 Aug 42	Spitfire	P R Davies	
	5 Apr 43	18 May 43	Spitfire	V H Elkins	
41	28 May 40	8 Jun 40	Spitfire	H R Hood	Now based
	26 Jul 40	8 Aug 40	Spitfire	H R Hood	at RAF
	3 Sep 40	23 Feb 41	Spitfire	H R Hood	Coltishall
				R C Lister	with Jaguars
				D O Finlay	
54	15 Jan 30	28 May 40	Siskin	W E Bryant	Now based
			Bulldog	S L Pope	at RAF
			Gauntlet	I M Rodney	Coltishall
			Gladiator	G D Daly	with Jaguars
			Spitfire	R G Lewis	but temporarily
				J R Jones	on UN operations
				C A Bouchier	from Turkey
				H M Pearson	
				E A Douglas-Jones	
				J A Leathart	
	4 Jun 40	28 Jul 40	Spitfire	J A Leathart	
	8 Aug 40	3 Sep 40		J A Leathart	
				D O Finlay	
	23 Feb 41	17 Nov 41	Spitfire	R F Boyd	
				N Orton	
				F D Scott-Malden	
64	10 Nov 40	16 May 41	Spitfire	A R MacDonnell	Disbanded
				B Heath	at RAF
	19 Nov 41	9 Dec 42	Spitfire	D Kain	Leuchars
				B J Wicks	1991
				W G Smith	
				F A Gaze	
				C F Gray	
	2 Jan 43	28 Mar 43	Spitfire	W V Crawford-Compton	
				M G Donett	
65	1 Aug 34	2 Oct 39	Demon	F O Soden	Now based
			Gauntlet	H W Pearson-Rogers	at RAF
			Gladiator	C F Grace	Coningsby
			Spitfire	D Cooke	with Tornados
	28 Mar 40	28 Aug 40	Spitfire	D Cooke	
				H C Sawyer	
				A L Holland	
66	8 Nov 43	23 Feb 44	Spitfire	K T Lofts	Disbanded at RAF Seletar, Singapore: 20 March 1969
74	21 Sep 36	14 Aug 49	Demon	D S Brooks	Now based
			Gauntlet	C E Sampson	at RAF
			Spitfire	FL White	Valley
				A G Malan	with Hawks

80	6 May 44	19 May 44	Spitfire	D H Barlow	Disbanded at RAF Bruggen: 28 Sep 1969
81	15 May 42	1 Sep 42	Spitfire	P R Berry	Disbanded at RAF Tengih, Singapore: 16 January 1970
92	9 Jun 40	18 Jun 40	Spitfire	P J Sanders	Disbanded at RAF Wildenrath, 1991
111	1 Apr 28	12 Jul 34	Siskin Bulldog	K R Park F O Soden L H Slatter E R Openshaw M B Frew	Now based at RAF Leuchars with Tornados
116	2 May 45	26 May 45	Hurricane Tiger Moth Oxford Anson		Disbanded at RAF Watton: 21 August 1958
122	1 Apr 42	18 May 43	Spitfire	F Fajtl L Prevot J R Kilian D E Kingaby P W Wickham	Disbanded at RAF Dalcross: 1 April 1946
129	28 Jun 43	17 Jan 44	Spitfire	H A Gonay P V Tripe	Disbanded at RAF Church Fenton 1 Sept 1946
132	2 Oct 42	9 Oct 42	Spitfire	J R Ritchie	Disbanded at RAF Kai-Tak: 15 Apr 1946
154	7 Jun 42	1 Sep 42	Spitfire	D Carlson	Disbanded as 'Bloodhound' Missile Squadron at RAF Hunsdon: 31 March 1945
222	28 May 40 29 Aug 40 19 Jul 41 29 Apr 43 10 Mar 44	4 Jun 40 11 Nov 40 18 Aug 41 30 Dec 43 11 Apr 44	Spitfire Spitfire Spitfire Spitfire Spitfire	H W Mermagen J H Hill R C Love E J Harrington G J Stonhill R F Inness	Disbanded at RAF Woodhall Spa: 30 June 1964
229	24 Apr 44	19 May 44	Spitfire	N F Harrison	Disbanded at RAF Coltishall: 10 January 1945
234	16 Sep 43	15 Oct 43	Spitfire	M G Barnett A Bocock	Disbanded at RAF Geilenkirchen: 15 July 1957
239	21 Jun 43	15 Sep 43	Mustang	P M Evans	Disbanded at RAF West Rayham: 1 July 1945
264	22 Aug 40 29 Oct 40	28 Aug 40 27 Nov 40	Defiant Defiant	P A Hunter G D Garvin G D Garvin A T Sanders	Disbanded as 'Bloodhound' Missile Squadron at RAF North Coates: 30 Nov 1962
266	14 Aug 40	21 Aug 40	Spitfire	D G Spencer	Disbanded as 'Bloodhound' Squadron at RAF Rattlesden 30 June 1964
274	24 Apr 44	19 May 44	Spitfire	J F Edwards	Disbanded at RAF Warmwell: 7 Sept 1945
278	13 Nov 44	15 Feb 45	Walrus Warwick Spitfire		Disbanded at RAF Exeter: 14 Oct 1945

No.			Aircraft	Commander	Notes
287	3 May 45	15 Jun 45	Oxford Martinet Beaufighter Tempest Spitfire		Disbanded at RAF West Malling: 15 June 1946
313 Czech Squadron	15 Dec 41	8 Jun 42	Spitfire	K Mrazek	Left RAF Manston for Prague and disbanded there 15 Feb 1946
340 Free French Squadron	28 Jul 42	23 Sep 42	Spitfire	B Duperier	Disbanded at RAF Fassberg: 25 Nov 1945
349 Belgian Squadron	26 Oct 43	10 Nov 43	Spitfire	1 G de Bergendal	Disbanded at RAF Fassberg: 24 Oct 1946 Transferred to Royal Belgian Air Force
350 Belgian Squadron	23 Sep 42	1 Mar 43	Spitfire	D A Guillaume	Disbanded at RAF Fassberg:
	13 Mar 43	23 Mar 43	Spitfire	A L Boussa	15 Oct 1946
	13 Oct 43	31 Oct 43	Spitfire	A L Boussa	Transferred
	30 Dec 43	10 Mar 44	Spitfire	A L Boussa L O Prévot	Royal Belgian Air Force
403 Canadian Squadron	4 Aug 41	25 Aug 41	Spitfire	A Lee-Knight	Disbanded at Soltau: 30 June 1945
411 Canadian Squadron	22 Nov 41	15 Mar 42	Spitfire	R B Pitcher P S Turner R B Newton	Disbanded at Utersen: 21 March 1946
	22 Apr 42	7 May 42	Spitfire	R B Newton	
453 Australian Squadron	23 Sep 42	15 Nov 42	Spitfire	F V Morello	Disbanded at RAF Hawkinge:
	27 Mar 43	28 Jun 43	Spitfire	J R Ratten K M Barclay	31 May 1945
485 New Zealand Squadron	18 Oct 43	21 Nov 43	Spitfire	M R Hume	Disbanded at Drope:
	15 Mar 44	15 Apr 44	Spitfire	J B Niven	26 August 1945
504	19 Jan 44	30 Apr 44	Spitfire	H J Hallowed A Banning-Lover	Disbanded at RAF Wymeswold: 10 March 1957
567	14 Nov 44	13 Jun 45	Barracuda Martinet Hurricane Oxford Anson		Disbanded at RAF West Malling: 15 June 1946
600 'City of London' RAAF Squadron	2 Oct 39	14 May 40	Blenheim	Viscount Carlow J Wells D de B Clarke	Disbanded at RAF Biggin Hill: 10 March
	20 Jun 40	12 Sep 40		D de B Clarke	1957
603 'City of Edinburgh' RAAF Squadron	27 Aug 40	13 Dec 40	Spitfire	E H Stevens G L Denholm	Disbanded at Turnhouse:
	16 May 41	15 Dec 41	Spitfire	F M Smith M J Louden T H Forshaw	10 March 1957
611 'West Lancashire' RAAF Squadron	14 Dec 40	13 Nov 41	Spitfire	E R Bitmead F S Stapleton E H Thomas W A Douglas	Disbanded at Hooton Park, Cheshire: 10 March 1957
765	14 Nov 44	15 Jun 45	Wellington	D H Coates	Disbanded at RNAS Culdrose: 25 March 1957

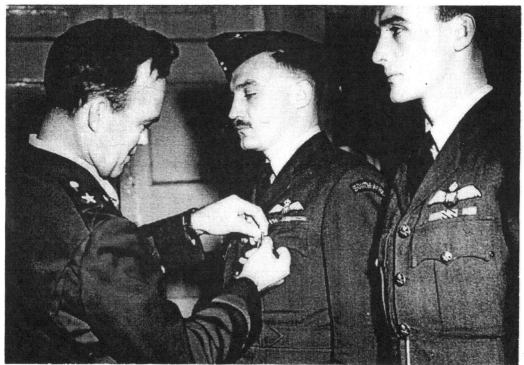

Group Captain Petrus Hugo and Wing Commander Anthony Lovell
receiving the United States DFC from Brigadier General D'Arcy, for
operations escorting U S 8th Air Force Fortresses and Liberators in
daylight raids

Wing Commander William Crawford-Compton in 1943
(*Imperial War Museum*)

AIRCRAFT FLOWN IN SQUADRON SERVICE FROM
RAF HORNCHURCH FROM 1928

Airspeed Ltd	Oxford	Hawker Aircraft Ltd.	Demon
Armstrong Whitworth Aircraft Ltd	Siskin		Hurricane
A V Roe & Co. Ltd	Anson		Tempest
Boulton Paul Aircraft, Ltd.	Defiant	Miles Aircraft Ltd.	Martinet
Bristol Aeroplane Co., Ltd.	Beaufighter	North American Aviation, Inc.	Mustang
	Blenheim	Saunders Roe, Ltd	Walrus
	Bulldog	Supermarine Division of Vickers-Armstrong	Spitfire
de Havilland Aircraft Co., Ltd.	Tiger Moth	Vickers Armstrong, Ltd.	Warwick
Fairey Aviation	Barracuda	Vultee Aircraft, Inc.	Vengeance
Gloster Aircraft Co., Ltd.	Gauntlet		
	Gladiator		

WING COMMANDERS (FLYING) AT RAF HORNCHURCH

Following the appointment of Air Vice Marshal Trafford Leigh-Mallory as Air Officer Commanding No. 11 Group, Fighter Command, the squadrons were grouped in Wings of three or four squadrons. At each Sector Station a Wing Commander (Flying) was appointed, responsible for leading the Wing into combat.

These men were among the most proficient airmen of their time. Thirteen Wing Commanders (Flying) served at RAF Hornchurch between 15 March, 1941, and 29th February, 1944. They were

Farquhar, Andrew Douglas	15 Mar 41	2 Jun 41	Emigrated to South Africa after the war and farmed there. He died in the 1960s
Kayll, Joseph Robert	2 Jun 41	25 Jun 41	Shot down over Hazebrouck on 25th June 1941 and became a prisoner of war. Escaped, but was re-captured. CO of 607 (County of Durham) Squadron AAF, 1946
Stapleton, Frederick Snowden	27 Jun 41	3 Dec 41	Retired from RAF in 1967 to Melbourne, Australia. He died in 1974
Dawson, H L	4 Dec 41	16 Jan 42	
Powell, Robin Peter Reginald	17 Jan 42	26 Jun 42	Suffered fractured skull during sweep over France, 26th June, 1942. He died on 28th January, 1970
Finucane, Brendan Eamonn	27 Jun 42	15 Jul 42	Hit by machine gun fire from French beaches on 15th July, 1942: too low to bale out. Died when his aircraft ploughed into the Channel
Hugo, Petrus Hendrik	18 Jul 42	31 Aug 42	Posted to North Africa. Retired from RAF in 1950 and died South Africa 1986
Thomas, Erie Hugh	31 Aug 42	27 Nov 42	Subsequently Wing Commander (Flying) at RAF Biggin Hill. Released from RAF in 1944 and died in 1972
Bentley A M	27 Nov 42	29 Mar 43	
Kilmartin, John Ignatius	30 Mar 43	30 May 43	Retired from RAF 8th July 1958
Ratten, John R	31 May 43	28 Jul 43	Commanded 453 (Australian) Squadron at Hornchurch prior to appointment as Wing Commander (Flying)
Crawford-Compton, William Vernon	30 Jul 43	18 Dec 43	Remained in RAF and captained RAF Skiing Team in 1967, when he was 51. He died in 1988
Simpson, Peter James	18 Dec 43	29 Feb 44	Retired from RAF in 1968. He died in 1987

1928
　　General Italo Balbo: Italian Under Secretary of State for Air - with 10 aircraft
1930
　　Air Vice Marshal Hugh Caswall Tremenheere Dowding
1933
　　Sir Philip Albert Gustave Sassoon: Under Secretary of State for Air
1934
　　HRH the Prince of Wales
　　Sir Edward Ellington: Chief of Air Staff
1935
　　Sir Philip Sassoon: Under Secretary of State for Air
　　Air Chief Marshal Sir Robert Brooke-Popham
1936
　　Air Chief Marshal Sir Hugh Dowding: AOC in C Fighter Command
　　Air Vice Marshal Sir Victor Goddard
　　Air Vice Marshal E Leslie Gossage: AOC in C, 11 Group
　　Sir Ludlow Hewitt: Deputy Chief of Air Staff
1937
　　The Maharajah of Nepal
　　Nagendra Men Singh: Prime Minister of Nepal
　　General Milch: German Secretary of State for Air
　　General Stumpff: Luftwaffe General
　　General Udet: Head of Luftwaffe Technical Department
　　Major Polte: German Air Attaché in London
　　Sir Philip Sassoon: Under Secretary of State for Air
　　Viscount Swinton: Secretary of State for Air
　　Air Chief Marshal Sir Hugh Dowding: AOC in C Fighter Command
1938
　　Sultan of Muscat and Oman
　　Sir Kingsley Wood: Secretary of State for Air
　　Rt Hon Leslie Hore-Belisha
　　Jean Batten: lady aviator
1939
　　Major Horn: CO of 54 Squadron in 1914-18 War
　　Air Chief Marshal Sir Hugh Dowding: AOC in C Fighter Command
　　Air Vice Marshal E L Gossage: AOC in C, 11 Group
1940
　　HM King George VI
　　Air Commodore HRH the Duke of Kent
　　Marshal of the Royal Air Force Lord Trenchard
　　Sir Archibald Sinclair: Secretary of State for Air
　　Sir Robert Brooke-Popham: Inspector General
　　Sir Edmund and Lady Benthall: East India Fund
　　Mr Rowan Hodge: East India Fund
　　Air Chief Marshal Sir Hugh Dowding: AOC in C Fighter Command
　　Air Vice Marshal Keith Park: AOC in C, 11 Group
　　Captain Balfour: Under Secretary of State for Air
　　Air Marshal W C Fielden
　　Air Marshal Nichol

BIBLIOGRAPHY

Adam, Ronald: We rendezvous at ten (Universal Tandem, 1970)

Adam, Ronald: Readiness at dawn (Gollancz, 1941)

Barclay, George: Fighter pilot (Kimber, 1976)

Barfoot, John: Over here and over there; Ilford aerodromes and airmen in the First World War (Ian Henry, 1998)

Bateman, Dennis: Home Commands of the RAF since 1918 (MoD Air Historical Branch (RAF)

Bowyer, Chaz: Fighter pilots of the RAF, 1939-1945 (Kimber, 1984)

Collier, Richard: Eagle day (Hodder & Stoughton, 1966)

Crouch, Marcus: Essex (Batsford, 1969)

Deere, Alan: Nine lives (Hodder & Stoughton, 1959)

Forrester, Larrie: Fly for your life (Collins, 1960)

Freeman, Roger: The Mighty Eighth (Macdonald & Janes, 1970)

Freeman, Roger: Mighty Eighth war diary (Janes, 1981)

Grieve, Hilda: The great tide (Essex CC, 1959)

Halley, James: The squadrons of the RAF (Air Britain, 1980)

Halpenny, Bruce: Action stations, v.8 (Patrick Stephens, 1984)

Hillary, Richard: The last enemy (Macmillan, 1942)

Hooper, Bill: Pilot Officer Prune's picture parade (HMSO, 1991)

Jackson, Robert: Strike from the sea (Arthur Barker, 1970)

James, John: The Paladins (Macdonald, 1990)

Johnson, Johnnie: Wing Leader (Chatto & Windus, 1956)

Longmate, Norman: The doodlebugs (Hutchinson, 1981)

Mason, Francis: Battle over Britain (McWhirter Twins, 1969)

Morris, Joseph: The German air raids, 1914-1918 (Pordes, 1969)

Perfect, Charles: Hornchurch during the Great War (Benham, 1920)

Perfect, Charles: Ye old village of Hornchurch (Perfect, 1917)

Pope, Rodney: Andrews Field (Ian Henry, 1990)

Ramsey, Winston G: After the battle, no. 2 (1973)

Ramsey, Winston G: The Battle of Britain then and now (After the Battle, 1980)

Rawlings, John: Fighter squadrons of the RAF (Macdonald & Janes, 1969)

Robinson, Douglas: The Zeppelin in combat (Foulis, 1966)

Rimmel, Ray: Zeppelin (Conway Maritime, 1984)

Salmagi, Cesare *and* Pallavisini, Alfredo: 2194 days of war (Gallery, 1988)

Sutton, H T: Raiders approach (Gale & Polden, 1956)

Taylor, J W R *and* Moyes, P J R: Pictorial history of the RAF (Allan, 1969)

Thetford, Owen: Aircraft of the RAF since 1918 (Putnam, 1958)

Vader, John: Spitfire (Pan/Ballantine, 1969)

Wallace, Graham: RAF Biggin Hill (Putnam, 1957)

Wood, Derek *and* Dempster, Derek: The narrow margin (Hutchinson, 1961)

Wright, C E: The fate of the Zeppelin L-32 (Chanticleer, 1977)

Wynn, Kenneth: Men of the Battle of Britain (Gliddon Books, 1989)

Hunt, Leslie: Various aviation articles in *Essex Countryside* and *Romford Times*

Havering: a Recorder souvenir. Romford Recorder, 1965